T. T Leberthon, A Taylor

The City and County of San Diego

Illustrated and Containing Biographical Sketches of Prominent Men....

T. T Leberthon, A Taylor

The City and County of San Diego
Illustrated and Containing Biographical Sketches of Prominent Men....

ISBN/EAN: 9783337019150

Printed in Europe, USA, Canada, Australia, Japan

Cover: Foto ©ninafisch / pixelio.de

More available books at **www.hansebooks.com**

THE
CITY AND COUNTY
OF
SAN DIEGO.

ILLUSTRATED,

AND CONTAINING

BIOGRAPHICAL SKETCHES

OF

PROMINENT MEN AND PIONEERS.

SAN DIEGO, CAL.
LEBERTHON & TAYLOR.
1888.

PREFACE.

I HAVE been asked to sketch the history, topography, resources and progress of the city and county of San Diego, up to date. To do so in full is to write a ponderous book whose size would at once seal its fate. To sketch the whole in brief and readable form, giving due importance to all parts, omitting unimportant details fit only for an advertising pamphlet, is a greater task than to write the whole in full.

Neither history nor geography is of any value if one-sided. There is little use in writing anything unless written in a way that will make the reader believe it. The day has long passed when a one-sided tale about California can be palmed off on an intelligent reader. As a mere matter of policy, to say nothing of honesty, such writing is unwise.

A fair account of the whole necessarily requires the statement of some cold facts. It is difficult to see any reason why these should not now be given. They are certainly a part of our history. Heretofore they have generally been concealed. Surely the time has come when all may afford to laugh at them. If a sorrow's crown of sorrow is remembering happier things, so is the memory of the dark and stormy waves a pleasure when the bark is once safe in port. There is little credit in a fight won against no enemy; slight glory in a field where there were no odds. The trials of San Diego really brighten the triumph of to-day, and form a setting for the picture that it would be foolish not to use. T. S. VAN DYKE.

San Diego, March 1, 1888.

BIOGRAPHICAL.

THE biographical sketches of the prominent and pioneer citizens of San Diego that appear in this volume, have all been prepared from data furnished by those interested. If we have, in some instances, enlarged and embellished this material, it has been because we believed that the subjects were deserving of it. It would be difficult in any part of the country to find a group of men more worthy of praise, to whom the community where they make their home owes more, than the older citizens of San Diego. For many long years they waited patiently for the coming of the day that was to bring a realization of their hopes; when the world was to acknowledge what they had long contended, that here on the shores of the Bay of San Diego was the fitting place for a great city—a metropolis. That day has come, and is it to be wondered at that they feel proud of their constancy, their faith in the future? T. T. LEBERTHON,
A. TAYLOR,
Editors and Publishers.

San Diego, Cal., March 1, 1888.

CONTENTS.

	PAGE.
The Early Days	9
Progress of Farming, etc.	13
Beginning of Fruit and Vine Culture	16
Rise of San Diego City	18
The Long Sleep	21
The Awakening	25
The Bay Region	30
The Interior	34
The Lower Coast Division	39
The Northern Division	44
The Mountain Division	48
Water	52
Production	58
The Climate	69
Out-of-door Amusements	72
Miscellaneous	75
Morse, Whaley & Dalton Building	210
First National Bank	211
The Consolidated National Bank of San Diego	213
The Pierce-Morse Block	214
Villa Montezuma	214

(v)

LIST OF BIOGRAPHIES.

	PAGE.
Biographical Sketches	83
A. E. Morton	83
E. W. Morse	87
Judge O. S. Witherby	91
M. Schiller	93
Thomas Whaley	96
Hon. James McCoy	102
Andrew Cassidy	104
Robert Kelly	106
Colonel C. P. Noell	109
J. S. Mannasse	112
Charles A. Wetmore	114
George B. Hensley	118
William E. High	120
Aaron Pauly	122
D. Choate	125
Judge McNealy	129
Robert Allison	131
Philip Morse	133
R. G. Clark	136
Daniel Cleveland	139
George W. Hazzard	142
William Jorres	145
Charles J. Fox, C. E.	147
A. Klauber	150
S. Levi	152
Bryant Howard	154
John S. Harbison	156
Col. Chalmers Scott	159
Charles Hubbell	162
George William Barnes, M. D.	170
O. S. Hubbell	164
Joseph Faivre	167
Thomas L. Nesmith	172
Mrs. Mary J. Birdsall	175
D. Cave, D. D. S.	176
Dr. W. A. Winder	179
Judge M. A. Luce	181

LIST OF BIOGRAPHIES.

George A. Cowles 184
Dr. P. C. Remondino 187
N. H. Conklin 190
R. A. Thomas 192
Judge John D. Works 194
L. S. McClure 197
Governor Robert W. Waterman 199
Col. W. H. Holabird 203
Col. John A. Helphingstine 206
Willard N. Fos 208

CHAPTER I.

THE EARLY DAYS.

THE BAY of San Diego was discovered in 1542, by Cabrillo, and named in 1602 by Vizcaino, who made a survey of it at the time. From the survey of Vizcaino over a century and a half rolled over its unbroken face until the ships of Padre Junipero Serra anchored within it. It was several years before the Indians were fully subdued, but they finally succumbed to the peaceful arts of the missionaries. Soon after the establishment of other missions in California, and the quieting and gathering in of the greater part of the Indians around the missions, settlers from Spain and Mexico began to come in, and later on a few from the United States, England, and elsewhere. Nearly all of these settlers obtained grants of large tracts of land from the Mexican Government, which have since been the cause of much litigation, envy, and quarreling. These grants were simply Mexican homesteads, given to settle the country just as the United States homesteads are given, for practically nothing.

Instead of selling a man, as the United States then did, all the land he wanted for $1.25 an acre, the Mexican Government gave it to him by the square league. The grants were made large partly as an inducement to the settler to go into such a wild and remote country, but mainly because the raising of cattle for the hides and tallow being the only industry, a large range was absolutely necessary for profit as well as the support of the band of retainers necessary for profit and safety. Instead of abusing the owner of a grant as a monopolist and a robber, the man who felt bad because he did not own a slice of it, should have remembered that he or his father or grandfather might have had it just as easily. But they preferred the luxuries of civilization to a rude life in a foreign country, both wild and remote, and which, as everyone then believed, would never be anything but a wild cattle range. The man who endured years of privation for its sake, could scarcely be blamed for wanting something for it. In some respects these large holdings have been an injury to California. But it is equally certain that the results have not been one-sided. Such improvements as have been made at Coronado Beach, Escondido, and many other places in Southern California, would have waited fifty years, had the land been half covered with ordinary farms. Riverside, Pasadena, and nearly all that is of much value in Los Angeles and San Bernardino Counties, owes its value to the fact that the control of the water, highways, and improvements of all kinds were in one hand.

Nevertheless the first effect of these large grants was to retard settlement. The county of San Diego, in common with the rest of Southern California, was then believed to be a veritable desert of sand, cactus, and horned toads, fit only for stock range at the rate of about one hundred acres to each animal. The owners of the large ranchos, who knew better than this, still believed the land fit only for stock range; and as they practically owned all the outside range, they naturally looked with jealousy upon the incoming of any farmers either to overstock the ranges or to make cultivated fields, upon which the cattle would trespass and cause trouble. Hence, it was for the interest of all these large owners to keep up the cry that the land was of no use for anything but stock, even had they not really believed it.

Under these influences the county remained virtually an open stock range, covered with many thousands of cattle and horses, for about twenty years after the admission of California to the Union. A very few persons had come in and attempted farming, some on large and some on small scales, but made a poor headway against low prices, wild cattle and their own ignorance of the land's peculiarities. Much quarreling and bad feeling between the new settlers and the old necessarily resulted. On the one hand the ranchero claimed that his lines embraced all available Government land in his vicinity, and ate out the crops of the granger with his cattle. In this he was aided by the sheep-man,

Summer Scenes in San Diego.

who had for some time been a power in the land and who wanted all the public grazing for himself. On the other hand, too many a "granger" ignored all lines, declared all grants frauds, denounced his Government for recognizing vested rights, squatted in force upon what was unquestionably within the grant lines, and shot the ranchero's cattle not only in his grain fields, but in the hills. The cattle shot in the fields were left where they lay, but the beef upon which some of the new settlers kept fat came from the hills.

The "granger" increased so fast under the impetus given by the founding of New San Diego, the fact—first proved by J. S. Harbison, of Sacramento, who brought the first bees into California and into this county—that enormous quantities of fine honey could be raised here, and the fine climate, that he soon became a power in the land. The squatter, or "esquatero," as he was contemptously called by the sheep and cattle-men, finally walked off with the country, as he eventually will with the great cattle ranges of the great western basins. About 1870 he worked through the Legislature a law which broke up the old free range system which had been in use in all the new States of the West in their early days. Under this system damages for trespass by cattle could be had only upon proof that the land was protected by a fence of a certain size. The new law, or "no-fence law," as it was called, made the common law of England, by which every man must keep his cattle on his own land, the law of this county.

This law soon reduced the raising of cattle and horses to a minimum, because it was too expensive at that time to fence the large ranchos, and because the free range upon which cattle had heretofore run was practically destroyed. The sheep interest did not suffer, but improved in consequence of the law. Being under the care of a herder day and night, sheep could not trespass, and the amount of free range on public land was increased by the withdrawal of the cattle and horses. From this time sheep-raising, bee-keeping, and general farming became the leading industries, though on a few of the large ranchos, such as Santa Margarita and Santa Rosa, the cattle were retained. The ranchos remained, however, closed to settlement, as the owners did not care to admit a few small farmers, and there was then no probability of getting settlers enough to make subdivision profitable. El Cajon, San Dieguito, and La Nacion were for many years the only ranchos open to settlement, and the farmer had to seek such spots as lay around the grants or in the small valleys in the surrounding hills. Some very valuable tracts, such as Poway, Fallbrook, and San Pasqual, never were included in grants and were speedily taken up. Hundreds of other small tracts were scattered over the land in pieces of from one hundred to a thousand acres or more, and of these the smaller ones were gradually settled, until it became nearly impossible to find forty acres of good, arable Government land west of the desert divide. San Jacinto was opened to general settlement in 1882, Escondido in 1886, Ex-Mission in 1885, Santa Maria in 1886, San Marcos in 1887, Temecula in 1883. But many of the large grants still remain closed, though it will be but a short time before all of them are upon the market in small tracts.

CHAPTER II.

PROGRESS OF FARMING, ETC.

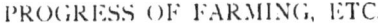

IF ever a country needed good plowing it was San Diego County. If ever a country failed to get it, it was this same San Diego. The long tramp, tramp, tramp, of immense bands of sheep over the ground while it was wet had packed it to the hardness of an adobe brick. Even the alfileria and burr-clover, which endure more ill treatment than almost any other vegetation, failed to reach half their natural size. In many places they were nearly destroyed by being eaten off while growing, and foxtail and other kinds of poverty grass and rank weeds were in their places. The desolate appearance given the land by the bands of sheep, can scarcely be imagined to-day by those who look only upon the cultivated vineyards of El Cajon, or the alfalfa fields of San Jacinto.

"Tickle the earth with a plow and it will laugh with a harvest," some well-meaning goose had written of California, in the days gone by. Unfortunately for the land this was true in many seasons. In fact, in three seasons out of ten, grain sown upon an old road or abandoned brick-yard will do about as well as anywhere. In two years more out of ten, the mildest scratching will suffice. As the great California weather prophet remembers only his predictions that turn out correct, so the new farmer remembered only his successes, and scratching in grain with a cultivator, harrow, or even a brush-drag, became the rule. Even where a gang plow was used, there was no plowing, the plows being so numerous that no team could draw them if deeply set. For years the single plow was never seen in use, except to make a road or break brushy ground. Many defended this style of farming on reasoning that appeared sound. "If it is a good year I will get a good crop anyhow, no matter how carelessly put in. If it's a bad year, I won't get a crop no matter how well it is put in. By scratching I can get in four or five times as much ground as I can with good plowing, and the chances of a good season are always six out of ten."

The crops raised under this system were sometimes enormous, exceeding the heaviest yields ever known east of the Rocky Mountains, and when combined with a good price, often yielded a heavy return over expenses. But in the long run this style has been a failure. It soon made the soil foul with weeds, cheat, etc., reducing the quality and quantity of the grain, so that it became necessary to lose an occasional year by summer fallow. And in the years of light or average rainfall, the want of good plowing told too heavily. In the mountain belts, where there was always rain enough in dry years, there was too much in years when there was enough along the coast. Fine crops were raised there in such severely dry years as 1877 and 1883, but the cost of hauling to market was too great.

The smaller farmers, who sowed small areas with grain, did better work and had better crops. But their work was generally a failure in the long run for another reason: The big farmers did everything by machinery and hired labor, and it was beneath the dignity of the small farmer to do otherwise. There was not a cradle, flail, or threshing floor among the Americans in the whole county; and if a man had only twenty acres of grain, he must have it cut with a header and threshed with a threshing machine, no matter how much spare time he or his boys might have. When harvest came a small army of ravenous hands and horses would descend upon him, generally on Saturday night, so as to insure rations for Sunday. Instead of cutting around the field with a cradle to make a way for the header, the ponderous machine smashed its own way around the first swath or up the center of the field. The knives, sharpened apparently but once a year, tore and stripped many a stalk instead of cutting it, and many a head of grain was so badly cut that it fell under the machine instead of in the receiver. From fifteen to twenty per cent of the crop was thus wasted, and there was no gleaning of the stubbles except with the live stock. When threshing-time came around, the same wasteful extravagance was repeated on a still greater scale. By the time the farmer had his grain sacked and hauled to market, he was often in debt and seldom much ahead.

In many other respects, San Diego County farming was about the worst in the world. Make no machinery that you can buy, and do nothing yourself that you can hire anyone else to do, seemed to be the cardinal principle. Nearly all were farming, not for something to eat or use on the farm, but for something to haul many miles to market to sell at a low price, to buy provisions at a high price, to haul all the way home again to eat. Never did it take men so long to learn anything. One man would lose a hundred chickens by wild cats and cayotes before he would learn to shut the coop at night. Another would lose his garden or young vines two or three years in succession before discovering that a rabbit-proof fence was the first and not the last requisite. Other farmers seemed to forget everything they ever knew before. Men who, in Illinois, planted corn forty inches apart in rows straight both ways and cultivated it constantly until it was too high to drive through,

planted it here in rows but twenty inches apart, crooked both ways, and never afterward touched it. The same was done with potatoes and all kinds of produce planted in hills or rows. And though Heaven rewarded their folly as it deserved, yet year after year, as the spring came around, they went through the same old ceremony, as if trying a new experiment in a new country. The same thing may be seen to-day in too many places. Yet, in spite of all this carelessness, coupled with high rates of interest and high prices for all manner of goods and machinery, the farmers of this county generally lived better, had more spare time, more spare change, and fewer mortgage foreclosures than the farmers of any other State. The absence of rain, hail, etc., in summer and the difference in the cost of getting through the winter, more than overbalanced all else.

For several years, beginning about 1869, bee-keeping was immensely profitable, and in the warm days of winter and spring, the air above the spangled earth was a steady hum. About 1878 the price of honey began to decline, with a decided falling off in the certainty of production. The use of glucose for adulteration, in the East, has probably broken the price. The decline in production has been explained in various ways, all of which are unsatisfactory. These styles of farming continued up to about 1880, when slight changes for the better were noticed, and from that time to the present, the inflow of new-comers, with the advance of new ideas and principles worked out in the counties north of us, has brought about a decided revolution, which is fast spreading.

CHAPTER III.

BEGINNING OF FRUIT AND VINE CULTURE.

FOR a long time it was supposed that fruit and grapes, as well as garden-stuff, could not be grown in California without irrigation. The irrigation facilities of this county, being generally expensive, were not developed to any extent. Even in the few places where water was cheaply obtained there was no encouragement to raise anything. A wagon load of any kind of fruit would drug the San Diego market and shipping it farther was out of the question. Some made a few dollars by selling to their neighbors; but most of the neighbors preferred to wait until they could get it for nothing. To raise fruit or even vegetables for one's own use was not only expensive but vexatious, on account of birds, rabbits, squirrels, etc., which concentrate upon an isolated patch of anything green in summer; and the farmer soon concluded it was cheaper to buy from someone else, or go without, than to bother with such things. A few, however, as far back as ten years ago, had orchards and gardens not excelled to-day. At Fallbrook, the place of V. C. Reche, was a perfect oasis of the richest green; apricots, oranges, lemons, peaches, apples, quinces, and what not of the finest quality, abounded. At Julian, Mr. Madison and others were raising deciduous fruits and berries of the finest kind. On Mesa Grande, Mr. Gedney was doing the same; others throughout the county were beginning to follow them. Around San Diego Bay, especially in and around National City and Chollas Valley, fine orchards and gardens twelve years ago had answered the sneers of those who said that the land was fit only for stock. A few vineyards at long intervals already foretold the coming land of the grape, and at the old missions a few old trees proved abundantly what the olive could do with half an opportunity.

Irrigation was confined to a few spots on the river bottoms or lowlands and was of the old-fashioned kind, a drenching of the ground every few days, with no cultivation whatever. The greater part of the water was used only by Indians, and where used by the whites was principally for corn, melons, garden produce, or grapes, which were then supposed to need plenty of water even on low ground. Some irrigation with windmills was attempted in a few places, and was as near a success as windmill irrigation pumping against a long lift can be. But the quality of the fruit, especially oranges and lemons, was inferior, because water was used as a substitute for cultivation, and the best varieties were not yet planted. In the North the plow had for years been creeping from the low-lands, which for a time were supposed to be the only lands available for culture, farther up the slopes. It had been discovered that the slopes and uplands were not only better for vines and many kinds of fruit, but would, with close and constant cultivation, retain moisture enough during the summer to raise fair crops of grapes, deciduous fruits, and other produce. This discovery spread South through the different counties, and about 1880 began to dawn as a new idea in San Diego. Some people imagined that they were the discoverers, others that this power of the soil was confined to their special locality. By 1882 the idea had become widespread, and from that time truly dates the rise of fruit culture in San Diego County, although in some favored localities good fruit had been grown without irrigation many years before.

In 1882 R. G. Clark produced in El Cajon the first raisins cured in the county; their quality was so fine that they attracted the immediate attention of Riverside growers, who at once bought a large tract of land in El Cajon. Geo. A. Cowles and others in different sections had in the meantime set out vineyards, and the following year sustained the reputation of the raisins so well that it has scarce been questioned since. About the same time oranges and lemons from the National Ranch and Janal began to excite wonder at the fairs of Riverside and Los Angeles. The lemons were soon conceded to be superior and the oranges puzzled the best judges. With the exception of specimen fruits raised in this way by people who could afford to play with them, little has been done until the past two or three years. The local market was too small and shipping long distances at a profit in small quantities was out of the question. Now, thousands of acres are coming into bearing, and thousands more are planting. The oil-press is at work turning out the finest of olive oil; and hundreds of tons of raisins are yearly dried. It will be but a short time before the railroad will run refrigerator cars and then the great market of the world will call forth a pent-up energy that is now little dreamed of. The capacity of the county in the way of raising fruit is immense; but until there are transportation facilities, people will not plant to any extent. This failure to plant, of course, delays the building of railroads, etc. Each one reacts for a time upon the other, but the see-saw is finally broken and the outlet is furnished.

CHAPTER IV.

RISE OF SAN DIEGO CITY.

THE first settlement made in California was on San Diego Bay. In July, 1769, the first mission in California was built at Old San Diego, now called Old Town, some three miles west of the present city, and the old ruins on the hill above the town are the oldest relics of the first year of civilization in this State. Old Town is also the oldest municality in the State. In January, 1835, the city government was organized. Ten years afterward the city lands, to the extent of forty-seven thousand acres, were surveyed and mapped and granted to it by the Government of Mexico. This grant was afterwards confirmed and patented by the United States, and hence the magnificent proportions of the present city limits.

For many years the only business done at Old Town was the shipment of hides and tallow. The population was then almost entirely Mexican, though a very few Americans and other foreigners were there. When California was admitted as a State and divided into counties, Old Town became the county seat and remained so for many years. A few more Americans came about the same time; some of the most prosperous and respectable of the present citizens of San Diego, E. W. Morse, James McCoy, O. S. Witherby, Thomas Whaley, Joseph Mannasse, and others were among the first to settle there. For many years Old Town contained all the life upon San Diego Bay, and the old plaza and old adobe buildings surrounding it could tell high tales of the olden time if they could talk. Until after the establishment of New San Diego, it remained substantially a Mexican town. Spanish was the principal language spoken, and the tinkle of the guitar, the jingle of spurs, and the clink of coin on the monte blanket were the principal sounds of civilization. The country was then full of cattle, which, after the inflow of the gold-seekers in the North, brought for years a good price. Money

A View in Santa Rosa, San Diego County.

was abundant, coming easily and going easily, and kept well in circulation through the active medium of cards and horse-races. The old Spanish settlers were lavish and reckless, borrowing at any rate of interest, and many of the best ranchos thus passed into the stranger's hand.

As early as 1850, an attempt was made to colonize the present site of San Diego. Several houses were then built near the present Government barracks. The barracks were built about the same time for a depot of military supplies, the soldiers being then quartered at the old mission. San Diego was then the base of military supplies for Fort Tejon, Fort Yuma, and other points to which wagon trains were run from San Diego. About this time the first wharf on San Diego Bay was built at this point by William Heath Davis, for which he received a grant of land around it from the city. This first settlement was made without any railroad expectations and solely on the strength of harbor and climate. The old Californian of that day saw the importance of these and sought even then to realize on his foresight. But he shared the common fate of foresight when not sufficiently backed with such little aids for waiting as youth and wealth. The excitement soon died out, most of the houses were moved up to Old Town, the wharf speedily fell before the teredo, and the cayote and wild cat were again left in possession. In the year 1867, foresight again appeared upon the scene in the more substantial shape of A. E. Horton. For twenty-six cents an acre he bought one hundred and sixty acres where the central part of San Diego now stands, and laid out the city. In the meantime two or three railroads had been projected, one of them as far back as 1854, but little had been done beyond organizing a company. Soon after the founding of the new city by Mr. Horton, the projected Memphis and El Paso Railroad began to look like a certainty and the first "boom" in San Diego began. Railroad meetings were the order of the day, the steamers brought many new-comers from the North, and many of the present old residents came here first upon the strength of the bright prospects. The new city grew rapidly to a town of twelve or fifteen hundred, when suddenly the shining bubble burst. There was then but little settlement in the back country to support a town, and but for the numerous quails and rabbits about town, there would have been more than one slim larder in the new city.

In 1871 the Texas Pacific Railroad was organized and the luxuriant mushroom of brief hope again sprung up. A handsome subsidy was voted Colonel Scott for the road, ten miles of it were graded—much of which may still be seen—strangers poured in, and the population rapidly grew to nearly four thousand people. During this time the Horton House, Horton's Hall. Horton's Bank, and several other buildings, beside a large wharf, were built by Mr. Horton, and various enterprises and churches were aided by his liberality. Many buildings were built which look highly respectable beside the more modern ones of to-day. Some of these were very large for the size of the city at that time, and some on an extravagant scale, such as the building now occupied by Hamilton & Co., which was built for a city market and was large enough for a city of ten times the size. In the meantime the county seat was moved from Old Town to "New Town" and the present Court House built. Most of the American settlers and many of the Mexican residents moved down to the new city and Old Town became more of a curiosity than a town. Some of the older American residents have still clung to it, partly because of past associations and partly because it has the best climate on the bay. When the old adobes and other ancient rookeries are removed it will be very desirable residence property, but these now stand in the way of its progress.

Soon after the city was begun by Mr. Horton, Frank Kimball and Warren Kimball had also a severe attack of foresight, which was quite as well founded as that of Mr. Horton. The lands of the National Ranch were better in quality and more free from gravel, gullies, etc., than those immediately surrounding Mr. Horton's new city. Four miles south of New San Diego was as good a water front, with as deep water, with thousands upon thousands of acres of fine land sloping gently away into lofty and fertile table-lands. The Kimballs saw that some day those slopes would be covered with fine residences, surrounded with groves of orange and lemon and everything that in Southern California can be grown at all. They bought the rancho, containing some twenty-seven thousand acres, built a fine wharf and several other buildings, put the tract on the market, laid out National City, and made many sales. For a time it looked as if it would be a formidable rival of San Diego, and a foolish envy then sprung up, which for years has been an injury to both places, but which is now about dead. Many settlers came in and bought the lands, and the first attempts made by the Americans to raise anything upon the coast lands were made in Paradise Valley upon the rancho and in Chollas Valley adjoining it. In the brighter light of to-day those first experiments appear extremely crude. Nevertheless they were a sufficient answer to the laughers and sneerers, who for a time had things all their own way and declared that nothing could be grown here even with water. The finest places and best orchards, vineyards, and gardens to be found upon the bay of San Diego, are to be found upon that rancho to-day; not because they cannot be equaled on the fine table-lands about San Diego, but because the lands of National City were so much lower that water was easily obtained by windmills.

CHAPTER V.

THE LONG SLEEP.

S the best target shot with the rifle finds the estimating of distance a source of error that he can never wholly master when shooting at game, so the keenest foresight fails to master that provoking variety of distance known as time. The eye of faith is true, the atmosphere is clear, the outlines of the game can be seen. Through the mirage of heated imagination it dances entrancingly near, and the labor of the day is staked perhaps upon a single shot which falls a long way short.

What the Texas Pacific might have done for San Diego it is useless now to inquire. The financial crash of 1873, beginning with the failure of Jay Cooke, crippled the resources of Colonel Scott. He went abroad to borrow money and failed. He has been blamed by many as a swindler, but there seems every reason to believe that he was acting with the best of faith. In such a crisis the best enterprises cannot borrow, for the simple reason that capital dare not lend to any great extent no matter what the security.

The population of both San Diego and National City rapidly declined to a few dozen at National and about twenty-five hundred at San Diego. The real estate offices were deserted; the hotels had more waiters than guests; empty stores and vacant houses became numerous on all sides. Day after day and year after year the bright sun shone upon quiet streets and store-keepers staring out of the door at an almost unbroken vacancy. Many a man in San Diego during those long years that followed sat and looked at nothing long enough to have made a fine lawyer, doctor, engineer, or a fine literary scholar if he had only substituted a book for the empty door-way.

Still a large majority clung with undying faith to their investments. They found in the soft and steady sunshine of San Diego a comfort they had never before known, and most of them would have remained even had they known that their dying eyes would close upon empty streets and vacant lots. The painful duty of an impartial historian requires the writer to record the farther fact that more than one representative of the great "progressive, enterprising citizen whose undying faith in San Diego has made him rich" (as we occasionally read in the papers of the day), has become so on the rise of town lots that he tried for years in vain to sell for money enough to get out of town with.

Many whose faith in the future of San Diego was unshaken had to leave for better (temporary) fields, and most of these have returned. Many more shook the dust of San Diego forever from their feet and spent most of their time thereafter in pouring out all the bitterness that disappointed fancy could conceive. The misfortunes of San Diego during all this time served as a whetstone for the newspaper wit of the State, a sure resource when everything else failed. Their jokes were quickly accepted as fact, and along the whole coast the most absurd stories were told all travelers with all the solemnity that the consciousness of duty to fellow-man imposes. One of the favorites of that day along the coast was the following:—

"What? you a-going down to Sa-a-a-ndy Ago?" (Questioner backing off and surveying from head to foot and back again the rash mortal who had mentioned San Diego as his possible destination.) "Do you know where in —— you are going to? Why you pick up a handful of dirt down there and in two seconds half of it is gone. That's fleas. In a minute more the rest has slipped through your fingers. That's sand. Why, that's what it gets its name from, Sa-a-a-a-a-ndy Ago."

Another common and convincing derivation was "Sandyague," from sand and ague, which were supposed to be the leading features, next to rattlesnakes and tarantulas.

It must be admitted that in favorable breeding seasons San Diego, like San Francisco and Los Angeles, has a flea or two, but the disintegrated granite soil, which in washes looks like sand, has proved to be, next to its climate, the greatest treasure Southern California possesses. The ague talk, like all the rest, was a perfect absurdity.

In 1876 an attempt was made to get Congress to guarantee the bonds of the Texas Pacific Railroad. Mr. Horton and Mr. Felsenheld spent most of the winter in Washington lobbying with Colonel Scott. But the cry of " no more subsidies to railroads" arose in the East, and was at once taken up by the Northwest, which wanted no Southern line. The clamor of these two sections, aided by the power of railroads, that already had all the subsidies they needed and never did need any competing line, overcame the strong pressure brought to bear by the South, which was wholly in favor of the measure.

This movement awoke no life in San Diego, and it slept on until 1881, unbroken, except, in 1879, by a slight excitement of a few days caused by an unfounded railroad rumor. Out of this one real estate man made enough to justify the ordering of a new buggy from San Francisco, but no one else was damaged in the upper story.

San Diego County Fruit Display.

In 1881 Frank A. Kimball, of National City, who had been about the most tireless and liberal of all workers in behalf of the bay region, and has received for it the least credit of anyone, proposed to go to Boston to see if he could not induce the Atchison, Topeka and Santa Fé Railway to come to San Diego. He was answered with a general guffaw from all the wise ones, and many of the leading citizens refused to contribute a cent toward his expenses. His reply was that he was able to pay them himself. He went and bearded the great lion in his den, amid the sneers of the public, who never can learn that it is very unsafe to say what a man cannot do when he tries.

He met nothing but rebuffs and cold shoulders. Nothing daunted he sat down for a prolonged siege. To his splendid offer of seventeen thousand acres of the best land on the bay, belonging to himself and his brother, Warren Kimball, over half of the National Ranch, capital at last bent a listening ear and sent out two directors of the road—Messrs. Platt and Wilbur—to investigate. The investigation was satisfactory; the donations of land were increased by several thousand acres from other parties. The California Southern was organized and finished to Colton in San Bernardino County in 1882.

During the building of this railroad the population of San Diego increased by some fifteen hundred people. National City, the terminus of the road, grew to a population of about one thousand. Bright hopes were held in both places, but in both they were doomed to a blight as speedy and severe as ever before. The railroad had no Eastern connection; almost every man in San Bernardino and Los Angeles Counties and on the line of the Southern Pacific Railroad made a specialty of abusing San Diego and warning travel away from it. For over a year after the completion of the road the through travel from Colton scarcely averaged five passengers a day, of which two or three were either "drummers" or "dead heads." So slight was the amount of business that in running through the huge flocks of geese and ducks which then used to rise beside the train in Santa Margarita Valley, the train was stopped, as a matter of course, if any game were shot from the car. On one occasion the engineer shot with a pistol at an acre or two of geese some three hundred yards away, and accidentally hit one. He stopped the train and walked leisurely over and bagged it.

Meanwhile National City lost about one-half its newly acquired population and San Diego more than all that had come in. To crown the trouble 1882–83 was a very dry winter on the coast, with a general failure of crops on all the unirrigated low-lands. In the fall of 1883 the vacant buildings in both San Diego and National City seemed to be fully one-half of the whole number, while the streets of San Diego seemed more deserted than ever.

On the 16th of February, 1884, the greater part of the railroad in

Temecula Cañon and Santa Margarita was washed out by a flood. It had been built too low by Boston engineers, who thought it never could rain in San Diego, who sneered at all advice of old settlers, and were too wise even to examine the drainage area of the stream or look at the rain records of the country. Such destruction has rarely been seen, and nearly nine months were required to place the track on better ground and get trains running. Then were dull times indeed.

The rebuilding of the road had little or no immediate effect in helping matters. There was little increase of travel for some time, until it became known that the road would be extended to a junction with the Atlantic and Pacific Railroad at Barstow, on the Mojave Desert.

CHAPTER VI.

THE AWAKENING.

THROUGHOUT the long line of lovely days that dawned and died on San Diego Bay without shining on a new roof or a happy face, the interior of the country was steadily settling. But stores in the country kept such even pace with the growth that there were few if any more wagons in town in 1884 than in 1875. Considerable trade was of course done, but mainly with eight or ten-mule teams and two or three wagons that loaded quietly and departed, making little stir upon the streets of San Diego. Settlers crept from National City up the Sweetwater Valley and from San Diego to El Cajon, which rancho was opened to settlement as early as 1869. The mines discovered near Julian about that time brought in many miners; a little town was started there, and a few settlers took up some of the rich little valleys around it. The tracts of Government land surrounding the large ranchos were soon sought out by the new-comers. They scaled the rugged hills that surround Bear Valley, climbed the heights of Mesa Grande and even the high Volcan and Palomar. A few of these were ex-boomers from San Diego who saw more money in bees than in corner lots. Some were old forty-niners from the North in search of anything new. Others were restless wanderers moving farther West and looking for a home of any kind in this farthest West. Many others were people more or less impaired in health, in search of a mild and comfortable climate where they could make a living by some light out-of-door work. In this way the American population outside the city of San Diego increased from a few hundred in 1868 to some twelve thousand or nearly five times that of the city in 1884. Yet the effect upon the city was almost inappreciable.

In the early part of 1885 work was begun upon the extension of the California Southern to Barstow. This was quickly construed to mean that the great Santa Fé railroad system would make San Diego its Pacific terminus. In the spring of the same year the first one of the series of extensive water systems that are shortly to make San Diego County the most attractive county in the State, was begun on the San

(25)

Diego River on a scale so immense that the usual number of sages made the usual number of predictions about what cannot be done by people who are determined to do something.

During all these years that San Diego was waiting and watching, the counties of San Bernardino and Los Angeles were increasing in population at a much greater rate than San Diego County, and with a far greater proportion of people of wealth. From very early times people had been coming to California on account of its climate. But for many years their numbers were very few and confined to the class of decided invalids. After the completion of the Central and Union Pacific lines a few began coming to spend the winter just as the many went to Florida. For a long time the impression among them was that they must flee as a matter of course at the opening of the spring, just as they would from Florida. San Diego from its first start had a few of these. In the winter of 1875-76 for a few weeks the Horton House and all the adjacent lodging-rooms around the plaza were full and a large and fashionable boarding-house kept by J. O. Miner on the Cajon had at one time some twenty-five guests at twelve dollars a week. This travel resulted in no settlement or improvement except a very temporary one in the pockets of hotel and livery stable keepers, barbers, saloons, etc. But in Los Angeles and San Bernardino Counties there was a decided difference. The early development of water there and its surprising results captured a goodly proportion of the visitors, many of whom bought and built, while the fairest portions of San Diego, for lack of water development, which was here more costly, showed nothing of what they can readily do. The new settlers on the north quickly discovered that instead of paying a high price in summer for the luxury of the winters they had actually gained quite as much by the change from the Eastern summer as by the change from the Eastern winter. A remarkable feature of the whole was that though few, if any, of the fine vineyards or orchards or beautiful places paid anything on the investment, and most of them, owing to the lack of transportation to market, were a dead loss, yet the owners were perfectly satisfied. Not one in fifty could be driven out of Southern California. If anyone wished to sell it was only to get money to buy another place with, and for everyone who wanted to sell a dozen were ready to buy. There the lands commanded a price which purchasers with eyes wide open plainly saw was far too great, if values are to be measured by the interest that can be made from the land. There was then for lack of transportation little prospect that it ever would pay full interest on the investment. Yet they bought and improved and the faster prices rose the more numerous and eager became the buyers. It was plain that they were in fact buying comfort, immunity from snow and slush, from piercing winds and sleet-clad streets, from sultry days and sleepless nights, from thun-

A Mountain Ranch, 4,500 Feet Above Tide Water, San Diego County.

der-storms, cyclones, malaria, mosquitoes, and bed-bugs. All of which, in plain language, means that they were buying climate, a business that has now been going on for fifteen years and reached a stage of progress which the world has never seen before and of which no wisdom can forsee the end. The proportion of invalids among these settlers was very great at first; but the numbers of those in no sense invalids but merely sick of bad weather, determined to endure no more of it, and able to pay for good weather, increased so fast that by 1880 not one in twenty of the new settlers could be called an invalid. They were simply rich refugees.

In 1880 the rich refugee had become such a feature in the land and increasing so fast in numbers that Los Angeles and San Bernardino Counties began to feel a decided "boom." From 1880 to 1885 Los Angeles City grew from about twelve thousand to thirty thousand, and both counties more than doubled their population. But all this time San Diego was about as completely fenced out by a system of misrepresentation as it was by its isolation before the building of the railroad. Much of this misrepresentation was simply well-meaning ignorance; but the most of it was—pure, straight lying so universal from the editor to the brakeman on the cars and the bootblack on the street that it seemed to be a regularly organized plan. So thorough was its effect that at the opening of 1885 San Diego had felt scarcely any of the great prosperity under full headway only a hundred miles north.

But when the extension of the railroad to Barstow was begun and recognized as a movement of the Santa Fé railway system to make its terminus on San Diego Bay, the rich refugee determined to come down and see whether a great railroad was foolish enough to cross hundreds of miles of desert for the sake of making a terminus in another desert. He came and found that though the country along the coast in its unirrigated state was not as inviting as the irrigated lands of Los Angeles and San Bernardino, there yet was plenty of water in the interior that could be brought upon it. He found there was plenty of "back country" as rich as any around Los Angeles, only it was more out of sight behind hills and table-lands, and less concentrated than in the next two counties above. He found a large and beautiful bay surrounded by thousands and thousands of acres of fine rich slopes and table-lands, abounding in the most picturesque building sites on earth. He found a climate made, by its more southern latitude and inward sweep of the coast, far superior to that of a hundred miles north, and far better adapted to the lemon, orange, and other fine fruits. He found the only harbor on the Pacific Coast south of San Francisco; a harbor to which the proud Los Angeles herself would soon look for most of her supplies by sea; one which shortens by several hundred miles the distance from the lands of the setting sun to New York; a harbor which the largest merchant vessels can enter in the heaviest storm and lie at rest without dragging an anchor or chafing paint on a wharf.

The growth of San Diego now began in earnest, and by the end of 1885 its future was plainly assured. A very few who predicted a population of fifty thousand in five years were looked upon as wild, even by those who believed most firmly in its future. Even those who best knew the amount of land behind it and the great water resources of its high mountains in the interior believed that twenty-five thousand in five years would be doing well enough. Its growth since that time has exceeded fondest hope. It is in truth a surprise to all and no one can truthfully pride himself upon superior sagacity, however well founded his expectations for the future may be. At the close of 1885 it had probably about five thousand people. At the close of 1887, the time of writing this sketch, it has fully thirty thousand with a more rapid rate of increase than ever. New stores, hotels and dwellings are arising on every hand from the center to the farthest outskirts in more bewildering numbers than before, and people are pouring in at double the rate they did but six months ago. It is now impossible to keep track of its progress. No one seems any longer to know or care who is putting up the big buildings, and it is becoming difficult to find a familiar face in the crowd or at the hotels.

It may well be doubted if any city has ever before had such a growth of the same character. Mushroom towns there have been of course. Mines and railroads have built up some towns with great speed. But the buildings, the improvements and the people have all shown that it was but a temporary gathering liable to dissolve at any time.

Not so with San Diego. The hundreds of costly residences, the thousands of less expensive but still luxurious homes, the scores of solid business blocks, the great wharves, machine shops, and warehouses, the miles of street railway, water and gas pipes, tell of a different class of people from those that settle ephemeral towns. The electric lights, the hundreds of thousands of dollars spent in grading the streets, cutting down hills and filling up low ground, the perfect system of glazed-pipe sewers costing four hundred thousand dollars, indicate a people who are not building for to-day. The shipping in the harbor, the millions of feet of lumber landed every week, the loaded wagons and cars that daily start for the interior, have no temporary look about them. The number of the new residents who are very wealthy is certainly such as no new city ever before received in so short a time.

The whole bay region of which San Diego is the center is enjoying to a great extent the same prosperity and settling with the same class of people. Some forty miles of steam-dummy road now run in various directions around it and extensions of fully forty more are under construction. An electric road is now running to the farthest end of University

Heights and will have miles of branches; while a cable-road is about to climb the table-lands far out into the outskirts. The fine lands about National City are fast being covered with fine residences and the new water works, costing over six hundred thousand dollars and now complete, will hasten its progress. Coronado Beach has reached a stage of development that few ever dreamed of seeing, yet Pacific Beach, a few miles above it, is already close upon its heels with great and costly improvements, and the first day's sales of lots there amounted to two hundred thousand dollars.

Three things now appear certain:—

First, that the San Diego Bay region is, for a certain class of people, the most desirable residence on earth.

Second, that it is to be the greatest summer resort as well as the greatest winter resort on either coast of America.

Third, that it is to be the harbor and distributing point not only for its own interior, Lower California, which, under the work of the International Company of Mexico is now fast settling, but for San Bernardino County, and also for Los Angeles as soon as the short line of the Santa Fé, now graded to Santa Ana, is done.

The whirligig of time brings in its revenges but it is surely a strange freak of the wheel that turns into San Diego's back country the two counties that have so long retarded her growth by the oft-repeated story that she had "no back country." Yet the great Maker of harbors has so decreed.

CHAPTER VII.

THE BAY REGION.

SAN DIEGO BAY is the only harbor in California south of San Francisco. There are several roadsteads, fondly called *harbors* by the dwellers on the shore, where a vessel may anchor in fair weather, and discharge by lighters. But by the word *harbor*, the great world means a place that a vessel can enter with safety, tie up at a wharf and discharge her crew. A place where vessels have to hold themselves ready to put to sea at any moment for safety cannot be made a harbor by any stretch of fancy or Government funds. San Diego bar has twenty-three feet of water at low tide, and is so smooth that the largest vessels pass over it during the heaviest storms ever known. During the great storm of February, 1878, when the wind reached the highest point ever registered by the signal service at San Diego, the *Hassler*, a large steamer of the United States coast survey, lay during the whole storm directly upon the bar, taking soundings and surveying the harbor. During that same storm the coast line steamer *Orizaba* had to pass every stopping-place between San Diego and San Francisco, and lie off San Francisco three days before daring to cross its bar. At San Diego is often seen what is a rare sight at any seaport in the world, a full-rigged ship of the largest size entering under full sail, sailing all the way up the channel, turning around and sailing up to the wharf—all done without a harbor pilot or steam tug. And this is done too by foreign vessels, whose pilots have never before entered the bay.

The bay of San Diego is about twelve miles long, and from one mile to two and a half miles broad, with abundance of deep water for thousands of vessels. It has miles of good wharfage front, completely landlocked and sheltered. The report of the United States coast survey furnishes the most incontestable proof of all these facts, as well as much other interesting information about it. It is certain to be not only the principal port of Southern California, but will be the Pacific port of a line of steamers to China, Australia and Japan, being some five hundred miles nearer than San Francisco. The completion of any of the

Hotel Del Coronado, Coronado Beach, San Diego, Cal.

canal or ship railroad schemes on the Isthmus will also be certain to secure it a large commerce.

Surrounding this bay are miles upon miles of slope and table-land of fine quality lying in almost perfect shape for town sites, villas, and ornamental places, where beauty and profit may go hand in hand.

Next in size to San Diego is National City, four miles farther up the bay, also in the full enjoyment of the new prosperity. It, too, has a long and excellent water front, with plenty of wharf room in deep water. It is the terminus of the railroad, and has all the railroad shops, stores, and general offices. Its present population, including suburban places on the adjoining slopes and in the neighboring valleys, is about three thousand, which is rapidly increasing. It is situated upon the National Rancho, one of the most valuable ranchos in the county. To the wise liberality of the owners in giving about seventeen thousand acres of the choicest part of this tract to the railroad, San Diego County is indebted for getting it much sooner than it would otherwise have come. From the National Rancho have come most of the choicest products, that have shown what the county can do; the lemons that have captured all the premiums at the fairs of Riverside and Los Angeles; the oranges that took the premiums at New Orleans over the best of Florida; while its raisins, olives, and deciduous fruits are surpassed by none in the State.

The area of choice land surrounding National City, sweeps around the southeast side of the bay to the Mexican line in almost unbroken slope toward the water, terminating on the east in the high rolling Otay mesa, containing some five thousand acres of fine land; on the south in the rich valley of the Tia Juana River, and on the ocean side in a large alluvial tract of rich, warm soil, forming the upper end of the peninsula that forms the bay, part of which is now known as Coronado Heights. On this are also situated the new towns of Oneonta and South San Diego. This peninsula then runs northward for several miles in a long strip that shuts out the sea completely. Opposite the city of San Diego, it widens out into a large tract of about twenty-five hundred acres, almost divided by an arm of the bay called Spanish Bight. Upon the southern division of this, containing some eleven hundred acres, and over a mile in its narrowest diameter, a remarkable improvement is now almost complete. Within two years, nearly a million and a half of dollars have been expended in preparing this for residence. The whole has been cleared of the native vegetation, laid out and mapped, and water piped across the bay. A large steam ferry connects it with the main-land; a steam motor road carries the visitor across it in a few moments, where bath-houses are so arranged that he may bathe winter or summer, either in the surf or the bay, at his pleasure. A $1,000,000 hotel, first-class in every respect, and lighted by electricity, has just been built, water works and a perfect system of small pipe sewers are complete, everything needed for comfort or convenience, for either resident or traveler, is being provided as fast as money can do it; and Coronado Beach will soon be known as the most remarkable watering-place in America, if not in the world. There have been $2,600,000 worth of lots sold here within a year.

The high promontory on the north, known as Point Loma, runs out into the sea, sheltering the bay from the western winds, has abundance of good land upon its slopes and top, but is as yet but slightly settled, though a town called Roseville has been laid out in a very attractive and sheltered portion of it. When water is piped to it, and the street railroad now in progress reaches it, the southern slopes of this promontory will make fine residence property and be in high demand. Just beyond where Point Loma joins the main-land, lies Old Town. From here the land widens and slopes more gently away from the bay until it spreads out into San Diego proper.

Old Town is now connected with San Diego by a steam motor railroad, which will be extended to Roseville and along the north shore of the bay. This will make a continuous line of horse and steam motor railroad around the bay. Within some twelve miles of the bay, on the north, south, and east, there are fully one hundred thousand acres of arable table-land or mesa, most of which will in a few years be irrigated in the ways hereinafter mentioned. A little beyond Old Town is the new and beautiful suburb known as Pacific Beach, with the new villa sites of Morena lying midway between. Pacific Beach is in the hands of a company bent on making it rival even Coronado. A stupendous hotel, a fine college, electric lights, bath-houses, street railroads, and all else needed to make it attractive, are under way to be completed as fast as money can complete them. A few miles farther up the shore is La Jolla Park, a very picturesque spot. And on the western slope of the northern side of Point Loma lies Ocean Beach, also a new and attractive watering-place.

From all the shores and table-lands around the bay, a wide and varied prospect opens upon one, but the best is from the highlands of Point Loma back of Roseville. There the great ocean, its smooth face unmarred except by the high, rocky ridges of the Coronado Islands, thirty miles away, seems almost to embrace one, stretching so far and so vast, north, south, and west, with the bright waters of False Bay running around one on the north, and San Diego Bay reaching far inland on the south. For miles the placid face of San Diego Bay lies shining in the bright sunlight, broken here and there by a wharf, ship, or sail-boat, the plunge of the pelican or rolling of porpoises. Along the inner shore lie the two cities, fast spreading toward one another in a line of houses, and far away in the south can be seen the line of set-

THE BAY REGION. 33

tlements in the Otay and Tia Juana Valleys. Over the table-lands that slope from the bay, chains of lofty hills rise tier after tier, looking down upon the vast ocean up to the high, pine-clad lines of the distant mountains that bound the great desert. High, rocky spurs studded with bowlders, towering peaks of bare gray granite, soft, grassy slopes and timbered highlands roll away skyward into lofty ridges clad in cedar and oak. On the south, far away into Mexico, the whole dissolves in a hazy mist from which rise in long blue waves the outlines of its high mountains and table-lands. On the north, over one hundred miles away, lie the great, snowy tops of the San Bernardino Mountains, and a little to the east of them the yellow sides of Palomar swell a mile skyward into a long blue line of timber. And over it all lies an almost eternal sunshine, unbroken often for weeks by the faintest cloud, and over it ever plays a gentle breeze that never fails to fan one, yet never loses its temper.

CHAPTER VIII.

THE INTERIOR.

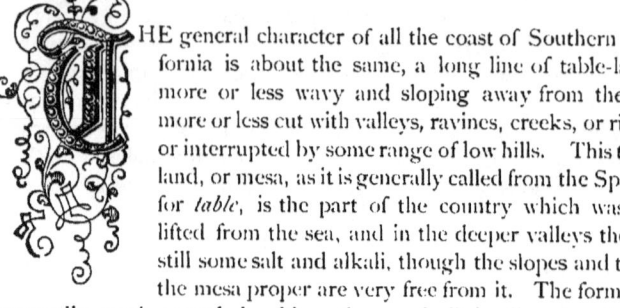

THE general character of all the coast of Southern California is about the same, a long line of table-lands, more or less wavy and sloping away from the sea, more or less cut with valleys, ravines, creeks, or rivers, or interrupted by some range of low hills. This table-land, or mesa, as it is generally called from the Spanish for *table*, is the part of the country which was last lifted from the sea, and in the deeper valleys there is still some salt and alkali, though the slopes and top of the mesa proper are very free from it. The formation is generally sand, gravel, bowlder, clay, and silt in all sorts of alternations beneath; but the top soil is nearly always of fine gray or red granite, sometimes both, though sometimes an adobe, which again is often mixed with fine granite. These mesas reach from five to twelve or fifteen miles from the coast, and are often found far in the interior as benches around some broad valley or plain. Where irrigable they command the highest price of all lands. Their value is generally dependent upon their elevation above the valleys or sea, the higher ones being generally more desired, and their value, not only for residences, but for fruit-growing, is constantly rising.

Over such a table-land you pass for some twelve miles in going from San Diego to the interior. Some of it looks hard and sterile, but nearly all of it is good land, needing only good plowing to equal the best valley land. Its climate, free by its elevation from frosts in winter nights, is tempered by the coast breezes from the heat of summer noons. Yet most of it is far enough from the coast to be free from the freshness of the sea, and is lifted to a point that gives a grand, far-reaching view of ocean and mountain. This mesa reaches far away to the north, broken by the cañon of the San Diego River, and far away into the south to the Mexican line, broken by the Sweetwater and Otay Valleys.

Some twelve miles back of San Diego, this mesa falls suddenly off about two hundred and fifty feet into a broad valley called El Cajon. In and around this valley and its connections are some twenty thousand

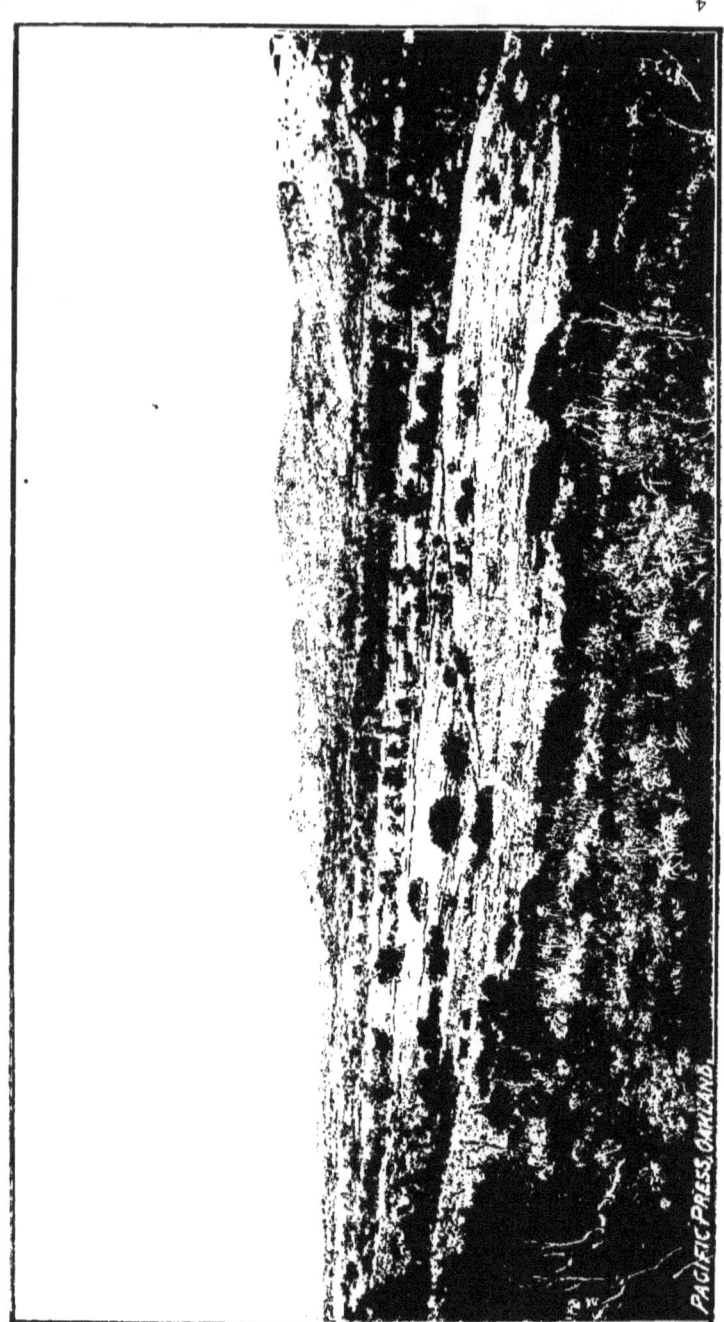

A View in Montserrat, San Luis Rey Valley, San Diego County.

acres of fine rich land. The valley land proper is well suited to the raisin grape, and Cajon raisins have within four years won an almost national reputation, and shown what the county can do. Around the main valley and its branches are thousands of acres of slope and small mesa, which are as fine orange and lemon lands as can be found, and unexcelled for residence property. El Cajon has a population of nearly three hundred and is rapidly growing.

Having seen El Cajon, the average tourist thinks he has seen the whole county; for the girdle of high, rugged hills by which it is embraced gives little indication of anything around or beyond it, yet valleys of various sizes lie just over the hills on all sides, with small mesas or slopes leading up to the higher hills. Six miles up a winding mountain road brings us to another broad valley of some fifteen thousand acres of fine plain and slope, twelve hundred feet above El Cajon, which averages only four hundred feet above the sea. This is the Santa Maria, an old Spanish grant. Here again the land breaks on the sides into hills, some quite smooth and rolling, others high, sharp, and heavily studded with bowlders. You notice that the roads show plenty of travel, but you see few people or houses, or cultivated farms; a feature you may note all over the county. This is because the large grants are as yet quite unsettled, many of them being still closed to settlement, while most of those that are open have been upon the market but a few months. The land is, however, being fast taken up, as you see here and as you saw in El Cajon, but the great majority of the settlers are on Government land around these large grants. As remarked before, these dark chaparral-clad hills or bowlder-studded ridges that seem to bound all that is tillable, are full of pockets, little valleys and parks in every direction, and in the girdle of hills around this one valley are stowed away over fifty farms whose presence one would never suspect, while just over the ridge on the right are about four thousand acres of fine plow land, between us and the tall mountain of granite that seems so near,—the rancho San Vicente.

Here you begin to see more timber than on the lower levels. The hills and slopes around this valley once abounded with great live oaks, but fire and the ax have swept away the most of them. But you can see a great change in the general appearance of the country. In almost every one of the larger ravines, and on the larger hill-sides, you may now find living springs, which you could not do along the coast. Everything indicates a land of much more rain than you have yet seen. And such is the fact, this valley being upon the second rain-belt of the county, where the winter rains are always ample for full crops. The new town Ramona lies near its eastern edge, in a fine location.

Leaving the Santa Maria by the Julian road, you pass through a series of smaller valleys, constantly rising one above another. Here you find running water in all the little brooks, timber increasing, and farms more like Eastern farms than you have yet seen; in short, evidences of more rain even than in Santa Maria. Soon the road runs into a larger valley of about two thousand acres including slopes and all. This is known as Ballena, and is the center of quite a settlement of some six thousand acres, of which, as before, the surrounding hills show no sign. It is twenty-five hundred feet above the sea, and about one thousand feet above the Santa Maria. Still up we go, passing again through small valleys, and among hills in whose hidden pockets whole farms may be stowed away, until at an elevation of three thousand feet we come into the valley of the Rancho Santa Ysabel. This is the central valley of the rancho, containing, with its branches and slopes, some four thousand acres of fine land, but used with the adjoining hills only for stock range, dairy, and cheese-making. Here are still more evidences of a heavy rainfall. Springs are on almost every hill-side, little streams in every ravine, while nearly across the center runs a creek that in the driest time of the year runs a large stream of the purest water. All these surrounding hills, like the main valley, are splendid stock range, affording abundance of feed. In fact, the very best feed is in those bad years when the winter rains along the coast have been little but light storms of drizzling mist. Yet scarce anything would appear less fit for general farming. It will be worth your while, however, to spend a whole day on that range of high rolling hills on the northwest dotted with live oak timber, and yellow with ripe wild oats and grass.

Up a long grade the road winds, until some five hundred feet above the main valley you reach a broad tract of several miles in width, rolling and tumbling in great swells of alternate hill and valley from thirty-five hundred to forty-five hundred feet above the sea. Part of this belongs to the Rancho Santa Ysabel, and is still held in stock range, but beyond the rancho line on the Government land you will find some thirty farms. This tract is called Mesa Grande, and contains some six thousand acres of splendid plow land. Here too you find plenty of springs and running brooks. The farms are still more like Eastern farms than those of Ballena, a scarcity of rain is unknown, all crops and fruits are a certainty, and the farmers have no anxiety except the fear of too much rain. The whole now looks like an eastern country with no resemblance whatever to the land thirty miles west, and three thousand feet below us; the country from which nearly all impressions of San Diego County are taken.

A glance at the distant sea shows that we are well up in the world, but almost as high again in the east loom rolling slopes, covered with grass and timber like those of Mesa Grande, and topped by dark, pine-clad hills. You have already seen enough of what hills may contain to warn you against assuming that you have reached the limits of settlement. Those hills too are worth inspection.

Crossing again the main valley of Santa Ysabel we take the road to Julian, and again our way leads upward. Through a few miles of tumbling hills containing abundance of grass, but otherwise of little use, we go where the land again opens into valleys and slopes covered with rank grass and scattered timber. The proportion of arable land is much greater than before, farms open upon every hand, but, as before, dozens more are hidden by intervening ridges. High hills, yellow with dried grass, and higher ones blue with timber, still rise ahead, and soon we roll into the little town of Julian, forty-two hundred feet above the sea. In and around the Julian region are some twenty thousand acres of tillable land, though most of it is partly covered by timber. The population of the town and immediate surroundings is about six hundred. Taking the short cut known as "Tally's road," from here to the Cuyamaca Rancho, we soon enter denser timber growing on gently rolling slopes, broken at intervals by open meadows clad in deep grass. Here you notice in abundance a new oak, much like the Eastern red oak, though this first appears as low down as thirty-five hundred feet. You also find an entirely new live oak, stately and shining, with trunk and bark much like the Eastern white oak. This is the mountain variety of the white live oak you have seen lower down, which now disappears. Through some miles of oak timber, mixed with an occasional pine, we ride until the road suddenly runs out into a broad open flat of several thousand acres, part of the Cuyamaca Rancho. At the lower end of this is one of the reservoirs of the San Diego Flume Co., covering about one thousand acres with a dam thirty-five feet high. On the east the timber now disappears, but on the west it bristles darker, taller, and denser on the three tall peaks that rise from fifteen hundred to two thousand feet above us, the elevation of this flat being about forty-six hundred feet above tide water. Once here it will well repay the trouble to climb the tallest of these peaks, it being very easily ascended. A wagon may be driven to within a thousand feet or so of the top. The road winds through rich meadows, and then through timber until you reach the "cold spring," a spring flowing about one hundred gallons a minute of the purest and coldest water. From here the way to the top on foot is quite easy. As you ascend, the common live oak of the lowlands disappears and only the red oak and white live oak are left. The "bull pine," whose massive trunks have hitherto lined our path, begins to disappear, and sugar pines as large as six feet in diameter take its place. The silver fir and the cedar, bright, stately trees with tall, trim trunks, also appear in abundance, forming in most places an almost solid shade. The extreme top is a pile of rocks, the highest point but one in the whole county and sixty-five hundred feet above the sea. From here on a clear day one can see with a glass the greater part of the southern half of the county, and can learn better than in any other way the conditions of its peculiar climate.

But a few miles from us on the east, the land falls off five thousand feet into the Colorado Desert, a sea of fiery sand broiling beneath an almost eternal sun, apparently as vast and level as the great shimmering plain of water fifty miles to the west. A hundred miles away the snowy scalp of Grayback of the San Bernardino range lies like a cloud two miles in the northern sky with San Jacinto, but a trifle lower beside it; while between them and us runs the long, lofty chain of blue and gray mountains that separate the western part of San Diego County from the great desert. Away on the south the range continues dark with pine, green with oak, or bluish with chaparral until lost in the hazy outlines of the highlands of Mexico. From here you can look down on hundreds of rolling slopes, golden with dry grass, wild oats, or stubble, or covered with scattered oaks like some old Eastern apple orchard; on hundreds of little valleys and parks, with little farms nestled in them; on larger plains, yellow with grass or stubble; on deep cañons filled with eternal shade, but having plenty of good land; and on broad rolling table-lands covered with chaparral, but as good land as any. High mountains rise in all directions; some broad-backed, like Volcan, just beyond Julian, or Palomar still farther northwest, both almost level with our feet, and crowned with forests, breaking away in long ridges clad with grass along the backs and sides, with dark, timbered gulches between. Others are lower and clad only in chaparral, or scattered trees, like the great granite dome El Cajon, or Lyons Peak. And both north and south, the whole land is tumbling and tumbling in long alternations of valley, slope, and hill, away to the distant sea. And now it is easy to see how so little is known of the county. Unapproachable on the east because of the desert, from the south because no American travel comes that way, only the coast line and a line of the northern edge can be seen by the ordinary traveler. These beautiful timbered mountains, and the long, rich slopes that lead away from them, and the fine valleys hidden among them, show nothing but barrenness from the desert side; while from the coast they look by distance even more dreary than the bare, rocky hills of the coast rain belt. The desert is, of course, uninhabitable, as is that of San Bernardino County, but we shall hereafter see it is worth more for its effect on climate than if its millions of acres of burning sand were Illinois prairie; while the inhabitable part of the county is a long slope fifty to sixty miles wide, rising eastward to a general level of five thousand feet, forming a rim of the great basin of the desert five thousand feet deep.

SCENE IN PARADISE ... OUNTY.

CHAPTER IX.

THE LOWER COAST DIVISION.

ASSING directly from the coast to the highest tracts of arable land in the county, the reader will now be prepared to examine it intelligently in detail. He will now understand the great difference caused by increase of elevation, and distance from the coast; how the good land in this county is broken and scattered into a thousand shapes; how a greater variety of climates can be found here than in any other county; and how a greater variety of productions can be raised in perfection. Ask any one of the old stockmen of Los Angeles or San Bernardino Counties where their horses and cattle were saved in such disastrous years as 1864. They will tell you it was not to their own mountains that they drove them, but to the highlands of San Diego. The reason is simple. In those counties when you pass an elevation of fifteen hundred feet above sea level, you leave below you about all the good land there is. Here, at that elevation you just reach the best, that is, from the old standard of values,—a standard that for many purposes is still useful. This county has ten times the area of arable land lifted into a region of certain and abundant rainfall, that both those counties together have; their highlands being generally quite barren, with a very few small mountain valleys, although the general elevation of those mountains is much higher than those of San Diego County.

Nevertheless, by the new standard, the lower lands here are the more valuable for some purposes, because the colder winter nights of the higher levels do not permit the raising to any extent of oranges, lemons, and other delicate fruits, because their greater rainfall makes them less desirable for the invalid, and because they are less easy of access. We will examine first the sections nearer the coast, returning to these highlands.

Beginning at the Mexican line, at a little above tide water, we find in the Tia Juana Valley some three thousand acres of fine gray granite alluvium, with water but a few feet below the surface, making the raising of all deep-rooted vegetation easy without irrigation. This soil, which is found in all the river bottoms, is the finer wash from the interior hills, wonderfully rich, and it can be plowed in any condition of moisture. It is always fine corn and alfalfa land, excellent also for vines, deciduous fruits and vegetables. This valley is all taken up with farms. There is no trouble here with our Mexican neighbors, the rowdy element that is spoiling for a fight being absent on both sides of the line, and the best of feeling prevailing.

The Otay mesa has already been mentioned. Between that and the National Ranch, at an elevation of from fifty to two hundred feet, lies the Otay Valley, containing, with adjacent slopes, some two thousand acres of good land, most of which is now cultivated and dotted with vineyards, orchards, and houses, nearly all done within the last two years. The upper part of this valley is included in the Otay Rancho, a fine body of valley, slope, and mesa from two hundred to eight hundred feet high, containing some four thousand acres of arable land, lying from eight to twelve miles from the coast.

On the northeast, a little farther from the coast, and separated from Mexico by the blue range of San Ysidro, is the Janal, a rancho already mentioned, containing about the same amount of arable land as the Otay, but with less valley land and more mesa and slope. Both this and the Otay are composed of red granite soil and a brown adobe of extraordinary richness, with an elevation of from four hundred to eight hundred feet above the sea. Some six miles easterly from the Janal, at an elevation of about five hundred and fifty feet, lies the Jamul Rancho, containing about five thousand acres of arable land, nearly all fine red granite soil. This is bounded on the east by a high rocky range from three thousand to four thousand feet high, which, like all other ridges, hides a score or more of mountain valleys and parks.

Between the Janal and the coast lies the tract of the National Rancho, already mentioned as given to the railroad. North of this we come to the valley of the Sweetwater, part of which is included in the National Rancho. Passing several miles up this valley, which contains several thousand acres of rich bottom land like the Tia Juana, with long, tillable slopes on either side, we come to the Jamacha Rancho, at an elevation above the sea of from two hundred and fifty to five hundred feet. This has some four thousand acres of fine red land and is about sixteen miles from the coast. Upon this is the new town of La Presa, one of the best and most picturesque of all the suburban town sites. Over the ridge on the north lies El Cajon. Behind the peak of San Miguel, which towers four thousand feet upon the south, lie the Janal and Jamul; and over the low hills on the northwest lies Spring Valley, a choice body of some three thousand acres of Government land, now cut up into farms and green with vineyards and orchards, lying about twelve miles from the coast and from four hundred to seven hundred feet above it. At its upper end is the new town of Helix.

First National Bank Building, San Diego, Cal.

Continuing up the Sweetwater several miles we pass farm after farm, and place after place where good farms can be made, and pass as usual numerous farms hidden from sight by hills or timber. About twenty-five miles from the sea the Sweetwater bottom narrows to a rocky cañon in which there is scarcely any arable land for nearly twenty miles. We leave the valley on the south, however, and turn north upon one of its tributaries along which are several farms and several places for others, until at an elevation of twelve hundred feet and twenty-five miles from the coast we reach Alpine District just east of El Cajon; a point to which we will again return.

North of the Sweetwater the coast lands are composed, as far as the San Diego River, some ten miles in all, of the mesa lands already mentioned as lying around and behind National City and San Diego, the elevation ranging from one hundred and fifty to six hundred feet above the sea. Back of National City the slope is very gentle. Back of San Diego the land rises at first faster than at National, and then from a general level of three hundred feet slopes gently inland. All these mesas are bounded on the east by Spring Valley and El Cajon.

The lower valley of the San Diego River, called Mission Valley, is well settled and contains some four thousand acres of gray granite alluvium, with slopes of red land on either side, in all some five thousand acres, all very rich. Some ten miles from the coast it narrows into a cañon, which about four miles farther east runs into El Cajon.

On the north side of the San Diego River the land rises again into a fine mesa from three hundred to seven hundred feet high, as yet but little settled, but containing long sweeps of fine land, with a climate equal to any. This reaches with but few breaks to Peñasquitos Creek on the north, and Poway and El Cajon on the east.

Poway is a well-settled interior valley like the Jamul, about fifteen miles from the ocean and about five hundred feet above it. It contains about six thousand acres of fine red land, but, like everything else we have seen, has numerous branches and side valleys, not discovered except by special search, which increase considerably the amount of arable land. Over the low ridge on the south lies El Cajon; over the high rocky range, from three thousand to four thousand feet high, on the east, lies the Santa Maria; hidden among the rolling hills on the west, lies Peñasquitos Rancho; and on the north is the rancho San Bernardo.

The San Bernardo, about twelve miles from the coast, and five hundred to seven hundred feet high, contains about twelve thousand acres of fine red land with several very thriving farms. It joins Escondido on the north and shares largely in the general advantages of that large valley. The greater part of it is rich mesa and slope and is above the frost belt of the bottom of the Bernardo River. Easterly from Bernardo, about eighteen miles from the sea and five hundred feet above it, lies the valley of San Pasqual, now well settled and containing some four thousand acres of bottom land and slope, all very productive and threaded by the Bernardo River.

Peñasquitos Rancho is a long, narrow valley nearly west of Poway, about twelve miles in length, and some four miles from the coast at its lower end. Its elevation is from one hundred to six hundred feet above the sea and it contains with slopes and all some four thousand acres of good, arable land. At its lower end it opens into Soledad, a small valley having considerable good land at its upper end. Just around the opening of Soledad Valley upon the sea lies the handsome seaside town of Del Mar, with some three hundred inhabitants. East and north of Del Mar, are two or three miles of mesa covered with brush but mostly good land, and then we descend into the valley of the San Dieguito River.

Here are some six thousand acres in all of fine alluvium with slopes of red land, and then the land suddenly rises into another mesa similar to the last. In about two miles this falls again into the valley of San Elijo, a small valley of rich land with slopes of adobe and granite loam and running back some six miles from the sea to an elevation of about three hundred feet. This again rises into a narrow mesa of red land, a part of the Encinitas Rancho, which descends again into the valley of Encinitas. Encinitas is a small Mexican grant of four thousand acres, of which twenty-five hundred are arable, consisting of rich gray loam, adobe, and red granite soil at various elevations from one hundred and fifty to five hundred feet above the sea and about four miles distant. West of the valley on a fine table-land is the town of Encinitas with some two hundred inhabitants. Passing Encinitas Rancho the land is rougher for a few miles, with salt washes reaching up from the coast with fine strips of mesa between, reaching to the very coast; that between Encinitas and the sea being especially fine.

A few miles farther on lies the Rancho Agua Hedionda lying immediately on the coast and running back some six miles to an elevation of five hundred feet. This contains some ten thousand acres in all of plow land, mostly red fertile mesa rolling and abounding in most picturesque building spots that look down upon the sea, with rich valley land between. Just north of this is Carlsbad, a new watering-place with a mineral spring whose waters are attracting much attention. A few miles north of Carlsbad is Oceanside, a fast-growing seaside town of over a thousand people.

East of Agua Hedionda is the San Marcos Rancho, a fine combination of valley, slope, and low mesa running from six to twelve miles from the sea at an average elevation of six hundred feet. It contains in all some six thousand acres of arable land. Upon this some six miles from the sea is the new town of San Marcos in a very fertile and picturesque spot.

Joining this on the east and San Bernardo on the south, lies the Rancho Escondido, generally known on the map as Rincon del Diablo, twelve miles from the sea and seven hundred feet above it. This has some eleven thousand acres of fine arable land mostly in valley alluvium, smooth plains, and low mesa land of fine red granite soil, the whole lying in an almost solid body. Escondido is rapidly settling and has now a population of about eight hundred, of which some six hundred are in the town.

Between Escondido, San Marcos, San Bernardo, and the coast the land is mountainous and rough for several miles, but scattered around in various parts of it are many settlers in small valleys and on mesas.

On the north San Marcos and Escondido merge in a wide range of rocky and brushy hills reaching to a height of some two thousand feet and running through nearly to the San Luis River, containing as usual numbers of hidden valleys in which are dozens of farms.

Northwest of San Marcos the land breaks away into low, smooth hills which speedily run into mesa and valley land, of which there are fully twenty thousand acres, all fine arable land lying between Agua Hedionda, the San Luis River, and the coast, the elevation ranging from fifty to five hundred feet. This is largely Government land and contains some of the finest mesa in the county, much of it commanding a view of the sea.

Included in this, however, are two small ranchos of about twenty-two hundred acres each, of which about two thousand in each are arable and of fine quality: Buena Vista, about eight miles from the coast and about five hundred feet high, and Guajome, same distance and from one hundred and fifty to four hundred feet high.

CHAPTER X.

THE NORTHERN DIVISION.

THE San Luis River Valley is a long strip of the same gray granite alluvium that forms the river bottoms generally with slopes of red land leading from the mesas and rolling hills on either side. About twelve miles from the coast this runs through the Rancho Montserrate, a fine tract of valley and mesa, containing some six thousand acres of plow land from three hundred to seven hundred feet above the sea, running on the north into the district of Fallbrook. Beyond Montserrate the river wanders through the high, rugged hills for some five miles to the old Mission of Pala, with valleys and low slopes among the adjoining hills, embracing from the sea up to Pala (exclusive of Montserrate) about six thousand acres of arable land.

Returning to the coast we find on the north of the San Luis the great rancho Santa Margarita, threaded by the Santa Margarita or Temecula River, and containing some fifty thousand acres of arable land. This rancho runs from the coast some fifteen miles back, reaching an elevation of about eight hundred feet on the south side of the river and on the north some three thousand feet. On the south it is nearly all high, rolling mesa; on the north of the river a long, low strip of fine mesa reaching to the line of Los Angeles County, rising gently from the sea for a mile or two, then swelling into high hills clad with scattered oaks and abounding in little valleys and parks of rich land. Along the river are some five thousand acres or more of rich bottom lands of granite alluvium.

South of the river the mesa continues beyond the line of the rancho and forms the settlement of Fallbrook at a general level of eight hundred feet above the sea and fifteen miles from it. Here are some five thousand acres of deep rolling red land, not including Montserrate, which here joins it. Fallbrook affords a good instance of the manner in which the average tourist and land hunter examines San Diego County. The railroad passes some six hundred feet below through a narrow, rocky canon. At Fallbrook the train stops twenty minutes for meals at a little station on about three acres of ground at the mouth of a narrow cañon

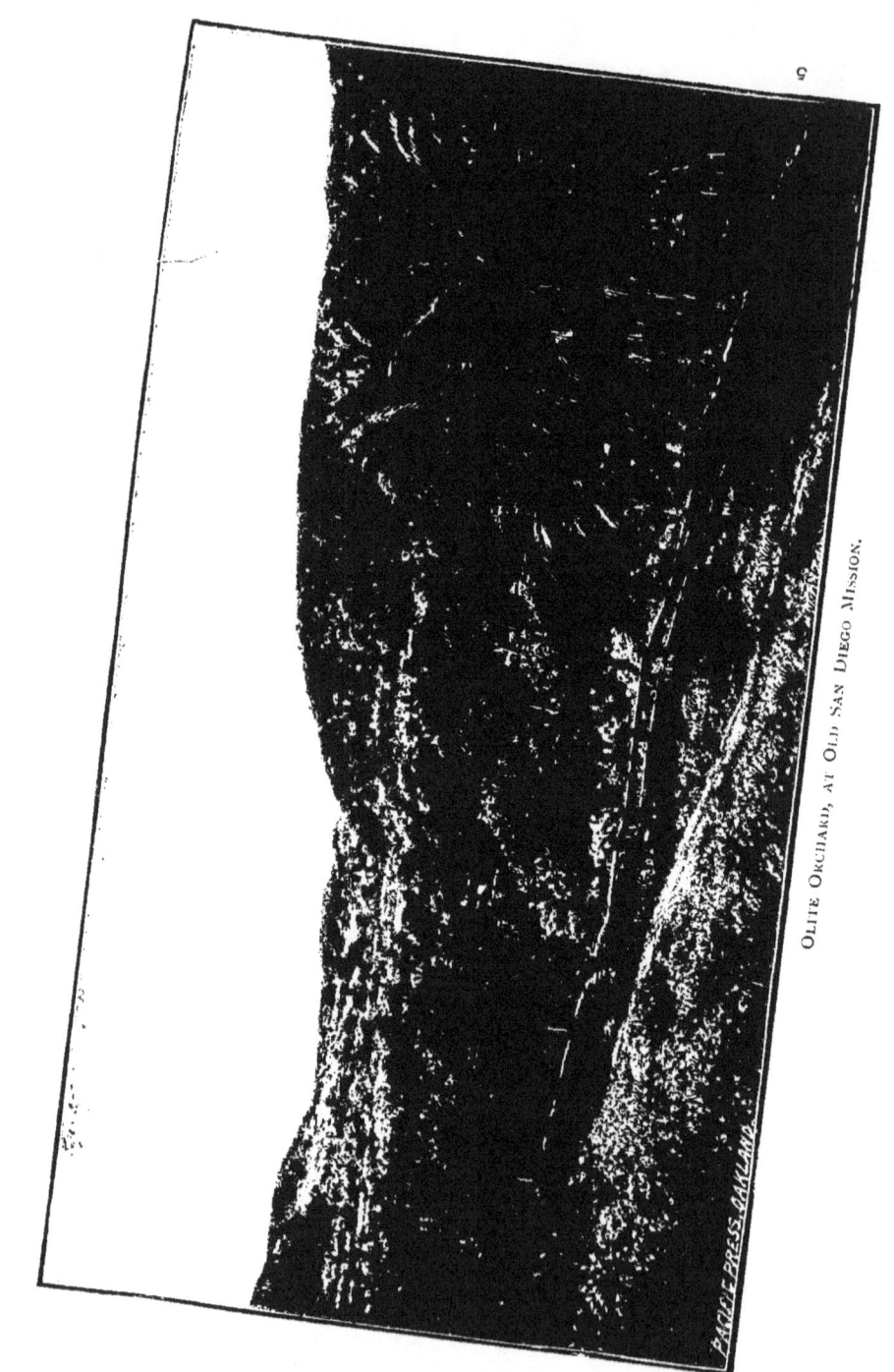

OLIVE ORCHARD, AT OLD SAN DIEGO MISSION.

up which the road leads a mile or so to the highlands above. Ye tourist alights, looks around the hills, and then contemptuously at the little bit of land around the station, and sagely remarks, "So this is Fallbrook, eh? Well, I don't want any of it." The district of Fallbrook embraces some twenty thousand acres of land lying some four hundred feet above the railroad and unsuspected by the traveler. Its population is about four hundred. The town has some three hundred people and is rapidly growing.

Northeast of Fallbrook some five miles lies a rich little valley of about one thousand acres, called the Vallacito; but most of the land from Fallbrook to Temecula on the northeast and Mount Palomar on the east is a succession of ridges and mountains, with but little arable land except a few little valleys and parks, in each of which two or three settlers are, as usual, stowed away out of sight.

Northeast of the Santa Margarita line on the north side of the river the lofty hills sink suddenly some twenty-five hundred feet to form a large amphitheater known as Corral de Luz, containing some twelve hundred acres of plow land on which are a dozen farms, but on the north these hills roll away in rugged, brush-clad ranges to the Los Angeles County line.

Northeast of de Luz the highlands of Santa Rosa Rancho suddenly mount to nearly two thousand feet, rolling for several miles in a charming alternation of grass-clad hills, slopes, and timber-filled valleys until the whole suddenly tumbles several hundred feet into the Temecula Rancho. Santa Rosa averages about twenty miles from the ocean and contains many thousand acres of arable land, the amount of which it is impossible to estimate closely on account of its being scattered into many small valleys and slopes, but probably five thousand in all.

Northwest of Santa Rosa the land rises to thirty-five hundred feet and over and continues on a dark jungle of chaparral mixed with bowlders and cut with ravines, with a few little valleys and parks, away to the county line of Los Angeles. But on the northeast the land suddenly sinks again and an open country consisting mainly of broad plains and low mesas, interrupted occasionally by a range of rocky or brushy hills, spreads away toward the great peak of San Jacinto ten thousand five hundred feet high and fifty miles away.

The Temecula Rancho, bounded on the west by the lofty slopes of Santa Rosa and on the east by low, open mesas, reaches from the Santa Margarita River, where it enters the cañon through which the railroad runs, some ten miles along the railroad. It contains about ten thousand acres of arable land, nearly all granite alluvium or red mesa, at an elevation of eleven hundred to fifteen hundred feet and about twenty-five miles from the sea. On the northern part of this is the town of Murrieta.

Just south of the Santa Margarita Creek at this point lies the Little Temecula Rancho, a small grant with some two thousand acres of plow land, at about the same elevation and distance inland as the other.

Northeast of this is the Pauba Rancho, about thirty miles from the coast and eleven hundred to eighteen hundred feet high, with some ten thousand acres of fine valley and low mesa, also nearly all granite soil.

Northeast of the Temecula, at an elevation of about twelve hundred feet and about twenty-five miles from the coast, is the Laguna Rancho, a long, narrow grant reaching nearly to the Los Angeles County line and embracing the largest lake in the county. Around this and southeast of it are some five thousand acres of good plow land mostly red granite and very rich. The lake is fed by the San Jacinto River. By this lake is the thriving town of Elsinore with nearly a thousand people, with Wildomar near by well on the road to overtake it. North of this river and between the railroad and the county line there is little but rough, rolling hills and rugged mesas, with the exception of a small strip near Perris. East of the railroad, however, sweeps a great plain of red granite soil, mile after mile to the east and southeast broken by small mountain ranges and rolling mesas. This is nearly all Government land with an average elevation of sixteen hundred feet. The amount of its arable land it is impossible to estimate closely; but including the Cohuilla Valley, Bladen, and a few other spots that appear before the land rises into the high range that bounds the desert, there are at the very least calculation forty thousand acres of land fit for the plow.

This tract is bounded on the north by the Rancho San Jacinto Nuevo, a grant containing some ten thousand acres of plow land, nearly all a broad plain of red granite soil about fourteen hundred and fifty feet high and some forty miles from the coast.

Joining this on the southeast lies the San Jacinto Viejo with about thirty thousand acres of arable land divided into valley land and mesa fifteen to forty feet above it. A large part of this mesa, like the bottom land, is alluvium, the rest of it being red land. This rancho lies about fifteen hundred feet above the sea level and nearly fifty miles from the coast, is threaded by the San Jacinto River and bounded on the east by the high range of the San Jacinto Mountains. On this valley land is the town of San Jacinto, with some sixteen hundred people.

This chapter and the last one include about all the lowlands of the county except a few tracts on each side of Mount Palomar better considered under the mountain division. The classification thus adopted has been more according to rainfall than to actual elevation; and even to this standard it is impossible to remain consistent without skipping around too much. Thus Fallbrook, Santa Margarita, and Santa Rosa have greater rainfall than most of the other sections mentioned, while San Jacinto is farther from the coast than Bear Valley, which has a much

Interior View of Consolidated National Bank, San Diego, Cal.

greater rainfall. Yet on the whole I have grouped together those whose climate most approaches that of the lowlands in general.

Between and around all the sections mentioned are small tracts of various sizes and so numerous that special mention of them is out of the question; though some of them, such as the country between Bernardo, Poway, and the mountains west of the Santa Maria, contain considerable fine land upon which are many prosperous farms.

The estimates thus made include only good plow land free from rocks, stumps, or swamps, and not rough land that may in future be cultivated when all else is taken up. It must not be supposed that all the other land which composes these large ranchos is worthless. I have omitted notice of it for brevity, but most of it is good stock range, nearly all of it is fair, and some of it excellent. The proportion of this to the arable land is often large, as in Santa Margarita, which has in all about one hundred and thirty thousand acres, of which not over fifty thousand would at present be considered arable. In other cases the proportion of arable land is in excess, as in Escondido, which out of twelve thousand eight hundred and forty acres has some eleven thousand of plow land.

There are also thousands of acres that will be considered good plow land in less than five years that would hardly be considered so to-day. To be on the safe side all such has been omitted. For instance, there are on Warner's Ranch (described in next chapter) some fifteen thousand acres of low, rolling hills free from rock, which can be plowed and which will in time make good fruit land. This would bring up the arable land to thirty-five thousand acres. Yet as it would scarcely be deemed good plow land to-day I leave it out. This plan will be followed throughout.

CHAPTER XI.

THE MOUNTAIN DIVISION.

SAN JACINTO, ten thousand five hundred feet high, is the highest point in the county. But this resembles the mountains of Los Angeles and San Bernardino Counties more than the general mountain part of San Diego. It has, however, a few valleys of rich land, but none of them are large enough for any purpose but stock range and isolated farms. The southern continuation of the range for many miles is of the same character until near the borders of Warner's Ranche. Between the edge of this range where it bounds the desert and Mt. Palomar, some thirty miles east, is a large tract bounded on the north by the Pauba Rancho and Cohuilla Valley and the San Jancinto plains and on the south by Warner's Ranche and the Coyote Mountains. The greater part of this is a very rough country, with numerous bare hills, steep, low, and ugly, having a few small valleys among them. This is also in many years a dry belt, the long and lofty Palomar cutting off most of the rain that comes from the coast. With the exception of a few spots like Aguanga and Oak Grove there is here little of value until we reach Warner's Ranche.

Warner's appears on the maps as San José del Valle and Valle de San Jose. It is composed of two Mexican grants lying at the southeast of Palomar with an elevation of twenty-five hundred to three thousand feet and about forty miles from the coast. It contains in all some fifteen thousand acres of fine plow land exclusive of that mentioned in the last chapter, mostly gray granite loam somewhat coarser than that found in the lower ranchos but of excellent quality for all kinds of fruit. The most of the ranche is rolling upland, but there is also considerable bottom land.

The southwest edge rolls upward a thousand feet or more in a long line of blue and yellow bluffs clad in grass, chaparral, and oak into the highlands of Mesa Grande, which we have seen before. On the south it rises over three thousand feet into the pine-clad heights of Mount Volcan, the eastern boundary of Santa Ysabel.

Northwest of Warner's Ranche the long, high back of Palomar runs away to Temecula. Palomar, commonly known as "Smith's Mountain," is about six thousand feet high and nearly twenty miles long. Its top and sides are partly clad in pine and oak, cedar and silver fir. Upon it are some six thousand acres of good plow land, fine meadows and little valleys abounding upon its top and along its sides. At the foot of its western slope, some four thousand feet below the top and upon the banks of the upper San Luis River, and some twenty-four miles from the sea, lie two Mexican grants, Pauma and Cuca.

The Cuca is a small grant about twenty-five hundred feet above sea level containing some six hundred or eight hundred acres only of arable land but of very fine quality, while Pauma, about fifteen hundred feet high, contains some four thousand acres of coarser grade than that of Cuca but still very desirable for fruit-raising.

South of the San Luis River at this point the land rises again into a broad tract from fifteen hundred to three thousand feet high running through on the southwest some twelve miles to the rugged hills that look down upon the fair Escondido, on the south some twelve miles to the edge of the deep cañon of the upper San Dieguito River, on the east some twelve miles from Escondido to the deep cañon in which Pauma Valley lies nestled, and rising on the other side with sudden sweep into the western highlands of Mesa Grande.

On the southeastern part of this lies the Rancho Guejito with some seven thousand acres of rolling mesa and valley all red granite soil, about two thousand two hundred feet above the sea and some thirty-five miles from it.

The rest of this inclosure that at a distance looks so rough and uninhabitable embraces a dozen or more valleys nearly all connected and having an average elevation of fifteen hundred feet with considerable mesa and slope. This is all known under the general name of Bear Valley and contains some seven thousand acres of plow land.

Crossing Santa Ysabel again we come to Mount Volcan, south of Warner's Ranche and five thousand to six thousand feet high. This is a broad-topped mountain with considerable arable land, grassy slopes and valleys and timber-clad ridges and gulches.

On the east this mountain suddenly falls some three thousand five hundred feet into the Rancho San Felipé. This contains some four thousand acres of fine arable land, most of it sloping away toward the desert.

Going up the cañon by way of Banner on the southeast we reach Julian and soon come once more to the Cuyamaca Rancho which we cross and go southward. The Cuyamaca contains some six thousand acres of arable land of which a part is included in the valley known as Guatay. West of the main peak of the Cuyamaca, among the forks of the San Diego River, which heads there, are some small valleys and mesas with several hundred acres of good land; but the mountains become rougher as we go south and plow land grows scarcer. South of the San Diego River we find no mountain valley larger than Viejas, which with its branches contains some twenty-five hundred acres of fine tillable land at an elevation of twenty-two hundred feet and thirty miles from the coast.

From Viejas the land falls away toward El Cajon on the east in small mesas, valleys and slopes known as Alpine District and containing a few thousand acres of plow land bounded by the deep, rough cañon of the Sweetwater on the south and on the west by the east line of El Cajon.

South of the Sweetwater the mountain valleys are smaller than on the north and steeper on their sides. Slopes and mesas of arable land are also smaller; Pine Valley, Lawson's Valley, Potrero, Cottonwood, and Milquatay are all small but very pretty and fertile valleys separated by rough mountains. A few small valleys and mesas are scattered among them and in the timbered range of the Laguna Mountains is considerable arable land. All this section is on a heavy rain belt and the arable land is very fine in quality often with good stock range between the tracts.

Upon the Colorado desert, which forms some three-fifths of the whole county, are thousands of acres of land of which the quality is good enough. Most of it cannot be irrigated at all, while much of it will some day be reclaimed by the waters of the Colorado River, by artesian wells and water from the eastern slopes of the mountains. But the rainfall is generally so light and the hot winds are so common that much cultivation is at present out of the question, and the desert is practically uninhabitable. For this reason the desert is never intended to be included when mention is made of San Diego County by any of its residents.

The estimate of arable land thus far made is a close one, rather under than over. It is greater than it would have been made five years ago and less than it will be five years from now. Yet I have taken pains to estimate it from the present standpoint. The time is not far distant when settlers will roll rocks out of the hill-sides and plant trees in their places, when hill-sides will be terraced for vineyards, and cobblestones will be raked from the soil and fences built of them, as has long been done in the East. But it would not be fair to include such lands in any estimate now, though they would add largely to the number of acres.

It will be safe to add to the acreage thus far described five per cent for small intervening tracts of which space will not permit special mention. We then have as the total acreage of fairly arable land in the county in the three divisions about five hundred and thirty thousand

SAN DIEGO COLLEGE AT PACIFIC BEACH, SAN DIEGO, CAL.

THE MOUNTAIN DIVISION.

acres. Adding five per cent we have in round numbers five hundred and fifty-five thousand acres, which exceeds the amount of fairly arable land in San Bernardino County estimated upon the same basis, and approaches very nearly that of Los Angeles County, excluding in both cases of course their share of desert.

CHAPTER XII.

WATER.

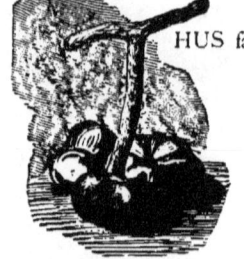

THUS far the land has been estimated as plow land pure and simple. Ninety-five per cent of it needs no clearing whatever, none of it at present needs fertilization and for many kinds of products never will need any. It does however need water. The ways and possibilities of watering are so numerous and varied, there is such difference in the distance of the underground water, such differences in the amount of rainfall, that it has been impossible within the limits of a reader's patience to consider the water question in connection with each tract. It will be necessary therefore to treat it generally using particular localities only to illustrate a principle.

As we have seen in our first trip from coast to mountain-top the rainfall increases with elevation. There are four different rain belts caused by this change, and the whole county is subject to its influence. We find however other changes for which we cannot account in this way. Thus Fallbrook has generally more rain than many other places having a greater elevation and distance from the coast; while the coast line above the Santa Margarita River has generally more than the coast below. Still the general rule is that the rainfall depends upon elevation, especially where a broad tract is elevated.

The general impression that San Diego is a dry country has been caused by the constant publication of the rain record of San Diego City to prove that it has the best climate in California, to wit, the driest. An ordinary reader would infer that this represented the rainfall of the county.

The following is the rainfall by seasons for San Diego City for fifteen years. This record is compiled by the signal service observer himself at the U. S. Signal Station at San Diego, and is the only accurate one yet published. All others are too low:—

YEARS.	INCHES.	YEARS.	INCHES.	YEARS.	INCHES.
1871–72	7.18	1876–77	3.65	1881–82	9.44
1872–73	7.41	1877–78	16.10	1882–83	4.92
1873–74	14.95	1878–79	7.81	1883–84	25.97
1874–75	5.48	1879–80	14.48	1884–85	8.60
1875–76	9.46	1880–81	5.20	1885–86	16.62

It will be seen from this that the rainfall is very variable. Such is the case all over California. The difference between the different rain belts is most apparent in the years of very low rainfall.

The second rain belt is best shown by the rainfall at Fallbrook, where we have a record of the last eleven years as follows:—

YEARS.	INCHES.	YEARS.	INCHES.
1875–76	17.51	1880–81	11.45
1876–77	8.75	1881–82	12.24
1877–78	24.84	1882–83	10.60
1878–79	8.52	1883–84	40.25
1879–80	20.45	1884–85	12.78
	1885–86	26.50	

Under this rainfall well-tilled land has never failed to produce good crops.

The third rain belt, best represented by Bear Valley, Santa Maria, Viejas, and similar elevations within that range, has about thirty-five per cent more rain than Fallbrook.

The fourth, or high mountain belt, is best represented by the rainfall of Julian four thousand two hundred feet high and about forty miles from the coast.

We have only five years of reliable report.

YEARS.	INCHES.	YEARS.	INCHES.
1979–80	30.63	1881–82	29.26
1880–81	25.89	1882–83	41.31
	1883–84	61.42	

A record of the snow was kept in only one of these years, 1882–83, when it was five feet, making seven inches of water, which are included in the 41.31 inches. Reference to the San Diego table shows this to be the driest winter on the coast since 1877. As a large proportion of the water at this elevation is every year precipitated in snow, especially in wet years, it will be safe to add about twenty per cent for snow to the other four years. In 1881–82 there were over five feet of snow at Julian in a single storm. This snowfall increases of course with elevation and on the high mountains it often takes weeks to melt off. Following the analogies of elevation from the coast upward it would be safe to add at least thirty-five per cent more for the next one thousand feet of elevation. It is well known that the precipitation at the Cuyamaca is considerably greater than at Julian. The average rainfall is doubtless fifty inches at five thousand feet.

This high rain belt embraces about forty townships, being one thousand four hundred and forty square miles, or nine hundred and twenty-one thousand six hundred acres of land. As most of this is quite steep hill-side with a tight soil, as the rain falls very rapidly and the snow melts fast under the warm sun, the amount of water that runs off is fully sixty per cent. Of the remaining forty per cent fully thirty per cent finds its way seaward under-ground, trickling out in thousands of springs and rivulets which in the mountains combine their water into little brooks and run all summer, but as they approach the coast sink in sand, or into the soft granite bed-rock or old under-ground channels and disappear.

The drainage of this broad highland area forms seven rivers which in wet winters often carry water enough all the way to the coast to float a large steamboat. They are often impassible for days at a time. During the summer they generally sink into their deep beds of sand and under-ground channels, and cease running above-ground, except in a few spots where a small thread may run for half a mile or so. Water may always be found in abundance a foot or two below the surface of the sand; but generally there is no flow above-ground worthy of mention until we reach the mountains, though in years of excessive rain these rivers flow to the coast all summer.

In many years of low rainfall the excess above the summer flow is only in the mountains, the water, though in abundance there, serving only to fill up the sand and under-ground channels below. In such years, large streams pouring from the mountains are swallowed up within ten miles or less after leaving the steep, rocky channels, and reaching the sand beds of the lower levels.

The irrigation possibilities of this county are far beyond what they are generally supposed to be even by old residents. The lowest rainfall recorded anywhere on this area of highland in fifteen years, was at Mesa Grande in 1877, where at an elevation of three thousand five hundred feet the fall was twenty-four and one-half inches. At Pine Valley, thirty miles south, and same elevation, the rain gauge for the same year gave twenty-five inches. Reducing the percentage of water running off to forty per cent we have about ten inches. Twenty inches being sufficient for full irrigation, we have water enough lost by surface drainage to irrigate four hundred and fifty thousand acres of land, to say nothing of the amount that afterward drains from below the surface. And this for the driest season yet recorded. As a matter of fact, however, water that will cover land ten inches deep will serve very well for irrigation, though it is not enough for the best results.

The proportion of this drainage that can be secured for irrigation cannot be easily estimated, as it is in most cases merely a question of what expense the present value of the land will justify. There are many places where large reservoirs may be made in the mountains to catch the flood waters there, many others where they may be made in the lowlands and water from the mountains led into them, many others in the lowlands where dams may be made to catch the waters of wet winters and hold them over for dry ones.

Several large schemes of this sort are already projected. The

A View of Sweet Water Dam, San Diego County.

Hemmet Valley Reservoir Company will build a dam one hundred and ten feet high in the San Jacinto Mountains and irrigate a part of the San Jacinto plains. The San Marcos Water Company will irrigate by reservoirs the fine country around Encinitas and on each side along the coast. In time the San Luis River will be brought upon San Marcos, Escondido, and the mesas about Oceanside. The San Luis Rey Flume Company is already at work upon this great project. The Otay Valley Water Company has been incorporated to irrigate by means of a large reservoir, with a dam of one hundred feet in height, the Otay Valley and adjoining mesas. The Fallbrook Water and Power Company is now at work to bring water from Temecula River upon the Fallbrook country.

The Sweetwater Valley Water Company is incorporated to build a twenty-five foot dam in the Sweetwater River at a narrow gorge upon the Jamacha Rancho, and irrigate part of the Jamacha and National Rancho below, conducting the water from the dam with a flume and pipes. This company has already made the necessary surveys and begun condemnation proceedings for right of way, etc.

The Land and Town Company have about finished a large dam in the Sweetwater, six miles east of National City, which is to be ninety feet high. From this the water will be taken to the best part of their lands below National City, and will also supply National City with water for household use. The Mission Valley Water Company is at work to bring water from the San Diego River upon the Mission Valley.

These four last enterprises, in connection with the one next mentioned, will reclaim four-fifths of all the dry lands within ten miles of the bay, and whenever it will be safe to trust a flume outside of the American line, the Tia Juana may be brought in from Mexico to reclaim some twenty thousand more.

The most advanced of all these projects is that of the San Diego Flume Company, which intends taking the waters of the San Diego River thirty-five miles back from the coast. This line is now under rapid construction, the two principal dams are done, and the whole line is graded and tunneled, sixteen miles of flume built, and the whole will be done to San Diego by June 1, 1888. The Santa Maria Land and Water Company will put in a large dam above Ramona to irrigate the lands thereabout, although very little is needed on that rain belt.

In addition to these large systems there are numerous ways in which water enough for a few hundred or a thousand acres may be had. In almost every valley water may be stored to some extent.

Long, low dams may be made of simple earth, as in India. These are quite safe up to about twenty feet without any puddle wall, and can be made by home labor, without any engineering skill. In the higher lands there are scores of small streams whose waters may be piped or flumed out. There are hundreds of springs whose waters piped into a cistern and saved will irrigate all the land one needs. Hundreds of others may be tunneled out and the flow of water increased from ten to fifty-fold. Water may be pumped, or drawn by under-ground pipes, from wells sunk in river beds or washes, and horizontal wells may be driven into a thousand hill-sides and reach a fair supply of water where none now shows upon the surface. Artesian water has been found in some places, and doubtless exists in more. At San Jacinto there are now one hundred and five flowing wells, made by boring into old river beds about one hundred and fifty feet below the present banks of the river.

All over the valley lands water is easily found at from ten to forty feet in abundant supply, for windmills or other power, and nearly all valleys have some wet ground where irrigation is unnecessary for any purpose. The average depth of water in wells is less here than in the East, owing to the different formation of the country. Irrigation is also unnecessary on nearly all the highest lands, and on the highest rain belt might be only a detriment for most things. Many of the lowland valleys and slopes do surprisingly well with nothing but good cultivation, especially when the subsoil is clay or red granite, which hold water like sponges. On the lowlands generally, irrigation is, however, necessary for some things, and on the mesas is needed for nearly everything except grain, which is irrigated nowhere south of the San Joaquin Valley. As a rule, whatever can be done without irrigation can be far excelled by it, provided it be not done to excess and be accompanied by thorough cultivation. Los Angeles County, where they have practiced irrigation and cultivation side by side, combined and separate, for many years, upon all kinds of soils, and generally under abundant rainfall, is the best place to study the various applications of the two systems of irrigation and cultivation only. Both are invaluable in their way, but their proper combination leads to the most marvelous results on earth.

It is not always necessary that irrigation be continued all summer. It is not to keep things alive through months of rainless weather that irrigation is needed in California. There is little trouble in doing that. Many things need no irrigation later than June, and many more do well enough with the ground well wet down by the middle of May. In many places where water cannot be obtained in summer plenty may be had in winter and spring, and in many others where a summer flow would be too expensive to maintain, a winter flow is easily and cheaply secured.

A careful estimate made by the writer places the amount of land irrigable in this county by all systems, of both winter and summer irrigation (except vertical and horizontal wells or tunnels) at about three hundred thousand acres. This supposes the first cost to be not greater than $50 an acre. Generally it will not exceed $30 for the first cost,

A Scene in Sweet Water Valley, San Diego County.

WATER.

with an annual cost of about $4.00. The amount irrigable by wells and tunnels and small dams can hardly be estimated at much less than two hundred thousand acres more, as it is solely a question of expense.

When we recollect that the greater part of the splendid prosperity of Los Angeles County is due to about ninety thousand acres of irrigated land, it is easy to see what the future will do for San Diego County. And at the ever-increasing ratio in which people of wealth, weary of Eastern winters, and determined to have a home in Southern California at any cost, are pouring into it, the development of all irrigation facilities is not far ahead. Thus far only simple methods have been used all through South California. But these have drawn about all the water obtainable in those ways, and the whole South is about entering a water-development era that will leave the past in the shade. When that time is complete San Diego County will stand in the front line.

CHAPTER XIII.

PRODUCTION.

WHILE San Diego County can raise almost anything as well as any other part of the State there are some things that it can raise much better. It is now conceded at Los Angeles and Riverside that San Diego County lemons lead their very best. Over and over again they have taken the highest premiums at the fairs of Los Angeles and Riverside, a thing that could not be done except by merit so great as to override at once all possible doubt.

While very few pears have as yet been grown here they too lead the coast. The following list of awards to the Kimball Brothers, of National City, at the great exposition at New Orleans in 1884–85, is a judgment from which at present there is no appeal. If San Diego County in its infancy can win such a judgment, there will be little use in contesting it when she is older.

No. 2.—Best collection, ten varieties, oranges from ANY STATE OR FOREIGN COUNTRY IN THE WORLD—First Degree of Merit (Silver Medal and $50).

No. 3.—Best collection, fifteen varieties, grown in THE STATE OF CALIFORNIA—First Degree of Merit (Silver Medal and $75).

No. 4.—Best collection, ten varieties, oranges grown in THE STATE OF CALIFORNIA—First Degree of Merit (Silver Medal and $50).

No. 5.—Best collection, five varieties oranges grown in THE STATE OF CALIFORNIA—First Degree of Merit (Silver Medal and $25).

No. 6.—Best General Exhibit of Citrus Fruits, other than oranges from THE STATE OF CALIFORNIA—First Degree of Merit (Silver Medal and $50).

No. 7.—Best orange, "Acapulco"—First Degree of Merit and $5.
No. 8.—Best orange, "Creole"—First Degree of Merit and $5.
No. 9.—Best orange, "Malise Oval," $5.
No. 10.—Best orange, "Osceola"—First Degree of Merit and $5.
No. 11.—Best orange, "St. Michael's"—First Degree of Merit and $5.
No. 12.—Best orange, "St. Michael's Egg"—First Degree of Merit and $5.

No. 13.—Best lemon, "Eureka"—First Degree of Merit and $5.
No. 14.—Best lime, "Giant Seedling"—First Degree of Merit and $5.
No. 15.—Best collection, five varieties, pears grown within the limits of PACIFIC DISTRICT—First Degree of Merit and $15.
No. 16.—Best plate of any variety pears grown in Pacific District—First Degree of Merit and $10.
No. 18.—Best "Hacheya" Japan Persimmons grown in the United States—First Degree of Merit and $10.

The first fourteen First Premiums were awarded to Kimball Brothers. The last four First Premiums were awarded to Frank A. Kimball. There are fully two hundred thousand acres in this county upon which lemons and oranges fully equal to these can be raised, and in many places even better ones are possible, and even on the National Rancho the best lands are not yet planted.

Had the apricots or raisin grapes of the county been in season so as to be on exhibition they too would have walked off with all the prizes. The apricots especially are so much superior in flavor to those of the North that no locality now pretends to question their eminence, while the raisins of El Cajon, the Sweetwater Valley and other places have been pronounced by the best judges the best in the world. And there are thousands of acres in every direction where equally good ones can be raised.

Apples, peaches, and plums fully equal to those of the North are grown along the lowlands here; but those of the mountains excel those of the coast. The same is the case with all berries and small fruits. Most of these can be grown nearly to perfection on the lowlands but in the mountains all that can stand heavy frosts reach their fullest excellence. Cherries, raspberries, blackberries, gooseberries, currants, strawberries, etc., can all be seen at Mesa Grande bearing in abundance large fruit of the finest flavor, and without irrigation. The same is done at Julian and can be done as low down as Santa Maria and Bear Valley. The superiority of nearly all deciduous fruits and vegetables grown in these mountains will in time make them extremely valuable; for the wealthy Californian is the spoiled child of luxury and will have the best, cost what it may.

All sorts of fancy fruits grow in this county to the finest stage of excellence: the guavas, the Japanese persimmon, the pomegranate, and a score of others. Some of these, like the guava, will soon have a commercial value for jelly or canning, while others, like the Japanese persimmons, Japanese plums, etc., will always be an excellent addition to the list of table fruits. The almond is not a prolific bearer anywhere in the South, though otherwise a beautiful tree; but the English walnut has done marvelously well at Agua Tibia, El Cajon, and other places where it has been tried, while all varieties of fig trees hang full of excellent fruit and often do so without irrigation, cultivation, or any care. Like the fig, the olive thrives almost anywhere on the lowlands without care or water, though like the fig and everything else it will do better with both. Peaches also do very well, though those of the mountains are much the best as well as the most prolific.

Fancy trees, bushes, shrubbery, flowers of all varieties, the camphor tree, rubber tree, banana, palms, and a thousand other things seen only in green-houses in the East, grow here with little or no trouble, though such things as the banana require a place quite free from frost, and also from wind.

Most kind of vegetables grow in winter and many kinds, such as peas, turnips, onions, beets, cabbage, carrots and cauliflower then grow the best. The tomato, if planted above the frost belt, becomes a perennial, growing year after year, climbing often over a small house and bearing the year round. Melons, beans, corn, egg plant, and similar tender things must generally be grown in summer; for though they may live in winter the nights are too cool to allow them to thrive. But other tender plants like the potato are raised in the dead of winter if planted on slopes or mesas above the frost line of the valleys. Many products have not yet been tried and the capabilities of the land are not yet half known. Nor will they be for many a day, because it by no means follows that if a plant fails in a certain kind of soil, or at a certain elevation, or at a certain distance from the coast, it will fail anywhere else.

Some fruits here bear ripe fruit all the year, like the tomato and lemon. Others half the year, like the strawberry when well treated, though the strawberry may bear a little all the year round. But most things have their regular seasons as in the East, though it is often much longer, as with grapes, melons, etc.

There are now growing in the county according to the latest returns of the assessor: 58,208 lemon trees, 102,013 orange, 51,571 olive, 35,086 apple, 26,849 pear, 30,918 peach, 3,595 quince, 72,719 fig, 3,317 prune, 2,359 cherry, 1,217 nectarine, 4,254 plum, 93,572 apricot.

San Diego County has shipped in one season the enormous quantity of two million seventy-five thousand pounds of honey. Immense shipments of wool, wheat, cattle, hides, etc., have been made in the past; but the day for all such things is over except as mere accessories to other things. The whole county is being fast devoted, like the rest of Southern California, to more profitable and pleasant industries and the making of luxurious homes.

The reader may be surprised at the small amount of arable land in the county in proportion to its whole extent. An Eastern State or county having such a great amount of untillable land would generally be pronounced very poor. Yet San Bernardino County is, in this re-

PIERCE-MORSE BUILDING, SAN DIEGO, CAL.

spect, far worse than San Diego County. Santa Barbara and Ventura are no better, and Los Angeles County, with all its wealth, is almost as bad.

The name "Southern California," or "South California," is now generally limited to the three lower counties. These embrace nearly all the choice fruit belts and finest climates, and all the other advantages which are now drawing such a stream of wealthy settlers. Yet these three counties, with an acreage of about twenty-seven million acres, cannot muster much over two million acres which from present standpoints can be fairly called tillable.

But what a two million they are! Nowhere else does the sun shine upon their like; and nothing approaching them lies outside of California. Fifteen years ago fully one-half of these was considered almost worthless except for stock range. To-day that half is far more valuable than the other, and the most readily saleable at from three to five times the price the other half will bring. A land where such a change of values could be so sudden and so great is certainly beyond any ordinary standard of value. It erects its own standard, and compels all old-time political economy and business principles to bow to it. There is but one South California on earth; a residence there is a luxury. The amount of its land is limited; people will have it; therefore it commands the price of a luxury and not of mere farming or garden land. It is quite useless to quarrel with these prices, to repeat the ancient joke about buying climate with the land thrown in. It is quite immaterial whether it is the climate or the land. The prices are nevertheless paid, and the stream of climate-seekers keeps increasing. The rich refugees have been coming so long in such constantly increasing force, so many of them are delighted with the land, buy, build, and do all they can to induce their friends to do the same, that climate now forms a solid basis of values with the advantage of being quite unchangeable except by some grand convulsion of nature. Such climate beneath the flag of the United States is an article whose supply is limited yet with an ever-increasing demand. Those who are fast building towns on lately bare plains, and perching fine houses on slopes and mesas that nobody would have a few years ago, have come here mainly for climate. The soil and its capabilities are of secondary importance. If a beautiful place under a fine climate can be made profitable, so much the better; but if it cannot, no matter; the residence and its climate must be had.

Two consequences necessarily arise from this kind of settlement: First, higher prices than the land might seem to justify as mere farming or gardening land; second, a large amount of production, often experimental, often fancy and even extravagant, which is of course unprofitable. From this a visitor too often infers that the prices of land are too much inflated, and that all production is necessarily expensive.

The limited amount of land, and the steadily increasing demand for it, sufficiently settle the question of inflation. If such conditions do not create value there is no such thing as intrinsic value, and every value rests only upon fancy.

While farming and fruit raising often cost a little more than in some parts of the East, they cannot be called expensive, and certainly are profitable, where conducted on any business principles. So many experiments have had to be made, and so much trouble has been had with transportation facilities, commission merchants, and various other things, that production has not always been profitable in the past. But a great change has of late taken place. Until three years ago not an orange from California went east of the Rocky Mountains. Railroads suddenly concluded that living rates were better than prohibitory rates, and a reduction started shipments. In 1885 twelve hundred car loads found a ready and paying market from St. Paul to St. Louis, and far to the east of both. In 1886 the shipment has been far greater, and regular fruit trains are now run on express time to the East. Before this the only market was San Francisco, which of course was easily glutted. Moreover, the finer varieties of oranges had not been long enough planted to produce much, and the proper mode of cultivating even the old trees had but just been discovered. It was much the same with lemon growing, with the additional disadvantage of not knowing how to preserve lemons until the foreign lemons were out of the Eastern market—a thing just discovered within two years and now a complete success. Raisin-growing has gone through much the same stages. Growers had to learn how to prune, to irrigate, to cultivate, to pick, to pack, to label and to market, and had to learn it all from their own experience. Few people have ever learned so rapidly as the fruit-growers of Southern California, and although some things remain to be known, four-fifths of the work is done. In growing, picking, packing, selling, etc., as well as canning, wine-making, drying, or curing of any kind, the present now has the experience of the past without the expense of the education; and the orchards and vineyards of Southern California are now among the most profitable of the world, the yield of many of the older ones now almost surpassing belief. Space will permit no tables of estimates of profits. They can be found in a hundred immigration documents, and if the reader will take the pains to annex qualifications, which a moderate amount of experience and common sense will readily suggest, he cannot be misled by them. The most extravagant of them is generally literally true, but may represent especially favorable conditions. All of them represent work and sound business principles, to which they are generally due more than to peculiar conditions. You will find no land where work is more indispensable to success than here, and none where it will bring the same heaping measure of results. Where you see unprofitable farming or fruit-raising you will nearly always find a man who came to California to make money without work, or who, having means to hire labor, has plunged into some new thing on too large a scale instead of feeling his way, or who, loaded with Eastern conceit, has disregarded the experience of others, or one who has run a ranch as a baby would run a candy shop.

Ordinary farming is in such a transition state, so many of the effects of the old systems still remain, that a new-comer who is not careful in his observations may get very wrong impressions. The great effort of the old-time farmer was to make money at farming; not a living with a little money over, as most successful farmers do the world over, but money, and plenty of it. And this was, of course, to be done with the least possible amount of work. There can be but one result of such farming anywhere. This State is no exception to the stern laws of nature. On the other hand there is no State where the four first requisites of successful farming,—diversification of products, hard work, close economy, and strict attention,—produce more certain or fuller results. Nowhere else will the same acreage produce such a variety and quantity as on the irrigated lands of Southern California. Even where the whole tract cannot be irrigated fine results can be secured. Ten acres of land with the water that an inch-and-a-half pipe will carry from a stream, spring, or ditch, and the work that a successful gardener in the East puts upon ten acres will, with thirty acres of dry land outside, not only support a family, but leave more money over than the best one-hundred-and-sixty acre farm east of the Rocky Mountains. Three acres in alfalfa, well irrigated, will keep two milch cows, a dozen hogs, and a score of chickens the year round, with all their increase. Half an acre more will raise all the vegetables a large family can use in a year, while the rest in raisin grapes, fine oranges, or a dozen other varieties of fruits, will yield a fair income. On dry lands outside of this, thorough plowing with irrigation will raise plenty of the best hay, which is made of grain cut in the dough or milk; also olives, apricots, wine grapes, figs, and many other things that bear well with cultivation alone. Irrigation will, of course, improve the yield of all such fruits, especially in some years, but very little water is needed and fair results may be had without any. Many things that are sure to be profitable in the future are very easily raised. The olive, for instance, grows on dry land with very little attention, is a hardy, prolific, and steady bearer, and outlives its owner's family. As soon as enough are grown in the vicinity to supply an oil press the profits are large and constant. Pickled when ripe they form an article of food which the whole family soon learns to like, as substantial as potatoes, and infinitely better to the taste than the foreign olives, which are pickled green to preserve a stylish color. It is a tree whose value is daily becoming more striking; and as a standby for the future, as a thing to work in with other products with scarcely any trouble, and to use unirrigable lands; its value in the future can scarcely be estimated.

To run through the list of trees, vegetables, grains, and berries that can be grown here with their special modes of cultivation and their profits would take a volume. Suffice it to say that about everything can be raised in San Diego County that can be grown in the temperate zone at all, with many of the best products of the tropics. The profits will depend upon the industry, attention, and business capacity of the producer.

Many things outside of common farming and fruit-growing have been raised at great profit in San Diego County, and many of them may still be raised to advantage in connection with other things. In nearly all parts of the county there is an abundance of bee pasture. Apiaries need little or no care except during working time, and in most years are very productive. Abundance of stock range, generally public land, lies outside of most of the arable tracts, and is used by many to keep a few head of stock, which can be done with very little trouble. Abundance of goat pasture lies on the hills, which are easily fenced in, and a cross of the Angora with the common goat makes excellent meat. Large numbers of sheep have been raised at a good profit, but raising them on a small scale, as in the East, has not yet been attempted. It can, however, be done much better here, as it is never necessary to protect sheep from the weather, and they thrive well upon the native grasses and are easily fenced in. There is no better country for raising hogs and chickens, none where they pay any better when half cared for, and none where they can find more feed for themselves. Hogs can be raised well upon alfalfa hay and will harvest a stubble-field until the last head of grain is gleaned.

The farmer here has many advantages over the Eastern farmer. He needs no out-buildings except a roof for his horses and cover for his wagon and machinery, more to protect it from the sun than from the rains. Grain stands ripe for months with no danger of sprouting, moulding, falling, or shelling, safe from rain, hail, wind-storms or lightning. The farmer needs little fire wood except for cooking, has no "fall work" to do, no winter to get ready for, except to plow and sow. He has twice the amount of fair weather in which to work that the Eastern farmer has, and need never work from daylight to dark in hot weather to get his hay or other crops out of danger of rain. If he will only work well and work steadily, and not put off things for days because there is plenty of fine weather ahead, he will have more and better food to eat, a better home, and more money to spend in luxuries, with much less actual work and less worry than the farmer in any other country.

The great and overwhelming advantage, however, that San Diego

A VIEW IN ESCONDIDO, SAN DIEGO COUNTY.

County now has for one who is determined to live in South California, is the very low price of land compared with prices farther north. Especially is this true of irrigable lands. Thousands of acres of land exactly like that which at Riverside brings, with a water right, $600 an acre, unimproved, and at Pasadena $1,500 an acre, may be had here for one-third of those sums. The mountain lands too, and the moist valley lands that need little or no irrigation, are far cheaper than elsewhere. This difference in price is a necessary consequence of the late opening of the lands to settlement, and of course it is a difference that cannot last long.

Prices of land in this county vary so with locality, rainfall, and irrigation facilities, that it is quite useless to attempt to give any scales. Plenty of fine land may yet be had at $50, and in the mountains the surest land in the world for crops may be had for $20 to $40, and even as low as $10 in remote places.

The experience of the last ten years shows that there is no such thing as a fall in prices of good, irrigable land in Southern California. Town lots may possibly shrink even in a growing city as they do elsewhere in growing cities, but the price of good fruit land and fine residence property is steadily upward. This results necessarily from the steadily increasing demand and the limited supply. Town lots in abundance can be laid out for years to come, but the acres that make beautiful places, surrounded with varied and luxuriant vegetation, and the acres that yield the enormous crops of the world's finest fruits, are rapidly going and cannot be replaced.

CHAPTER XIV.

THE CLIMATE.

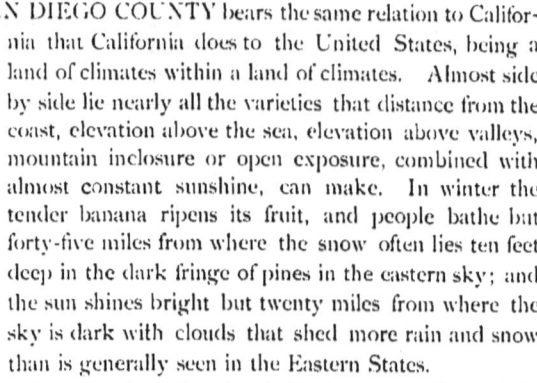SAN DIEGO COUNTY bears the same relation to California that California does to the United States, being a land of climates within a land of climates. Almost side by side lie nearly all the varieties that distance from the coast, elevation above the sea, elevation above valleys, mountain inclosure or open exposure, combined with almost constant sunshine, can make. In winter the tender banana ripens its fruit, and people bathe but forty-five miles from where the snow often lies ten feet deep in the dark fringe of pines in the eastern sky; and the sun shines bright but twenty miles from where the sky is dark with clouds that shed more rain and snow than is generally seen in the Eastern States.

It is unanimously conceded by its most envious neighbors on the north that this county has the best climate of the State. This is not caused by its more southern position alone, but also by the wide inward sweep of the coast to the east. The effect of this, which gives Santa Barbara such a different climate from that of San Francisco, is continued to the lower line of the State, giving San Diego County the same advantage over Los Angeles County that Los Angeles County has over Santa Barbara County. A much less rainfall along the coast and a far greater number of clear days in winter is an important result of this, but is by no means the most important. Without perceptibly increasing the heat of summer it removes the land farther from the influence of the cold ocean current that, coming down the northern shore, makes the summer wind so cold at San Francisco, and causes the heavy fogs that hang along the upper coast. What is left of that current passes San Diego far out at sea, just near enough to cool off the hot air flowing over westward in an upper current from the Colorado desert, and send it back in an under current just cool enough for comfort and drier than the land breezes of the Atlantic Coast. What few fogs there are—and there is scarcely any sea-coast without some—come at night, and generally vanish with the first burst of sunlight over the eastern mountains, while the sea breeze has little of the dampness ot that of the upper coast. The effect of this is seen at once in the growing of some kinds of fruit. Even in Los Angeles County good oranges and lemons cannot be grown within ten or twelve miles of the coast. But the oranges and lemons that swept away so many prizes at the New Orleans Exposition were grown within six miles of San Diego Bay, and many of them within half a mile of it; the only exception being a few which were grown about fifteen miles back, between the Janal and Jamul. Within half a mile of the bay at National City may be seen groves of olives as clear and bright as in the interior, which only one hundred and fifty miles north would be half black with scale caused by the dampness of the sea.

Subject to these modifications in its favor and to special modifications caused by altitudes, etc., as before explained, the climate of San Diego County is that of Southern California in general, of which the main characteristics are:—

1st. Warm winters.

2d. Dry summers.

3d. Cooler summers than are found elsewhere on the same latitude, and, on account of the unfailing sea breeze, summers much more comfortable than can be found on the Atlantic Coast, even of the Middle States.

4th. An atmosphere much drier in winter than is found in summer on the Atlantic Coast, and as dry in summer as is consistent with a good growth of vegetation.

5th. Absolute freedom from malaria of any kind except where locally caused by excessive irrigation or foul cities.

6th. Absolute freedom from cyclones, tornadoes, or dangerous winds of any kind; and entire freedom from lightning, thunder-storms, and cloud-bursts, except occasionally upon the deserts and highest mountains.

7th. A climate where many children's complaints, such as the bowel complaint of the dreaded "second summer," are quite unknown, and nearly all others, such as measles, scarlet fever, etc., are very rare and very much modified.

8th. A remarkable freedom from insect pests of all kinds, except where locally caused, as mosquitoes around open water-tanks or fleas around ill-kept places.

9th. Cool nights in summer, caused by the rapid radiation of heat from the earth through the dry air.

10th. Warm days in winter from the opposite cause—the more rapid transmission of the heat rays through dry air.

Tables of temperature as generally used to show what the climate is give little idea of the winter weather of Southern California. Neither average temperatures nor the lowest ones are of much use. There is here no such thing as a "cold snap" such as is known in Florida. There it is the edge of a "polar wave" from the north and it may freeze all day. Here a "cold snap" is only a series of unusually cold nights caused by dry winds from the desert. The percentage of moisture in these winds runs as low as five per cent and the earth's loss of heat through air so dry is necessarily very rapid. When these winds come at the time when the nights are the longest, and especially when the high mountains through whose passes they come are clad in snow, the long continuance of the rapid radiation may lower the temperature a few degrees below the freezing point. But this will happen only in the two or three hours before sunrise. Then the reverse process begins and the sunlight falling through the dry air raises it to a pleasant temperature in two hours. Cold weather therefore on the lowlands can happen only at night and only on a clear night. In such case the succeeding day is sure to be clear and consequently warm. This daylight temperature, however, is subject to a great modification which tables of temperature never show. It is only in the bottom of valleys or on great plains surrounded by mountains that it thus falls. On nearly all the high slopes around the valleys and plains, and on all elevated table-lands along the coast, the temperature will be at daylight from ten to twenty-five degrees higher than it will be one hundred or two hundred feet below, there being a warm belt which is much less affected by radiation, the loss of heat being largely supplied in some way not yet fully understood. Here even a white frost is generally unknown while freezes and spring frosts are quite impossible.

Winter being in California called "the rainy season" an impression goes abroad that it is a season of rain. It is quite the contrary. From first to last rain, a period of about six months, the number of clear and fair days always exceeds that of an equal period east of the Mississippi River, whether taken in winter or summer. Too often there is not rain enough on the lowlands for a full growth of grass or grain, and not more than once in twenty years is there too much. Government tables of rainfall generally count as "rainy" all days on which rain falls, whether the fall be by day or night. Fully three-fourths of the rainfall is at night and on the lower rain belts is almost invariably followed by fair or half clear days, sometimes having occasional light showers, but generally half clear until sundown, when the sky again closes in for work. So that winter, instead of being a season of rain, is merely the season when it may rain, as distinguished from the six months when it is quite certain not to rain enough to speak of.

The noon temperature of the clear days in winter is generally from sixty to seventy degrees on the coast and from sixty-five to eighty degrees in the interior. The noon temperature of the rainy days is

Orange Orchard in Cholla Valley, San Diego County.

about the same in both places, from fifty-five to sixty-five degrees, generally about sixty, with little or no fall of the mercury during the night unless the sky clears. The lowest midday temperature recorded at the United States Signal Station at San Diego during eight years is fifty-one degrees, and this but once. In those eight years there were but twenty-one days when the temperature at noon was not above fifty-five degrees. During that time there have been but six days when it was lower than thirty-six degrees at any time of the night, and but two when it reached thirty-two degrees, the lowest point ever reached there. On one of these two days the mercury rose to fifty-one degrees at noon and on the other to fifty-six. This was in the great "cold snap" of December, 1879. One hundred feet higher up the slope from where this record was taken it would not have been lower than forty degrees at the lowest point; while on the mesa eight miles back of town and five hundred feet above the bay and the surrounding valleys, it would have been about forty-five degrees at daylight and seventy degrees at noon.

"If the winters are so warm what must the summers be?" remarks Old Wisdom sweltering under the damp air of the East.

"I'd like to come and see you but it's as hot here as I can stand," wrote a very intelligent gentleman in St. Louis during the hot spell there last July to a friend in San Diego.

Such ignorance is quite natural. The writer himself moved here only for the winters, expecting to pay a fearful price for the luxury when summer came. Nothing in California surprised him so much as the summers of San Diego County, and if he had to spend three months East he would take the winter for the trip rather than the summer, so far as mere exchange of comfort is concerned. The reason is quite simple. The cool ocean current that makes San Francisco uncomfortably cold in summer, makes this far southern coast comfortably cool. Sixty miles from the sea just over the high mountain range lies the great basin of the Colorado desert, with its eight thousand square miles of fiery sand sending aloft, under an almost eternal sun, a daily column of hot air containing scarcely five per cent of moisture. This cannot flow over upon Arizona; for these is a rising column of air quite as hot and much larger; nor on the north, for there the great Mojave Desert of San Bernardino and Los Angeles Counties has the same effect. Nor can it flow out on the Gulf of California, for it is too narrow to receive all that hot air with that of Sonora and the west side of the peninsula of Lower California coming in before it. It must flow out over some cooler stratum of air and this is found in any considerable extent only on the west. Over it goes in a vast upper current toward the sea, causing by its rising a suction equally great below. Once over the cool surface of the sea it loses its heat and quickly descends to return in an under current to supply the place of the air still rising from the desert and the western slope of the land. Hence the sea breeze is here no sea wind laden with moisture. It is a dry breeze partly moistened close to the coast by its contact with the sea but drier above. A few miles inland the upper and drier strata become more mingled with the others, and the consequence is an air so dry that strips of meat two inches thick hung up in the breeze quickly cure without either salt or smoke. Even on the coast there are no damp walls, damp bed-clothing, rusting of guns, etc., as on the Atlantic coast, and thick strips of meat and fish will cure in the air, though not so quickly as a few miles inland.

Everyone who has traveled in the dry air countries or has marked the difference between a damp hot day and a dry hot one in the East knows the effect of dry air in hot weather. Cool nights follow of course from the rapid radiation; the backbone of the hottest day is broken at four o'clock; by six it is pleasantly cool, and by nine, cool enough for blankets. More rapid radiation of heat from the body and faster evaporation of perspiration and consequent absorption of heat from the skin also follow, and all the depressing effects of hot, damp weather are absent. On the very hottest of days one who has nothing to do but seek comfort can always find a luxurious coolness in the shade and breeze; while horses do more work than in the East and men work in the harvest-field without suffering and without the slightest danger of sun-stroke.

In the interior any given day will of course be warmer at noon than on the coast. Yet even there the number of summer days when the mercury does not pass seventy-five degrees is surprising. At Oakwood, United States station at Fallbrook, fourteen miles from the coast and seven hundred and seventy feet above the sea, the thermometer in five years reached one hundred degrees but twenty-three times, and ninety-five degrees but twenty-nine times (exclusive of the other twenty-three times). This fairly represents the heat of the interior.

Perhaps the most remarkable feature of the climate, next to the entire absence of hydrophobia, is the entire absence of dangerous winds and the almost entire absence even of unpleasant ones. The highest wind ever registered at the United States Signal Station at San Diego was but forty miles an hour and that but once. During the eight years the record has been kept, the wind exceeded twenty miles an hour but one hundred and fifty times. Of these one hundred and fifty there were but forty-seven over twenty-five miles an hour, but thirteen over thirty, only five above thirty-one, and but one over thirty-six.

Summer produces here no such bowel complaints or fevers as it does in the East. The entire absence of malaria, where not locally caused, makes one doubt whether one ever owned a liver. Gravel and all other kidney diseases, with rheumatism, neuralgia, etc., are quite unknown even in the old settled places, and very much modified or cured

A View in Spring Valley, San Diego County.

in cases that have come here with them; while catarrh is quite certain to disappear and hay fever is rarely known to return even to an old victim.

It is by many supposed that a climate so free from cold must abound in all sorts of reptiles and insect pests. It is, however, quite the reverse. Various reptiles are found but it takes a considerable search to see one, and the number of persons annually injured in the whole State by poisonous reptiles or insects of all kinds does not equal the number annually killed in most Eastern States by hydrophobia alone.

Neither yellow fever nor cholera has ever made a lodgment here, nor is there any special complaint of any kind peculiar to the climate.

There is after all no better test of a desirable climate than the number of days one can spend out-of-doors. The following record kept by the writer for his own information during his first winter in California, is extraordinary for a country where one can live and raise anything. Yet it was the unusually good season of 1875-76, when six thousand acres of wheat in El Cajon, scratched in with a harrow, yielded an average of twenty bushels to the acre, and the honey crop and other crops were immense. The record was kept in El Cajon, to see how many days could be spent out-of-doors in hunting, etc. From first to last rain, one hundred and fifty-nine days, there were one hundred and twelve days warm and clear. Noon temperature sixty-five to seventy-five degrees. There were thirteen days cloudy but warm; clear and cool, eight days; cloudy and cool, six days. Noon temperature of cool days fifty-five to sixty-five degrees. Rainy all day, ten; showery, ten. The lowest noon temperature was fifty-five degrees. The days marked "showery" were days of clearing-up showers after rainy nights, and were exactly like "April showers" at the East,—days when one could not venture out for a whole day, or perhaps a *whole* half day, but could still spend one-half the day out-of-doors. Here were one hundred and thirty-nine out of one hundred and fifty-nine days that one could spend entirely out-of-doors, and but ten days that one need spend wholly within. And this was a year wetter than two-thirds of the years in all Southern California. Of course all the rest of the year one could spend the whole day out-of-doors.

CHAPTER XV.

OUT-OF-DOOR AMUSEMENTS.

AN DIEGO COUNTY always abounded in resources for the sportsman and camper, and these attractions first brought here and secured as permanent residents such men as H. L. Story, E. S. Babcock, Jr., and many others who have aided largely in its development. There probably never was a more pleasant land for camping and traveling than this county has been. Good feed, fire wood, and water were abundant everywhere in the interior; the settlers were courteous and hospitable in the extreme; one could travel almost anywhere with a wagon, and anywhere on horseback, and camp almost anywhere without any danger of being disturbed or having anything stolen. The county was in fact about the safest part of the United States for either life or property. With the ocean on one side, the desert on the other, and Lower California on the south, it was a very difficult place to escape from. The tramp, the cowboy, the rustler, and all manner of hoodlums and malefactors quickly discovered that it was a fine place to get caught in and gave it a wide berth.

The valley quail of California abounded in numbers quite inconceivable to Eastern sportsmen. One hundred and fifty to two hundred a day was an ordinary bag for a good shot, and in any of the cañons within a mile from the post-office one could quickly load himself down with all he cared to carry back on foot. Fifty or sixty were a common score for one shooting only from a wagon in traveling from El Cajon, or Spring Valley, to San Diego in the morning or evening, and that many have often been shot there by one who knew nothing of wing shooting. This quail was found as high as six thousand feet above sea level, though not very abundant above three thousand feet, and most abundant along the coast, where they could always be found in great numbers with absolute certainty. No attention was paid to the law, and no impression was made upon their numbers until the building of the railroad brought in a host of market shooters. These generally hunted in pairs, and two men have shipped in one winter, from San Diego, thirty-five thousand quails, nearly all killed singly.

The small hare, commonly called "cottontail," and the large hare, or "Jack rabbit," also abounded in incredible numbers. Morning and evening they played over every acre of mesa, hopped in scores around the edge of every brush-clad hill or patch of cactus. A bushel or two of them could be shot from a wagon in a few miles' drive along any of the roads. But three years ago one hundred and thirty-five were counted along the road in a single trip from San Diego to Old Town, about three miles. By nearly everyone they were considered a great nuisance, and they certainly were destructive to gardens, and vines, and young trees. There are, however, few of the old settlers who would care to exhibit a balance-sheet with rabbit meat on the credit side at even three cents a pound. The flesh of the cottontail is as white and fine as chicken, in no way resembling that of the Eastern rabbit. It runs with a swift, zigzag motion that makes very pretty shooting, especially on bright moonlight nights, the flickering white tail making a fine mark for snap-shooting.

Turtle-doves and meadow larks were also very numerous, the former especially, though not so abundant as the quail.

Ducks of nearly all varieties were found in every lagoon and slough. In many places, such as Warner's Ranch, Temecula, San Jacinto, Elsinore, and Santa Margarita, geese and sand-hill cranes were very plenty during the winter. They covered the mesas and valleys of Santa Margarita at times by the hundred thousand.

The sloughs and bays along the coast were lined with curlew, snipe, willet, dowitchers, plover, etc., and there was no prettier sight than the thousands of water-fowl riding on the smooth face of San Diego Bay on a bright winter day. Where nearly all is now a watery blank and where even the sea-gull scarcely dares to fly, pelicans, divers, mergansers, shags, ducks of nearly all varieties, brant, sea-gulls, fish-hawks, terns, and what-not were everywhere. So tame were they that from the wharf one could watch the divers beneath him swimming along under water behind a school of little fish, picking them up right and left with dexterous motion. The black brant, the finest of American water-fowl, not known on the Atlantic Coast and rare on this coast south of Oregon, dotted the bay far and wide. Down Spanish Bight, the dividing inlet of Coronado Beach, where one may now watch for a month without seeing any, from fifty thousand to a hundred thousand could be seen at the ebb-tide coming into the bay from the sea. Reckless, idiotic shooting, the white man's hoggish disposition to waste and destroy, has reft this bay of one of its chief attractions.

The antelope played over the plains of San Jacinto, Temecula, and the mesa between Otay and El Cajon. The last of the latter band was killed about five years ago, the last of the Temecula band about two years ago, and the sole survivor of the San Jacinto band was killed this last fall.

The deer roamed from the coast to mountain-top. Though never so abundant as in the North, deer were still plenty enough for good sport. The variety is the mule deer, like that of Arizona, and not the black-tail of the North.

Though settlement and the increase of hunters have reduced the numbers of ducks, geese, sand-hill cranes, and quails to a scarcity, which few of the old residents ever expected to see, very good shooting, compared with that of most other States, still remains. The quails and hares can never be exterminated, and though the labor of hunting them is much increased fair bags may yet be made. The deer hunting is still very good in most seasons and will remain so for many a year.

There never was much trout fishing in this county. Trout were killed out of the Santa Ysabel Creek many years ago by the Indians, by the use, it is said, of "soap weed." They were swept out of Temecula Creek by the flood of 1862. A few yet remain in Pauma Creek, though sadly dwindled in both numbers and size.

Fair fishing may yet be had in San Diego Bay, and the fishing outside the bar is about as good as ever. The barracouda and Spanish mackerel afford fine trolling, are gamy, ravenous, and very plenty in season. In the kelp is found an abundance of rock-cod, red-fish, and other good fish, which can be caught in great quantities about all the year around.

There is no better place for rowing and sailing than San Diego Bay. The breeze is always certain, and equally certain to be never so strong as to be dangerous. Upon the great ocean the frailest boat may generally ride with safety, and the bar is nothing to cross.

No country ever had better natural roads for riding and driving than this county before the travel became too heavy. Even now they could be kept good if scraped in winter when damp, a thing that will probably soon be done in all directions. Even as they are they make pleasant drives for the greater part of the year.

Headworks and Diverting Dam of San Diego Flume.

CHAPTER XVI.

MISCELLANEOUS.

THE arable soils of San Diego County, though very varied, may be classed under two heads, the granite and the adobe, though there is sometimes a mixture of the two that at first glance resembles pure adobe.

The adobe is mainly clay, and is of four prominent colors, though these sometimes shade into one another. These are dark, light-grayish brown, red, and dark brown. The general character of all is the same. They are all very strong soils, probably standing longer cropping without fertilization, rest or rotation, than any other soil in the United States. They are, however, all hard to work unless taken in the right stage of moisture, when they are very tractable, and then, if well cultivated, they retain moisture as well as any soil. With sufficient moisture they raise the heaviest grain, and for some kinds of vegetables, such as beets, and for such fruits as pears, they cannot be excelled. But in general they are not as desirable as the granite soils.

The granite soils are all formed from the disintegration of the soft red, or gray granite, which forms the bed-rock of most of the interior hills. If dissolved in water, mica will be seen shining in the finest of them, and sometimes fine quartz crystals are mixed with it. With it all is an abundance of vegetable matter, but more in a state of pulverization than of decay; so that this soil generally lacks that fine rich shade which elsewhere is deemed a sure test of goodness. The eye cannot be relied upon as a judge of any soil in Southern California. Even that which appears to be pure sand, when well treated to seed and water, under the California sun, will give results that will astonish the most experienced farmer or gardener from any other land. These granite soils run through all shades of color between dark red, caused by the presence of iron, and light gray, and through all degrees of fineness, from the fine red soils which show no mica, unless dissolved in water, to heavy gray sand, coarse enough to make a gravel walk.

None of these soils as yet need any fertilization, although some, such as the coarse granite last mentioned, would, for many things, be improved by it; and the time will doubtless come when all of them will be bettered by it, especially for those trees and vines which bear heavily and need fruit of full size to be marketable, such as oranges and raisin grapes. Scarce any of these soils require any clearing that is at all expensive, and no "breaking," such as is needed in many countries—a common plow readily turning up the soil ten inches or more after the first rain. Under the pipe system of distribution, which is fast being adopted in the land to prevent waste of water and improve its delivery, scarce any of these soils now require leveling or any preparation for irrigation. Probably nowhere in the United States can virgin soil be so quickly and cheaply prepared for cultivation, while all the expense of preparing, watering, and keeping in order, does not equal the expense of clearing and fertilizing in Florida.

Though California is probably the only State in the Union where crops and many other kinds of produce can sometimes be grown without any plowing at all, it is probably also the only State where rich land often refuses, for no apparent cause, to bear, while unplowed, even a moderate crop of the native grass, or other vegetation, though the same land when plowed will raise anything in luxuriance. Still, other tracts may be covered with a dense growth of grass or brush and be rich for some things, yet may be very inferior for many of the most valuable products that can be grown. Hence it may be safely said that from the absence of native vegetation nothing can be inferred against the land; while any inference drawn from its presence may possibly be delusive in another way. Within a few years, such wonderful results have been obtained by careful cultivation, with judicious irrigation, that it may be said that there is no such thing as poor land in Southern California, provided it can be plowed at all and watered. And at the present rate of development of land, but five years ago deemed worthless, it may be almost predicted that in ten years more, water, climate, and prospect will give a high value to land that will require an outlay of $100 an acre to clear of bowlders and cobble-stones.

San Diego has a line of large steamers to San Francisco, and also to Mexico and Guatemala. The county now has over three hundred miles of railroad, of which nearly one-half belongs to the Southern Pacific, and lies upon the desert. The California Southern enters the habitable part of the county near Riverside, and terminates at National City. A branch line from Perris to San Jacinto will soon be finished. The branch from Oceanside through San Marcos to Escondido is already done, and that from San Diego to El Cajon will be built at once, and continued on through the interior. The continuation of the coast line from Oceanside to Los Angeles is nearly finished. All these are owned by the Santa Fe Company.

A new road is under way from Pomona to Elsinore, and the character of the incorporators indicates that it is no trifle. Elsinore is no terminus for any road, neither is Temecula, nor any other point north of San Diego. This means that San Diego is the objective point, and the road is without doubt the Southern Pacific.

The San Diego and Cuyamaca Railroad Company is preparing to build a narrow-gauge road to the beautiful Cuyamaca Mountains. This will open up the interior, as well as the finest summer resort in Southern California, the Cuyamaca Lake, and adjoining woods and hills.

A railroad will soon be built from San Diego to San Quintin, in Lower California. Lower California, for over three hundred miles below the line, is much like San Diego County, with the same climate, plenty of good land, and a high and broad mountain rain belt with plenty of water to take upon the table-lands of the coast. There are also numbers of well-watered valleys. It is a fine country. All the upper part for over three hundred miles is now in the hands of a strong American company called the International Company of Mexico, having a grant from the Mexican Government of eighteen million acres. This they are rapidly colonizing. Two steamers to Ensenada, some sixty miles below the line, are now running; also a steamer to San Quintin. The greater part of this fine country will be tributary to San Diego Bay and the railroads there centering.

Several very rich gold mines have been discovered in the county, and four are now being worked at a fine profit in the district around Julian. Gold-bearing ledges exist in various parts, but as yet few attempts have been made to develop them properly. The mines now paying so well at Julian were discovered several years ago, but were abandoned as of little value. When new owners came with more experience and improved methods, they soon proved them highly profitable. The change that proper management has wrought proves that in the matter of mines the resources of the county are yet quite unknown, while the number of places where rich quartz ledges are known to exist indicates that under proper methods a large number of mines will soon be worked at a large profit.

There are also other kinds of valuable mineral in various places, not yet worked, or even tested in any way that will prove whether they are profitable or not. Asbestos is found in abundance in the San Jacinto region; clay that makes excellent pottery is found near Elsinore in abundance, and exists in many other places. Lignite, so closely approaching coal as almost to prove a certainty of its running into it, is found near Elsinore in a vein of great thickness. So new is everything that all such resources of the county remain comparatively unexplored, and its inhabitants as yet know but little more than strangers of its under-ground wealth. San Diego strikes the stranger at first as a treeless country. But thousands and thousands of acres of fine timber lie in the high mountains, and fire wood is abundant enough above two thousand feet, and along the river bottoms. Eucalyptus, pepper trees, cottonwood, willow, sycamore, etc., can be grown in great quantity in a short time with a little water, or without irrigation on low ground, and all make good fire wood.

Hot springs, strong enough with sulphur, soda, and other minerals to suit anyone, are found in various places. Some, like those at Warner's Ranch, Murietta, and San Jacinto, are as large as those of Arkansas and of about the same character. Others are smaller, but hot enough and strong enough to please either taste or imagination. All are easily reached, and some of the larger ones have bath-houses and accommodations for travelers. The Murietta Springs are but three miles from the railroad. All of these will, in time, be fitted up in good style.

San Diego will soon have the finest educational advantages of any county in the State. Not only are good schools abundant in all directions, but good colleges are arising in several places. The colleges at Escondido and Ramona are already under way. The colleges at San Diego, on University Heights and Pacific Beach, will be a credit to any city. Both these are already heavily endowed with the most valuable city property in quantity enough to insure the building of magnificent buildings and a good annual income. They will be run on the most progressive principles, and not be stifled in any fog of bigoted orthodoxy.

Prices of living average about the same as in the East, some things being higher, others cheaper. Taxes are much less than in most parts of the East. Probably in the long run it costs less to live here, especially in the country, the difference in the expense of getting through the winters overbalancing all else. Southern California hotels and restaurants generally are much superior to those of the East for the same price, and $1.00 a day here will secure as good board and room as $2.00 will anywhere east of the Rocky Mountains, and without any bed-bugs thrown in.

There are, however, some things that by many who have never been here are considered drawbacks that are not so, such as the long summers of six or eight months. That feature of the land no resident would change if he could. Give San Diego County twelve inches of rain from December to April inclusive, and half reasonably distributed, and without another drop the land will excel in production, acre for acre, any other part of the United States. Unless sufficient for vegetation, summer rains would do more harm than good by injuring the dried grass and ripe crops. If sufficient, the chief beauty of the climate

A Scene in El Cajon Valley, San Diego County.

would be ruined; the land would be a tropical jungle full of malaria, with a sultry, enervating air, full of mosquitoes and other insect torments. There are other lands where one can spend a winter with comfort, but the chief glory of the California climate is that one may enjoy the winter, and instead of running away may remain and be more pleased with the summer.

It is the only southern land where a residence is more enjoyable at any time of year than anywhere east of the Mississippi River, and the great majority of those now covering the land with beautiful homes are held here as much by the summer as by the winter.

Neither are earthquakes a drawback. They are no more frequent than in the East, and are generally so light that a stranger will not know until told that there has been one. Since the coming of the Americans no house or person has been injured in the slightest, and the only case known before that was the falling of an adobe tower of a church eighty years ago. All the other old missions built of adobe, some of them like that of San Luis Rey, with high domes and towers, have never been injured in the hundred years they have stood.

There are no Indians here that anyone need fear. They are all brought up under the Catholic Church, are generally industrious, and trouble no one.

Neither are there enough Chinese here to interfere with any deserving white person. The few there are generally find employment, but it is at work that interferes little with the whites.

San Diego County has been called the Italy of Southern California. Though in one respect this comparison is as absurd as that of the newspaper poet who compared the sunset to the robin's breast, it is in the main correct. It is to Southern California what Italy is to Europe, the aggregation in its highest development of all its beauties and advantages. Whatever is beautiful, fertile, grand, sweet, or noble, in Southern California, one may find here heightened in effect by its more southern position and the varied elevations of its good land.

There are, of course, some objectionable features, as there are in every land. These may strike you all the more strongly because the whole of California has been absurdly overpraised. Your very first contact may be with these. But when you stay long enough to see the solid realities of the land, and learn that it is not to blame for your overwrought imagination, or the unwise enthusiasm of its friends, you will begin to like it. Year after year an affection that you cannot and would not resist winds itself ever more closely around your soul. Life comes so easily and so naturally; time flies so swiftly yet so softly. You feel the thread of life fly faster from the spindle, yet you hear no whizz. There are so few breaks or jars in the train of comfort as the long line of cloudless days rolls on; appetite and sleep hang around you so wooingly in the constant out-of-door life that you are enthralled before you know it. You feel yourself enslaved, but in a slavery from which you would not escape. The few who try it are only too glad to return to their chains after spending at their old homes a few weeks of either winter or summer.

BIOGRAPHICAL.

BIOGRAPHICAL SKETCHES.

A. E. HORTON.

It was the boast of Augustus Cæsar that he found Rome in brick and he should leave it in marble. With more regard to truth might Alonzo E. Horton, speaking in the figurative style adopted by the Roman Emperor, remark that he found San Diego a barren waste, and to-day, as he looks down from the portico of his beautiful mansion on Florence Heights, he sees it a busy, thriving city of 35,000 inhabitants. Probably there is no other instance in the history of our country, where great cities have grown from insignificant beginnings, where the presence of one man, unaided by abundant capital, has accomplished such wonderful results as have been achieved by A. E. Horton in San Diego.

To understand and appreciate, however, in its fullest sense, what Mr. Horton has accomplished, it is necessary to inquire into the antecedents and examine the characteristics of the man.

In the year 1635 the good ship *Swallow*, after a long and tempestuous voyage across the Atlantic, dropped her anchor in port at Hampton, Massachusetts. Among the passengers, who were all Puritans, was Barnabar Horton, a native of Leicestershire, England. From him, in the seventh generation, is descended the subject of this sketch. Alonzo Erastus Horton was born in Union, Connecticut, October 24, 1813. When he was two years of age his parents removed to Madison County, New York. Afterwards they took up their residence at Scriba, a few miles from Oswego, on the shore of Lake Ontario. Here his youth and early manhood were passed. During this time he was clerk in a grocery, learned the cooperage trade, and was a sailor on the lake, finally owning and commanding a schooner, in which he engaged in the grain trade between Oswego and Canada. When he arrived at man's estate he was in quite delicate health and his physician pronounced him consumptive, and said if he wished to prolong his life he must go West. Accordingly in 1836 he started for Milwaukee, landing there in May of that year. This was an era of speculation in the Western States; it began several years previously, and ended with the great financial crash of 1837. While in Milwaukee, turning his hand to whatever he could find to do, young Horton became possessed of the information that

(83)

the bills of certain Michigan banks would be received at the land office in payment of lands at par, and would be the equal of gold, and consequently command a premium of 10 per cent. He had a cash capital of $300, and acting on his secret information, he hunted out the holders of Michigan currency and was soon doing a brisk exchange business. This enterprise was a financial success. He returned to

A. E. HORTON.

New York State soon afterwards, but the year 1840 saw him again in Wisconsin. He bought a home in Oakland and married. After this for three years he was engaged in dealing in cattle and land, steadily adding to his little capital. He bought a large quantity of land warrants in St. Louis about this time and located 1,500 acres in Outagamie County, Wisconsin. Here he founded the village of Hortonville, and at the end of two years he sold out his investments at a profit of nearly $8,000.

It was in 1851 that Mr. Horton made his first journey to California. He spent a few months in the mines, but he soon found that he could make more money trading in gold-dust than digging for it. In this traffic his profits were quite large, during the last quarter of 1854 reaching as high as $1,000 a month. As the gold-dust business, however, got a little dull he engaged in an ice speculation. Locating some fine fields in the mountains, he cut and disposed of three hundred and twelve tons, which returned him a profit of $8,000. He now had a comfortable fortune for those days and he determined on going back home to his family. Accordingly in the spring of 1856 we find him a passenger on the steamer *Cortez*, for Panama. A few hours after the *Cortez* landed her passengers at Panama the terrible riots broke out in which the natives attacked foreigners wherever found, killing and plundering all who came in their way. Two hundred persons from the steamer were dining in the hotel when that building was attacked by the mob. A general rush was made for the upper story, where they hoped to escape their assailants. Among all the passengers only three had fire-arms and one of these was Horton. By common consent he was selected to command the garrison. The natives, who by this time had become crazy with rage and rum, attempted to carry the staircase leading to the upper story by storm and several of the leaders darted up the narrow passage. At the head of the stairs stood Horton, a revolver in each hand, perfectly cool and collected. In the room behind him were tenscore persons, including women and children; below were a thousand demons thirsting for their blood. It was a trying moment, but Horton did not hesitate. Those behind urged the foremost of the assailants forward; the leader mounted another step; there was a flash, a report, and he fell back dead. Two others took his place, but they dropped lifeless. Now the reports grew quicker and the flashes from the revolvers told of the sharp work being done. Horton had emptied his own weapons and had discharged most of the barrels of another that had been handed to him before the rioters fell back. Eight of their number were dead and four were seriously wounded. But the dangers of the besieged were not at an end. Although the mob had been repulsed they were not dispersed, and they were still vowing vengeance upon the passengers. The only place of safety was the steamer. Getting his little band in compact order, Horton distributing the revolvers to those whom he knew would use them judiciously, started on the retreat to the landing. This was reached in safety, though the mob followed them closely, and had it not been for the rare generalship displayed by Horton in getting the party embarked on a lighter instead of allowing them to rush, pell-mell, as they attempted to, on a small tug, many must have lost their lives. As it was, the lighter was towed out to the steamer and all were taken on board in safety. Mr. Horton's baggage, containing $10,000 in gold-dust, was lost, having fallen into the hands of the rioters. He saved $5,000, which he had tied around him in a belt.

Mr. Horton remained in Wisconsin until 1861, when he again started for the Pacific Coast, going with a party overland to British Columbia. He spent a season in the Cariboo mining district, and at first made money, but their claim, which had been considered a very valuable one, "petered out," and they finally disposed of it for $200 and started south. Mr. Horton then came to San Francisco, where he engaged in business of different kinds with varying degrees of success. In the early part of 1867, at a private literary gathering one evening, San Diego, its climate and harbor, was the topic of discussion. He was greatly impressed with what he heard. Here was the sight of a great city of the future; nature had done her share; all that was wanting was for man to develop it. The voice of fate seemed to call to Horton that this was his opportunity. He sold out his business in three days' time, and started on his pilgrimage southward. It was the 6th of April, 1867, that Mr. Horton reached San Diego. The few people that were settled here then lived at Old Town, but Mr. Horton after looking the ground over concluded that the true place for the city of the future, his ideal city, was farther down the bay. He first began the agitation of an election of City Trustees. Candidates were nominated and elected. There was no opposition. Then Mr. Horton had surveyed eight hundred and eighty acres which he desired to purchase. The property was advertised and sold at auction. There was but one bidder (Mr. Horton) and he bid it all in at twenty-six cents an acre. This property is now the main portion of the city of San Diego. Mr. Horton then had his "addition" platted, and started to San Francisco to dispose of it. At first he met with but indifferent success; people were suspicious of "Sandyago," as "John Phœnix" had dubbed it; the general impression was, it was very hot and was a place very congenial to the rattlesnake. But Mr. Horton was never discouraged; he had faith in the future. In 1867 his receipts were $3,000; in 1869, they had increased to $85,000. Since then the appreciation of his property has been steady until the last two years when the increase has been phenomenal. When we come to look at what Mr. Horton has done for the city of his creation, we cannot deny but that he has been a faithful and devoted parent. He has expended over $700,000 of his own capital in the improvement of San Diego. He built the first wharf, which was afterwards sold to the Pacific Mail Steamship Company, who in turn disposed of it to the present owners, the Pacific Coast Steamship Company. He gave to each of the religious denominations a lot for a church edifice, and some of them are now very valuable. The lots on which the Methodist Church building now stands at the corner of D and Fourth Streets, is valued at $60,000, and when the members of the congregation look upon it they are constantly reminded of Mr. Horton's munificence. If the real estate that he has given away was valued at the prices selling at this time (April, 1888) it would reach at least $1,000,000. In the days of the city's infancy he gave land to everyone who he thought would improve it. The promises made to him by the recipients of his bounty were not, however, always fulfilled. He gave a fine block of land to a man to build a hotel on, but the hotel was not built. He gave a block to a gentleman who now occupies a high position in the federal service, and two years afterwards bought it back for $4,000. He gave a block for a flour-mill and donated the block on which the court-house stands, to the county. In all he gave away fourteen blocks and innumerable lots, for the purpose of building up the city. For three years, when everyone but he had grown discouraged, Mr. Horton carried the town on his own shoulders, paying salaries of officials and all the expenses of the corporation. He was ready to help everyone who asked it of him, and married men could always get work from him to earn a living and support their families when all other employers failed them.

Personally Mr. Horton is one of the most genial of men. He is easily approached and is always as willing to give an attentive hearing to the man who earns his daily bread by the sweat of his brow, and if need be lend him a helping hand, as to listen to the schemes of the capitalist. Somewhat above the medium height, with a portly frame, he is in robust health, and his clear eye and pleasant countenance bear testimony to the fidelity with which he has complied with the laws of health.

E. W. MORSE.

THE visitor who reaches San Diego in a palace car, drives to a first-class hotel, and the following morning, from the seat of an easy carriage, looks down from the highest part of the city upon the beautiful bay and the enchanting landscape that greets his eye, breathing, meanwhile, the air that invigorates his entire system, is very apt to think that he has reached an earthly paradise. But it is doubtful if his enjoyment is as keen as is that of the man who, looking upon the same scene, and breathing the same atmosphere, calls to mind the fact that nearly twoscore years ago he stood upon the same spot and looked down, for the first time, upon the panorama which nature spread at his feet. There were no stately buildings before him then; the waters of the bay were not dotted with the hulls of merchantmen; it was indeed as nature had made it—neither marred nor adorned by the hand of man. The pioneer of the Pacific Coast possesses many of the qualifications of supreme happiness. He has seen the country emerge from a state of semi-barbarism into one of the most enlightened and progressive sections of the republic. He has seen old theories concerning agriculture, commerce, and transportation overturned. He has seen lonely hamlets made populous trade centers, and the desert to blossom as the rose. He has not only seen all these things, but he has participated in the many wondrous changes; and, if he has been usually economical, industrious, and persevering, he has kept

E. W. MORSE.

pace with the advance about him, and to-day enjoys a share in the general prosperity of the State. To this class belongs the subject of the following brief sketch:—

E. W. Morse was born in Amesbury, Massachusetts, October 16, 1823, in the house yet standing, and now over two hundred years old, in which his father, grandfather, and great-grandfather had been born before him. Until he was eight years of age he lived with his father and mother on the old farm. Then for the first time he left the parent nest, being sent to Newburyport to school. Here he remained for eight years, and by the time he was sixteen years old, he had acquired an excellent common-school education; just such a preparation for the work of every-day life as many a New England boy received at that time. Then, having a strong taste for an outdoor life, he went back to the farm, and until he was twenty-five worked steadily. He had apparently settled down to the steady-going life of a New England farmer. But an event was happening on the shores of the Pacific that was to make a change, not only in the career of young Morse, but in that of thousands of others. Gold had been discovered, and when the news was brought to the Atlantic States the wildest excitement was created. All eyes were turned toward the El Dorado. From no section of the Union did the argonautic fleet gain more zealous recruits than from New England. Young Morse caught the infection, and he joined a company, largely made up of his acquaintances and friends, who purchased the ship *Leonore*, and on the 4th of February, 1849, sailed away from Boston Bay in search of the golden fleece. The voyage was about the average of Cape Horn voyages, and they entered the Golden Gate on the 5th of the following July. They disposed of the ship, and all hands started for the mines, locating on the Yuba River. The work was hard, the weather was excessively hot, and after a few weeks the little band of gold-hunters that had left Massachusetts, strong and rugged, began to droop; many died, and the others, suffering from fever and ague, started for "the Bay." Morse was among these. Although the bracing air of San Francisco invigorated him somewhat, his system had become so impregnated with the malarial poison, that he felt that he must have a more complete change of climate if he would regain his old-time health and spirits.

Even in that early day the reputation of San Diego as a sanitarium was established, and Morse determined that he would make a trial of it. He accordingly took a sailing vessel, and after a pleasant voyage down the coast arrived in the harbor of San Diego. The settlement at that time was in what is now called Old Town. It was there that Mr. Morse engaged in the mercantile business and settled down to make his home. The climate he found to be all that was claimed for it; within a month after his arrival he was as strong and hearty as the day he left the old farm. The San Diego of that day differed greatly from the city of the present. The amusements were bull-fights, fandangoes, and *fiestas;* the buildings were all made of adobe; cattle, hides, and tallow were the chief exports, and beef and beans were the staple articles of diet. Young Morse, however, took readily to the new ways, learned to talk Spanish, and was soon a great favorite with the native population. Before settling down for good, however, he took a journey back East. In 1851 he started by the Nicaraugua route, and arrived safely at his old home. He then married Miss Lydia A. Gray, of Amesbury, and with his bride returned to San Diego. Five years afterward he was left a widower with one son, Edward W., who is now a resident of Merrimac, Massachusetts. In 1852 Mr. Morse was elected Associate Judge of the Court of Sessions of San Diego County, and the following year he was chosen a member of the Board of Trustees. He was afterward made Secretary of the Board, and held the office for twelve years. In 1856 he was admitted to practice in the courts of the Judicial District. In 1859 he disposed of his mercantile business, and went to Paloma, to engage in raising sheep. In 1861 he returned to San Diego, and again engaged in business as a merchant, also acting as agent for Wells, Fargo & Co. In 1865 Mr. Morse was married a second time, to Miss Mary C. Walker, a native of Manchester, New Hampshire. In 1869 he sold out his business in Old Town, and moved down to the new city of San Diego. In 1870 he was one of the moving spirits in the organization of the Bank of San Diego, the pioneer bank of the city. He also aided in organizing the Consolidated National Bank, and has always continued to be a director in that institution. In 1871 Mr. Morse went to Washington to look after the interests of the city in the case of the United States *vs.* city of San Diego, in regard to a disputed survey of the Pueblo. He appeared before the Secretary of the Interior, and argued the case so ably that a few weeks after Mr. Morse's return home, that official handed down his decision, which was favorable to the city. Mr. Morse has been Public Administrator and County Treasurer, and has always been identified with every enterprise that has been started to advance the interests of his adopted city. If he had never done anything, the erection of the magnificent block on the corner of F and Sixth Streets, which he undertook in connection with his long-time friend, the late James M. Pierce, would be an enduring monument to his public spirit. He has, in partnership with Thos. Whaley and R. H. Dalton, lately built another beautiful business structure on Fifth Street adjoining the First National Bank.

James M. Pierce left, by his will, the sum of $150,000 to found a home for boys and girls, and Mr. Morse and two other gentlemen have each contributed a like sum for the founding of institutions similar in character, which are to be established in the City Park, and will, together with Mr. Pierce's endowment, form a magnificent chain of benevolent institutions.

JUDGE O. S. WITHERBY.

IT is not alone to her wealth, the extent of her manufacturing industries, and the political influence she wields, that Ohio owes her proud position in the sisterhood of States. It is to the spirit of enterprise, business acumen, and go-aheadativeness of her sons that the wonderful progress of this wonderful State is largely due. Wherever great cities have sprung up, wherever there are projects requiring men of genuine ability to conceive, or capital to develop them, among the leading spirits of the community will be found the sons of Ohio. They have gone out from their mother State into the remotest sections of the Union, and carry with them everywhere the impress of progress that has become one of their fixed attributes.

One of Ohio's sons, who has aided materially in building up San Diego, is Judge Oliver S. Witherby. He was born in Cincinnati, February 19, 1815. He graduated at Miami University in 1836, studied law at Hamilton, and was admitted to the bar in 1840. Three years later he was elected Prosecuting Attorney for Butler County, an office which he filled for two terms. At the breaking out of the Mexican war he was First Lieutenant of Company K, in the first regiment of Ohio Volunteers, that left Cincinnati in May, 1846. After remaining with his company for about one year he was taken sick at Camargo, Mexico, and left there for home. On his return he resumed his duties as Prosecuting Attorney, and also acted as editor of the Hamilton *Telegraph*.

Judge Witherby came to San Diego in 1849, with the Boundary Line Commission, being Commissary of the commission, and after the labors of that body were finished he decided on locating on the shores of San Diego Bay. He was elected to represent the County of San Diego in the first Legislature that assembled at Monterey in 1850, and with his voice and vote assisted in moulding the laws of the State just created. He was elected the first Judge of the southern district under the first constitution, a position which he filled with honor until he was appointed, by President Pierce, Collector of Customs for the port of San Diego. Soon after the expiration of his term as Collector, Judge Witherby purchased a ranch, which is now called Escondido, and for over ten years he was a successful farmer. In 1868 he sold his ranch and returned to San Diego. During those early years Judge Witherby had judiciously invested in real estate. He is one of the few men who have had steady faith in the great future of San Diego. When others sold out their investments, discouraged at the prospect of the city's growth, he held on. As a result he is now one of San Diego's wealthy men. He is interested in many financial

JUDGE O. S. WITHERBY.

undertakings, and is a director in the Consolidated National Bank. Politically Judge Witherby has always been a Democrat, and he is looked upon as one of the leaders of the party in Southern California. He is a public-spirited citizen, liberal in his views, and his generosity is proverbial.

M. SCHILLER.

ONE of the pioneer residents and best-known citizens of San Diego is M. Schiller. Mr. Schiller was born in Vronka, in the Dukedom of Posen, in 1823. Until he was seventeen years of age he remained with his parents in his native town. Then he decided to branch out and see the world. He had as a playmate and intimate friend a youth of his own age named J. L. Falk. Young Falk had learned that somewhere in Scotland he had relatives living who had charge of a legacy left him a short time before. He determined to hunt them up, and, calling his friend Schiller into his counsels, without much difficulty induced him to join in the pilgrimage to Scotland. There is something romantic in these young boys starting out from a town in the interior of Europe to journey over land and sea many hundreds of miles in quest of a treasure that one of them had grounds for believing he might secure. They had but a small stock of ready money, and their stock of worldly experience was extremely limited. Nevertheless they had strong young bodies and brave hearts, and that made up for all else that was lacking. They first journeyed to Berlin, from there to Hamburg, and thence sailed to Hull, England, and from there took passage overland for Manchester. From Manchester they traveled to Liverpool, where they made a brief stop, and from thence pushed on to Glasgow, Scotland. In this city they were unsuccessful, and they spent several months journeying over Scotland in search of young Falk's relatives who held the key to the treasure of which they were in search. At last they became discouraged and resolved to return home. After many trials they again reached Liverpool. Upon arriving in that great city their money was entirely gone, they were without acquaintances, and they understood but little of the English language. Their situation was anything but comfortable. They started out along the docks, hoping that something would turn up to better their fortune. Here they met an old gentleman who was standing on the dock where a vessel was loading for America. He engaged them in conversation and at once seemed to take a fancy to young Schiller. He soon offered to take him with him to the United States. Schiller, however, refused to leave his friend Falk. Finally the old gentleman agreed to take them both. Accordingly they went on board and soon after set sail. When they landed in New York young Schiller at once started out in search of work. He was successful and obtained employment with a clothing and furnishing goods firm, with whom he remained four years. At the end of that time he formed a partnership with his old friend Falk, and together they engaged in the clothing business. They remained together several years, with fair success. Then they started for Tuskaloosa, Alabama, where they opened a clothing and furnishing goods store. At the end of three years Schiller removed to Talladega, Alabama, where he engaged in business

M. SCHILLER.

with another partner and continued two years. Then he went to Marion, Alabama, for about one year, and then removed to Augusta, Georgia, where he continued in business by himself for eight and one-half years.

He had heard a good deal about California, and the opportunities offered there for business, and he resolved to try the new country. He accordingly went to New York, and after a stay of six or seven months he purchased a stock of goods valued at $18,000 and shipped them to San Francisco around Cape Horn, coming himself by way of the

Isthmus. He reached San Francisco in 1853. When his goods were received they turned out to be too fine a quality for the market. He accordingly sold out his stock at considerable loss and bought a new supply of heavy goods. He then started for Nevada City, intending to locate there. In that year, however (1855), there was no rain and as a consequence times were very hard. Schiller was glad, therefore, to dispose of his stock at less than cost, taking notes at sixty and ninety days. Shortly after receiving these notes a disastrous fire broke out, which nearly devastated the town. Schiller, fearing a second conflagration, and afraid he would lose his money entirely if such happened, again disposed of these notes at a discount of twenty per cent for cash. With the avails he started for San Francisco. The weather was very severe and on the journey Schiller contracted a very bad cold. When he reached San Francisco his health was so poor that he decided to seek a milder climate, and accordingly came to San Diego, arriving here in 1856. He immediately went into business in Old Town, then the business center of San Diego, with M. Mannasse. At the end of a year he formed a partnership with J. S. Mannasse.

Later on they engaged quite extensively in the lumber trade, continuing their general merchandise business. They ran their own vessels and during 1872, the year in which they started the lumber business, in nine months they sent to one house in San Francisco $154,000 for general merchandise and lumber. This was the year of the Tom Scott boom. The firm then owned the Encinitas Ranch and part of the San Diegto Ranch, which they had stocked with some three thousand or four thousand head of cattle and over one thousand head of horses and other animals. They also had a vineyard on the ranch and a copper mine in which they sunk several thousand dollars. About this time a party of Mormons left their settlement at San Bernardino for the purpose of prospecting for coal along the coast between Point Loma and La Jolla. They found some good specimens of coal, but after they had been at work a little while they were ordered home to Utah by Brigham Young.

Schiller and his partner had furnished them with tools, provisions, and clothing, and had even advanced money to pay the hands. When they were ordered to Utah the firm naturally felt a little anxious about their pay. Mr. Schiller accordingly went up to San Bernardino, where he saw the leading Mormons. After stating the case to them they agreed to reimburse him and gave one hundred and forty-five acres of good land in settlement of the bill. About three years afterwards they traded the land off for the Encinitas Ranch. Nine or ten years ago they sold this ranch, sending their stock to Mexico on account of a drouth here. They still have three or four hundred head of stock in that country.

During all this time they were doing a large mercantile business and bought a good deal of land in Old Town and in New San Diego, considerable of which they still own. They own most of the Schiller & Mannasse Addition.

Mr. Schiller has contributed his full share to all public improvements and for many years there has been no movement started for the benefit of the city that their firm name has not been at the head of the list. No church has been built but they have contributed liberally; they paid $1,000 bonus to induce the telegraph company to build the first line here, and they subscribed handsomely to pay the expenses of the Texas Pacific lobby in Washington. They also gave twenty acres of land and the right of way through their addition to Tom Scott. Mr. Schiller was a stockholder and director in the old Texas, Gila, and San Diego Railway. He was a member of the Board of Trustees for two years, and during that time was instrumental in passing the resolution setting aside one thousand and four hundred acres of land for the city park. He is a director and on the Committee of Relief of the San Diego Benevolent Association, which has done so much to ameliorate the condition of the sick and poor. For thirty-four years Mr. Schiller has been a member of the Masonic Order. He joined the order in Augusta, Georgia. He was Master Mason of the Lodge here and has at different times held all the offices in the San Diego Lodge. He owns a comfortable residence on the corner of Front and A Streets, built fourteen years ago.

Mr. Schiller was married in September, 1861, at San Francisco, to Miss Rebecca Barnett. They have a family of nine children, four sons and five daughters.

THOMAS WHALEY.-

There is something at once interesting and fascinating about the life, character, and history of the California pioneers. They were, as a class, exceptional men, strong in most of the qualities that go to make up the typical American character. They were energetic, courageous, and far-seeing. The careers of many were full of incidents, and their life histories read like fiction. Thomas Whaley is a good representative of this noble class of men. He was born in the city of New York, October 5, 1823, a descendant of Revolutionary stock. His paternal ancestors emigrated from Ireland to New England in the early part of the eighteenth century. His grandfather, Alexander Whaley, of Bushwick Cross Roads, Long Island, New York, fought under the special command of General Washington, receiving at his hand a reward for brave and daring conduct, an account of which is given in the

BIOGRAPHICAL SKETCHES.   97

history of Brooklyn. His maternal ancestors were of the old English family of Pye, four brothers of which landed in New York about the year 1792, bringing with them his mother, then an infant. His childhood and youth were spent in the metropolis. He had the advantage of the best of schools, completing his course at the age of eighteen, at Washington Institute, New York City, which was named and dedicated

THOMAS WHALEY.

by Lafayette, in honor of his friend, George Washington, on the occasion of his last visit to this country. In 1842, before the establishment of steamship lines, he went with his tutor, M. Emile Mallet, to Europe and for two years traveled over England and the continent for instruction and pleasure. Upon his return he was variously engaged in mercantile pursuits, and at the time of the breaking out of the California gold fever, he was in the shipping office of George Sutton, owner of a line of packets running to Charleston, South Carolina.

The old ship *Sutton*, Wardle master, was at this time being fitted out to sail to the coast of California on a trading voyage. The preparations were interrupted, however, by the news of the discovery of gold, and it was decided, instead of sending the *Sutton* on a trading voyage, to fit her up as a passenger packet to carry emigrants to the New El Dorado. Young Whaley, brimful of pluck and enthusiasm, decided to join the fortune seekers, and took passage on the *Sutton*. The ship had quick dispatch, and on the first day of January, 1849, the *Sutton* sailed from New York Harbor. Snow was on the ground and Staten Island and the Jersey shore were wrapped in a mantle of white. Quite a crowd assembled at the wharf to see the first vessel from New York set sail for the gold fields of California. The greetings exchanged by friends were cordial and mutual and many were the requests for "chunks of gold, some as big as your head."

Among the passengers were A. C. Taylor, W. R. Wadsworth, George D. Puffer, Chas. S. Palmer, Chas. H. Strybing, A. Kuhner (the engraver of the great seal of California), Moseley, father and son, and Dr. Johnson and his nephew, Tom Grant. In all there were fifty-four passengers. They had rather a rough time of it after they got into the Gulf Stream, and all the way down to the line they experienced more or less heavy weather, so that it was found necessary to put into Rio de Janeiro for repairs. Here they remained for three weeks and during that time Whaley stayed on shore, having quarters at the old Hotel Ferrou. There were at least one thousand and seven hundred Americans in port from different ships, all bound for California, and many pleasant acquaintances were formed. Repairs being completed, Captain Wardle hoisted the "blue peter," and the *Sutton* was once more under way. They were a month doubling Cape Horn, having lost their reckoning and being unable to get an observation during that time. A sad accident occurred after rounding the cape. A number were, against the orders of the captain, in the stern boat fishing for "gonies." Owing to the weight, the boat broke away and a dozen or more were precipitated into the water. All were rescued except one shoemaker, who disappeared, battling with the gonies, who had picked into his brain, thus rendering effort useless. The sea was rough, the waves running high, and the man sank before help could reach him.

They stopped a week at Valparaiso for recreation and to obtain fresh provisions. On the 22d of July, nearly seven months after leaving New York, they neared the California shore, and passing within the Golden Gate, came to anchor amidst the fleet of vessels that had been more fortunate. Mr. Whaley remained on board the ship until the erection of a tent on the corner of Jackson and Montgomery Streets, near where the old Pioneer Hall stands. Their goods were landed at the foot of Washington Street, which then extended about a hundred feet below the corner of Montgomery. Whaley, with his friend Puffer, leased a portion of the store belonging to George S. Wardle & Co., erected a short time after his arrival in the city, and engaged in the mercantile business. In the fall of 1849 he leased a piece of land from Colonel Stevenson, agent of Henry Gerke, on Montgomery Street, opposite to George S. Wardle & Co.'s, for which he paid $450 per month; he sub-let a portion of this for $400 per month, and erected a two-story building containing ten rooms upstairs and two stores below, and leased one of the latter and occupied the other for his business. When Montgomery Street was graded this building was fifteen feet below the grade established. This proved disastrous, as all of Whaley's tenants left him and his business was destroyed. He then bought property on Rincon Point and erected a dwelling-house about opposite to where the U. S. Marine Hospital now stands. He engaged in business as a broker for a while and afterwards became a coffee merchant. In the summer of 1851 Lewis A. Franklin and George H. Davis chartered a vessel and with a cargo of goods started down the coast on a trading voyage. Whaley, who had an interest in the venture, remained in San Francisco, as their agent. Franklin and Davis stopped at various ports, finally at San Diego, and liked the prospects so well that they decided to locate. They wrote to Whaley and he came down, arriving here in the month of October, 1851. He then formed a partnership with Franklin, and together they opened a store on the plaza in Old San Diego, which they christened *Tienda California*—California Store. The following April their partnership was dissolved, and in connection with Jack Hinton, Whaley succeeded to the business of R. E. Raymond, in the *Tienda General*—General Store—also at Old San Diego. They remained in partnership for one year and during that time cleared $18,600 over and above expenses, a very large sum for such a business. In April, 1853, Hinton retired and E. W. Morse entered the firm. Whaley returned to New York about this time on a mission at once pleasant and romantic. On the 14th of August, 1853, he was married to Anna E. Lannay, of New York, a descendant of the De Lannay and Godtrois families, of pure French extraction. He then returned to San Diego, bringing his bride with him. They took up their residence in Old San Diego, which was then a thriving town, though primitive in its appearance and containing a mixed population of Spaniards, Mexicans, Indians, and whites. The change from the bustling metropolis to this quaint old town was novel and delightful, and the time spent with the hospitable people was particularly enjoyable.

In 1856 Morse retired from the business and Whaley continued alone, at the same time engaging in brickmaking in Mission Valley, near Old San Diego. He also erected a large brick building in 1856, the first built on the coast south of San Francisco. In 1858 he was engaged in mercantile business with Walter Ringgold, a son of Major George H. Ringgold, Paymaster United States Army, but in less than a year this store on the Plaza, Old Town, was destroyed by an incendiary fire.

At the breaking out of the Indian war in 1852, Whaley joined the Fitzgerald volunteers. There was a general rising of the Indians between Los Angeles and San Diego. Martial law was proclaimed in San Diego, and until their suppression by the capture and execution of their leader, Antonio Garra, the times were quite lively.

About January, 1859, Whaley went to San Francisco, and in March was appointed commissary storekeeper, under Capt. M. D. L. Simpson, United States Army, in which employ, under successive commissaries, he remained for several years. He then engaged in the shipping and commission business for nearly two years. After that, under Col. G. H. Weeks, Quartermaster, in charge of the clothing department, he was appointed storekeeper, and there remained till Colonel Weeks was relieved by Captain Sawyer, military storekeeper.

About this time the Russian Possessions, purchased at the instance of Wm. H. Seward, were to be turned over to the United States. Troops were to be sent up to Alaska under the command of General Jefferson and C. Davis, with Col. George H. Weeks Quartermaster, and acting Commissary of Subsistence, who procured an order for Whaley to take charge of the three Government transports, with stores, on their arrival at Sitka, as Quartermaster's agent. He proceeded on one of these transports and arrived at his destination September 26, 1867. The steamer *John L. Stevens*, Captain Dall, with General Davis and command, arrived October 10, and a few days thereafter the United States steamer *Ossipe*, having on board the Commissioners. Within an hour after their arrival the Territory was turned over to the United States by Russia. Whaley, in company with others, assisted in raising the American flag on the island of Japonski, opposite Sitka, simultaneously with the lowering of the Russian ensign, and the hoisting of the stars and stripes over the Governor's house at Sitka. Whaley remained in Alaska as commissary storekeeper and clerk until March, 1868. He was elected with Samuel Storer, W. S. Dodge, Lugerville, and one other, Councilmen of the town of Sitka, and helped to frame such civil laws for the government of the people as were permitted by General Davis, the Military Governor of the Territory. Whaley returned to San Francisco and then with his family went to New York. With the proceeds of a partial distribution of his father's estate invested in a stock of goods, he returned to San Diego and again engaged in business at Old Town. This was shortly after Father Horton had started his new town of San Diego, known as Horton's Addition. Everything then was booming in the Old Town. There were twelve stores, some of them carrying large stocks, particularly J. S. Mannasse & Co., fifteen saloons, four hotels, two express offices, the post-office, besides being the county seat. To secure a good location, in the spring of 1869, Whaley bought out his old partner Morse, who was doing a good business on the Plaza, and, in company with Philip Crosthwaite, continued business then till February, 1870, when it became evident that New San Diego was to be the point where the city of the future would be established, and the firm resolved to move their stock there; but the connection from beginning to end was a disastrous one to Whaley. In 1873 he again went to New York and remained there nearly five years, variously engaged. During this time he settled up the estate of his father, which, owing to the panic of '73, realized but the tithe of what he had expected. In 1879 Whaley returned to California. After passing a few months in San Francisco, he reached home, San Diego, in the latter part of 1879, poorer than ever he had been before. In the fall of 1880 there were prospects of a railroad, and a boom for San Diego. Whaley made a proposition to E. W. Morse to go into the real estate business, which was accepted and shortly afterward they admitted Charles P. Noell, the firm being Morse, Noell & Whaley, till February, 1886, when Mr. Noell sold his interest to R. H. Dalton, the firm being Morse, Whaley, & Dalton, till February, 1887, when Mr. Morse retired, leaving the firm Whaley & Dalton. Mr. Whaley bought considerable property in and around Old Town and at La Playa, the greater part of which he still retains. He has also acquired an interest in other property, known as firm property in different parts of the city, some of which, the Fifth Street property, is being improved from the sale of outside property belonging to the firm. He retired from active business last February to pass the few years remaining in peace and happiness with his wife, surrounded by loving children and grandchildren, dispensing the surplusage of his wealth for the relief of suffering humanity.

With the exception of being City Trustee in 1885, City Clerk in 1881 and 1882, Notary Public for the county of San Diego for six years, and Councilman for Sitka, Alaska, Whaley has never held any public office.

HON. JAMES McCOY.

THE pioneer American residents of San Diego were a marked body of men. Many of them are living here to-day, and the positions they occupy among their fellows denote that they possess qualifications that would make them leaders in any community. They were generally self-made men, who, by reason of their native force of character, succeeded in surmounting obstacles before which less heroic material would have been overwhelmed. These were the men who, when San Diego's future greatness was in embryo, sprang to the front, and with their push and determination started the young city on its progress toward commercial supremacy. One of the foremost among this class is the subject of this sketch.

James McCoy was born in County Antrim, Ireland, August 12, 1821. He lived with his parents, and worked on a farm for the first twenty years of his life. Then he began to yearn for that land of liberty beyond the sea, and in the summer of 1842 he took passage in the ship *Alexander*, for the United States, landing at Baltimore on the ninth of July. Here he found employment in a market garden, and afterward at a distillery. In these occupations he remained seven years. In 1849 he enlisted in the regular army, in Captain Magruder's Battery, which was under orders for the Pacific Coast. They sailed from Baltimore January 27, 1850, and landed in San Francisco on the tenth of August. They remained in that city about ten days, and then sailed down the coast for San Diego, which was to be their station. There was at that time considerable trouble with the Indians, and McCoy was sent, as a non-commissioned officer, with twelve men to San Luis Rey Mission, in the San Luis Rey Valley, about forty miles from San Diego. He remained at this post for two years and a half, and during that time his small force was often called upon to aid the settlers from Indian attacks. After leaving San Luis Rey he was sent with fourteen men to Jacumba, a station for keeping express horses and for mail carriers, on the road to Yuma. He remained there for about eleven months, until, his term of enlistment having expired, he was honorably discharged from the service. While at Jacumba he was often threatened by the Indians, and for better security he built a small fort. Here he was at one time attacked by a band of five hundred Indians, but his party were all picked men and trained to Indian fighting, and they succeeded in beating off their assailants.

He then went with a surveying party on the Colorado Desert to lay out townships. He was engaged in this business for two months and a half, and then was employed in the Government service driving teams between San Diego and Fort Yuma. He continued at this work for a little over two years, and then entered the employ of the San Antonio and San Diego Mail Line. He had charge of the mail between

HON. JAMES McCOY.

San Diego, and afterward between Yuma and Tucson. This was quite a hazardous service, and he had many narrow escapes from the Indians, besides suffering untold hardships in crossing the desert through which his route lay. In his trips from Yuma to Tucson he made some very rapid time. He once rode the distance of three hundred miles in three days and eleven hours and only changed mules twice. The man who rode with him, S. A. Ames, now lives at Riverside.

In the latter part of 1859, while carrying the mail, he was elected Assessor of San Diego County, and in 1861 he was elected Sheriff. He was re-elected five times, and remained in the office of Sheriff until he was elected to the State Senate, in 1871, when he resigned. In 1859, while Assessor, he became interested in raising sheep, and continued in that business until 1868. Mr. McCoy prides himself that he raised the best flock of sheep in San Diego County. In 1867 he bought the San Bernardo, a four-league ranch, for $4,000, and still owns a part of it. It is situated about thirty miles from San Diego. Mr. McCoy served one term of four years in the Senate, his term expiring in 1875. While in the Senate he used his best efforts to arrange for offering subsidies to induce the building of a railroad to San Diego. It was mainly through his efforts that the right of way was granted to the Texas Pacific. He also succeeded in having a bill passed authorizing the city to issue bonds to buy the San Diego and Gila Company —an old organization formed in early days. This company had succeeded in having two leagues of land granted them by the Legislature for the purpose of building their road. The bonds of the city were issued for the purpose of buying up the rights of this old company, as well as for purchasing the right of way for the Texas Pacific.

Mr. McCoy was one of the organizers and directors of the Commercial Bank of San Diego, and is now a director of the Consolidated Bank. He was also one of the organizers and a director in the San Diego Savings Bank. He was one of the organizers of the Commercial Bank of Los Angeles, since reorganized and now known as the First National Bank, in which he is a stockholder. He has been a City Trustee for fourteen years. There has been no public movement looking to the advancement of San Diego that has not had Mr. McCoy's active countenance and assistance. He owns considerable city property, and nineteen hundred and twenty acres of the San Bernardo Ranch, adjoining Escondido. He resides in Old San Diego, where he has a fine residence, erected eighteen years ago. Mr. McCoy was married in Old San Diego, May 17, 1868, to Miss Winnifred Kearney. They have no children.

ANDREW CASSIDY.

ONE of the pioneer residents of San Diego is Andrew Cassidy. He is a native of County Cavan, Ireland. When seventeen years of age he emigrated to the United States, landing at Boston. Having had the advantage of an excellent education in his native land, he was well prepared to accept of a position, which was offered him in the Engineer Corps, at West Point, under the immediate direction of George

B. McClellan. He remained at the Point for three years, and from there went to Washington, where he was employed in the Coast Survey office, under Professor Bates. He remained in that position about a year, when he was ordered out to the Pacific Coast with a party of five others, under Capt. W. B. Trowbridge, of the Engineer Corps, U. S. A. The party came by the way of the Isthmus, and landed at

ANDREW CASSIDY.

San Francisco in July, 1853. There they were engaged for about two months in putting up a self-registering gauge at Fort Point. Leaving one man in charge the others started for San Diego. They chartered a schooner and made a series of observations on the way down the coast. They entered the harbor of San Diego, and landed at Point La Playa, where they put up another gauge, and Cassidy was left in charge. He was stationed here in charge of meteorological and tide observations for seventeen years. During this period he made Old San

Diego his headquarters the greater part of the time. In 1864 he saw an excellent opportunity to engage in stock-raising and availed himself of it. He employed a man to take charge of the details, and only exercised a general supervision until he resigned his position in the Coast Survey. His ranch, which was then known as Soledad, situated twelve miles from Old Town, contained one thousand acres of exceedingly rich land. He had on this place at times one thousand head of cattle. The present town of Sorrento is upon this ranch. Mr. Cassidy continued in the stock business from 1864 to the beginning of the year 1887. He then sold out all his stock interests and subdivided his ranch, realizing a handsome sum from the proceeds of his land sales. Besides his interests at Sorrento he owns considerable city and suburban property. He served one term as city trustee in 1865, and again in 1871 was elected for two terms (four years).

Mr. Cassidy has been twice married, but is now a widower. He has one daughter, born to his second wife. Besides conducting his large farming interests, Mr. Cassidy has been a true friend to San Diego, contributing his share towards the city's material advancement. Personally he is very courteous, and his address marks him as one who has mingled much with men of the world. He is extremely popular among his acquaintances, and everywhere regarded as at once a progressive and substantial citizen.

ROBERT KELLY.

ONE of the pioneer residents of San Diego County is Robert Kelly. The ground where thirty-five years ago his cattle grazed at will, is now the site of a thriving city, and the bay on the shores of which he assisted in building the first wharf, is now thronged with shipping from all parts of the world. Mr. Kelly was born on the Isle of Man, Christmas day, 1825. His boyhood days were spent upon a farm, though when he was about fourteen he began to learn the carpenter's trade. When he was sixteen years old he left with his parents for the United States. They landed at New Orleans. Soon afterward his parents moved to Illinois, but Robert decided to earn his own livelihood and remained for a time in Louisiana working as a carpenter. He went from there to St. Louis, where he continued at carpentering and cabinet making, and in the evenings after his day's labor was over he attended school. Thus he acquired the rudiments of a fair education that was of great advantage to him in after years. From St. Louis he went to Galena, Illinois, and then to the Wisconsin pineries, where for about a year he was engaged, most of the time, in rafting timber on the Wisconsin River. At the end of this time, he went to Hancock County, Illinois, where he worked at his trade. In the summer of 1850 he started across the plains for

California. The party came by the southern route and their objective point was Yuma on the Colorado River. Here Kelly went to work for the Government and built a ferry-boat to cross the river. This craft was made out of cottonwood, the only timber growing there, which was sawed with a whipsaw.

After a few months he crossed the State to San Diego. Here he

ROBERT KELLY.

assisted in building the first wharf that was ever made in San Diego harbor. It was near where the Santa Fe wharf now stands. In the latter part of 1851 he went to work for the Government driving a six-mule team, hauling freight across the country to Fort Yuma. After several trips as a driver he was appointed wagon master, a position of greater responsibility, but more agreeable. In September, 1852, he went into partnership with Colonel Eddy on the Jamacha Ranch, where he engaged in farming and cattle raising. He planted rye, wheat, oats, barley and potatoes on three hundred acres and made a success of it. The ranch contained eight thousand eight hundred and seventy-six acres and was situated about twelve miles east of the present city of San Diego. At the time he sold out his interest in 1857, they had between two hundred and three hundred head of horses and one thousand cattle, and their stock often grazed on the shores of the bay, where is now the city of San Diego. Having sold out his interest in Jamacha he went into the mercantile business in Old San Diego with Frank Ames. He continued in this business for about a year. In 1860 he again engaged in cattle raising on the Agua Hedionda Ranch in partnership with F. Hinton. This ranch, which consisted of thirteen thousand three hundred and fourteen acres, is situated on the coast thirty-five miles north of the city. He now owns the whole of it, with the exception of three hundred and sixty-four acres, which he sold, and makes his home there. The ranch is all inclosed with twenty-five miles of fence. The California Southern Railroad Company has a station on the ranch.

Mr. Kelly has had quite an adventurous life. In early days he was one of the Judges of the Plains. These were men appointed by the Supervisors of the county to settle all disputes over the ownership of cattle. They naturally provoked enmity, especially from the lawless portion of the community. About dark on the evening of July 16, 1856, after a hard day's ride looking after some cattle, he was attacked on the Cajon Ranch by a gang of Mexican desperadoes who attempted to kill him. They succeeded in wounding him severely, three bullets taking effect: one grazed the top of his head, one struck him in the back of the neck, sideways, coming out about two inches above, and the other went through the muscles of his left arm. He carries the marks of these wounds to this day. He had the satisfaction of knowing that all of his assailants were killed a short time after in a revolution in Lower California, Mexico.

Mr. Kelly owns a good deal of real estate in the city and considerable outside property. He is one of the public-spirited men of the county and has contributed liberally to every movement tending to advance the public interests. He gave forty acres of land in the city and a money consideration, besides the right of way through his ranch, as his share towards bringing the railroad here.

Although over sixty years of age, Mr. Kelly is as alert and active as most men twenty years younger. The many days spent in the saddle and nights passed beneath the canopy of heaven have served to insure a state of health that many might well envy. He is firmly of the opinion that there is no place like San Diego, and as a climate for prolonging life it has no equal. Mr. Kelly is a bachelor.

COLONEL C. P. NOELL.

ONE could not have been in San Diego any great length of time up to the latter part of 1887 without having his attention attracted to a tall, fine-looking old gentleman, with silvery hair and a snowy white beard, slightly bent, as he walked along Fifth Street, having a pleasant word and a kindly greeting for all his acquaintances, and they comprised a large majority of those he met. This was Col. C. P. Noell, who was one of San Diego's oldest, most respected, and wealthiest citizens. He was born in Bedford County, Virginia, February 20, 1812. His parents were Virginians, and his grandparents were also natives of the Old Dominion. His early boyhood was passed in Lynchburg. He received his education at a school in Bedford County, about eighteen miles from Lynchburg. After leaving school he was engaged in mercantile business in Lynchburg until 1846. He then went to New Orleans, where he remained a few months, but the Mexican war was raging at the time, and as he had an opportunity to enter upon a profitable speculation by taking a stock of goods to Vera Cruz, where our troops, under General Scott, had, after a brief siege, become masters of the city, he availed himself of it. Having obtained an appointment as sutler, he remained in Vera Cruz for eighteen months. Disposing of his goods to advantage at the end of that time, he went to New York, and in a few months afterwards—in November, 1848—he sailed for California, doubling Cape Horn, in company with General Mason, the first military governor of our new acquisition on the shores of the far-away Pacific. The vessel in which he took passage was the *Silvie de Grasse*, and had been a packet running between New York and Havre, France. There were three other vessels sailing in the fleet, all loaded with troops. Noell was then in partnership with Samuel Hewes, who afterwards engaged in business in the young city of San Francisco, but was burned out several times and finally went to Australia. Mr. Noell landed in San Francisco in April, 1849. He had brought with him a stock of piece goods, which did not prove adapted to the market, so he shipped them up to Oregon City, and there disposed of them to advantage. He then returned to San Francisco and engaged in merchandising from July, 1849, to December of that year, when the first of the big fires that devastated San Francisco in its early days occurred, and swept away everything he had. In February, 1850, he came to San Diego, then situated at Old Town, and erected the first wooden building in the place. It is still standing there on the Plaza. This building was framed and packed in the East, and had been sent around the Horn to San Francisco. Colonel Noell saw it there, and purchased it, shipping it to San Diego by sailing vessel. In this building the Colonel carried on a general merchandise business for a year and a half, having as a partner Judge John Hayes. In company with M. M. Sexton and James Fitten, the Colonel bought a schooner in San

COLONEL. C. P. NOELL.

Francisco. He loaded it with a miscellaneous cargo and started down the coast. He sailed up the Gulf of California, and having disposed of his stock and vessel to advantage, he bought a large band of sheep in Sonora, and shipped them across the Gulf, from Guyamas to Moleje. From the latter point the Colonel started to drive them overland to San Diego. The country was a rough one, and for seventy-five miles there was no water to be had. They carried a little with them, packed in rawhide pouches, but, as might be expected, they were on short allowance. Over this arid waste progress was slow and fatiguing in the extreme, and many of the sheep dropped down and died. They started with thirty-six hundred, and on reaching San Diego had about three thousand. In 1853 the Colonel sold out his business in Old Town to his partner, Hayes. He was elected to the State Legislature by the Democrats, in the autumn of 1853. The Legislature assembled in Benicia, in December, and a month later removed to Sacramento. Here they remained in session continuously until May of the following year. There was no public business of importance transacted, the whole time of the session being occupied in an effort to elect a United States Senator. The Legislature was largely Democratic, but there was a strong wing of the party opposed to David C. Broderick, the leading candidate, and after months of debating, wrangling, and balloting they adjourned, unable to effect a choice. The next year Broderick overcame the opposition and was elected.

After his return from the Legislature Colonel Noell went to Central America, where he remained two or three years traveling through the country, in company with several others, prospecting for gold. He then went to New Orleans, going across the State of Honduras, and thence by the Carribean Sea. He remained a short time in New Orleans, and then went into Texas to visit his brother, with whom he remained several years. In 1870 he returned to San Diego, but remained only a short time, going back to Texas. Three years later, however, he came back to San Diego to settle down, after his many wanderings, for good.

In 1850 Colonel Noell, with ten others, bought the addition to San Diego known as Middletown. This proved a very lucrative investment. In addition to this he owned considerable real estate in other parts of the city. He was formerly a member of the real estate firm of Morse, Noell & Whaley, but retired from active business in February, 1886. Colonel Noell did his full share towards placing San Diego in connection with the outside world by means of the railroad, and had generally interested himself in all projects tending to benefit the city. He was a member of the Building and Loan Association, and a stockholder and director in the Old Town Electric Railroad. Colonel Noell was never married. He died in this city January 30, 1888, leaving a very valuable estate.

J. S. MANNASSE.

JOSEPH S. MANNASSE is another of those sterling pioneers who has seen San Diego grow from a sleepy adobe settlement to a thriving city. He has the proud satisfaction, too, of feeling that to the enterprise of men like him the present prosperity of the young metropolis is largely due.

Mr. Mannasse was born in Filehne, Prussia, August 3, 1831. His early boyhood was spent with his parents in his native town, but at the age of thirteen he began to think of supporting himself, and soon went to work to learn the trade of a furrier and cap maker. He served three years as an apprentice in Filehne. At the end of this time he began work as a journeyman at the salary of $20 a year. After serving two years he was given charge of the entire business of the establishment with twenty-five men under him, his pay being increased to $50 per annum. At the age of nineteen he left home for the United States, and landed in New York, October 15, 1850. When he stepped upon the wharf his entire capital amounted to one gold dollar. The very morning of his arrival he walked down Wall Street, and seeing the sign of a cap maker he entered the store of Eddy Brothers and asked for work. They gave him employment at once. The first year of his residence in New York he made $75. After a year or two he was promoted and was made cutter and manager. In April, 1853, he started for California, sailing on the steamer *Star of the West*, by the way of Nicaraugua. He was obliged to remain six weeks on the Isthmus, awaiting transportation. Finally the old steamer *Pacific* arrived, and he started with a large company of other passengers. Coming up the coast they entered the harbor of San Diego, coming to an anchor off La Playa. This was on Sunday, May 28, 1853. Mr. Mannasse with several others came ashore and visited the old town of San Diego. He little thought at that time it would be his future home. The same evening the steamer sailed for San Francisco. He was not as well pleased with San Francisco as he expected to be, and after remaining there a month he determined to return to San Diego. He left on the steamer *Goliah*, and after a four days' voyage down the coast, touching at the different ports, he arrived in San Diego the second time, June 28, 1853. His cash resources amounted to $200, and he determined to lose no time in engaging in some business. Accordingly he purchased a dry-goods box of Hinton, Raymond & Morse, then the leading merchants of the place, paying therefor the sum of $2.00. Out of this he made a shelf and a counter, and the next day he invested the balance of his capital in dry goods, etc. The first day after beginning business, his sales amounted to $98, and they continued to steadily increase from that time. He gradually enlarged his trading facilities and soon had a commodious store. In 1855 he was robbed of $100 in cash, but burglary was not a common crime at that day. In 1856 he formed a partnership with M. Schiller. In 1868 the firm started a lumber-yard at

J. S. MANNASSE.

the foot of Atlantic and E Streets, and soon did a large trade, carrying on their general merchandise business at the same time. In 1870 Tom Scott began his railroad and the demand for lumber was very brisk. They also had a large ranch at Encinitas, which was heavily stocked. In 1870 the drouth came, and in order to save their stock they drove it down into Lower California. The dry season had a most disastrous effect on everything. It was largely instrumental in causing the collapse of the railroad boom, and ruined a great many ranchers.

It bore very hard on the firm of Mannasse & Schiller, but they weathered the storm, although they lost $100,000, in various amounts, all of which is standing on their books to this day. Since then Mr. Mannasse has been engaged in various kinds of business with different degrees of success. At one time he happened to be so badly off that there was only only one firm in San Diego that would give him credit for a sack of flour.

Mr. Mannasse has always been one of the most liberal citizens, and there has never been a public undertaking to which he has not given his hearty indorsement. There has never been a charity proposed, or a church or a school started, that he has not contributed towards. He was one of the principal movers in establishing the Poor Farm and Hospital. He was a Supervisor for several terms, and has been elected a City Trustee two or three times. He was a member of the Board when Mr. Horton purchased his addition on which the business portion of San Diego is now located. He worked early and late to secure the building of the present railroad, and has been at different times interested in wharf and other substantial enterprises. He now owns a good deal of city property and country real estate. He is a part owner of the Mannasse & Schiller Addition, and in Mannasse & Schiller's subdivision. He is still interested in cattle and owns considerable live stock. His principal business now is that of a broker and collector.

Mr. Mannasse was married in 1867 to Miss Hannah Schiller, a sister of his partner, M. Schiller. They have one daughter.

CHARLES A. WETMORE.

ONE of the most energetic and public-spirited of San Diego's citizens is Charles A. Wetmore. He was born in Portland, Maine, January 20, 1847, but came to California when nine years of age with his mother and other members of the family, whither his father, Jesse L. Wetmore, who was one of the pioneers of the State and prominent in the early days in the development of San Francisco, had preceded them. In his business as a contractor he built the old Meiggs Wharf, and the first Music Hall in the city. Afterwards he was engaged for fourteen years in railroad building, and opening guano mines in Chili, Bolivia, and Peru.

In 1859 Charles, then twelve years old, while a student in the Hyde Street Grammar School, in company with R. L. Taber, edited, printed, and published the *Young Californian*, which was the first juvenile paper on the coast. He afterward attended the Oakland College School preparatory to entering the College of California in 1864, from

BIOGRAPHICAL SKETCHES.

which he graduated, being valedictorian of his class in 1868, at the age of twenty-one.

During the last year of his college course young Wetmore's activity of mind drew his attention to the labor problem and he became Secretary of the House Carpenters' Eight Hour League. He soon succeeded in organizing all the leagues of Alameda County into the Me-

CHARLES A. WETMORE.

chanics' Institute, of which he was elected President. While living at home he paid all his college expenses. During the last two years of his college course he was the Oakland reporter for the San Francisco *Bulletin*. His vacations were spent in exploring the State on practical missions. In the summer vacation of 1866 he took charge of the leveling party of an expedition which was conducted under a State appropriation, directed by Hon. Charles F. Reed, in the Sacramento Valley, to determine the practicability and cost of bringing the waters of the

Sacramento from Red Bluff, along the Coast Range, through the counties of Tehama, Colusa, Yolo and Solano. In 1867 he devoted the summer, at the request of the college authorities, to canvassing the central, northern and mining counties on behalf of the proposed erection of a State university. His success in awakening public sentiment was so great that, when at the next session the question came before the Legislature, there was practically no opposition to the plan of the founders of the College of California, whose magnificent property at Berkeley was accepted by the State as the first endowment of what is now the State University. As a testimony of their appreciation of his labors the trustees declined to accept any further payment of dues from Mr. Wetmore. He was also honored by having the degrees of Bachelor of Arts and Master of Arts conferred upon him. On the day of graduation he was elected Secretary and Treasurer of the Associated Alumni of the Pacific.

In 1868, immediately after his graduation, Mr Wetmore came to San Diego, which it was even then whispered was to be a future commercial metropolis. He had a strong taste for journalism and he intended to publish a newspaper, but changed his mind and established a real estate agency, the first one in the new city. He had had printed an outline map of the harbor and had copies of it placed conspicuously in San Francisco offices to attract attention. In company with Mr. Winfield Curtis he negotiated his first sale—the San Bernardo Ranch. At that time the first small house was being built on Fifth Street in Horton's Addition, and the business of the town was conducted in Old San Diego. There was no wharf and no railroad.

Studying law and searching records led him into partnership with Solon P. S. Sanborn, a very able lawyer, then practicing here. The members of the firm devoted themselves to unraveling and perfecting old land titles. There were a horde of squatters here then, who, influenced by unprincipled lawyers, were misled into seizing of the property of absent owners with the hope of defeating their titles. They claimed that the city lands had been improperly disposed of and a reign of confusion was threatened. Mr. Wetmore was one of the organizers and a leading member of the Pueblo League, whose mission it was to protect the interests of *bona fide* holders of property from the raids of these land sharks. An attempt was made at one time to steal Cleveland's Addition, and Mr. Wetmore, in company with Clarence L. Carr and Major Swope, armed for defense, rode up from Old Town, destroyed the string fences before they were completed, and stood guard all day to prevent further aggression. On another occasion, by his prompt and energetic action, he thwarted the scheme of a party of real estate pirates who attempted to steal one hundred and forty acres, including the present site of the court-house and all the land from the bay to Horton's Addition, on the north side of D Street.

This unequal contest became uncomfortably warm for all parties and a bill was drawn up by Messrs. Wetmore and Sanborn, confirming the act of the old Alcaldes and city trustees, and urged before the Legislature so strongly by Mr. Wetmore that it was passed. This put an end to the squatter controversy and laid the foundation for public confidence in land titles in San Diego.

During the dull period following the dry season of 1869-70 Mr. Wetmore joined his father in his railroad work in the Cordilleras of Peru, for one year. Upon his return to California he became attached to the editorial staff of the *Alta California*. He was soon sent to Washington as the special correspondent of that paper, and while at the national capital he had frequent opportunity to aid San Diego in her contests with giant monopolies. He secured for the ex-mission lands the United States Patents, which expedited the settlement of titles to our neighboring lands. During his stay in Washington he was a member of the Land Attorneys' Association.

In 1875 he was appointed by the Government special commissioner to report upon the condition of the Mission Indians in this county, and during a flurry of excitement along the Mexican border he secured an order of the War Department establishing the military post, which is still here.

In 1878 he was appointed delegate for the California Viticultural Association to the Paris Exposition. The letters written during his study of vineyards in France to the *Alta California* created a sensation throughout the country, and aroused the people to the importance of developing viticulture on a grander scale than had been dreamed of before.

On his return from Paris he married a young lady of Washington and abandoned journalism, returning to California to reside permanently. He perfected the organization of the State Viticultural Commission and for several years he devoted his whole time and all his energy to the development of the industry which he had aroused. As one of the members of the State Board, Vice-President and Chief Executive Officer and later President of the National Viticultural Association organized in Washington in 1886, Mr. Wetmore accomplished an amount of work in behalf of California's viticultural interests that it is almost impossible to estimate.

During all these years he managed to make occasional visits to San Diego, always looking upon it as his permanent home. The Escondido town site and vineyards were laid out under his influence by a company organized in Stockton, of which he was a member, but which subsequently transferred the property to the present management.

During the past summer Mr. Wetmore opened an office in San Diego, having resigned his position as Chief Executive Officer of the

State Viticultural Commission, and is once more an active citizen of San Diego. Here, surrounded by his family, he purposes settling down to enjoy the fruition of many years of past hopes. He has done much in the past towards laying the foundation that led to the development of the San Diego of to-day. In the future his active energy and indomitable pluck will aid in building up the great city that is bound to be.

GEORGE B. HENSLEY.

GEORGE B. HENSLEY.

ONE of the best known and most energetic of San Diego's business men is George B. Hensley. Mr. Hensley is a native of England, having been born in Cornwall, November 26, 1847. His early boyhood was spent in Cornwall and he attended school there until he was thirteen years old. He then went to work in the mines, where he remained five years. At the age of eighteen he started for the great city of London.

There he soon obtained a position in the office of a shipping and insurance broker. He remained in London for four years. The last business he was engaged in there was in a wholesale silk and lace house. In the spring of 1869 he left England for California by way of the Isthmus of Panama. He arrived in San Diego in the month of June and at once took up a ranch in Tia Juana Valley. In the early part of 1870 he became interested in mining with his brother, who discovered the Stonewall Mine at Julian. Three months afterward he went to San Francisco, where he remained a year. He then returned to San Diego, when he was appointed Deputy County Clerk, a position which he held until March, 1872. He then opened an abstract office, a business in which he was engaged till October, 1876. On account of his health he then moved into the country on a ranch, where he remained until the following year, when he was appointed United States Inspector of Customs on the Mexican line. This office he retained for seven years. In May, 1884, he went to Portland, Oregon, where he spent a year. Then he came back to San Diego and has since been engaged in the abstract and real estate business.

Mr. Hensley has been one of the most active promoters of the growth of San Diego. He has been identified with all public movements and has invested liberally in every enterprise having for its object the advancement of the city. He was one of the organizers of the San Diego Building and Loan Association and for two years acted as its Secretary. He is a stockholder in, and present Secretary of, the San Diego and Old Town Railroad Company, and a large stockholder and Secretary of the Pacific Beach Company. He is also an active member of the Chamber of Commerce. He always had strong faith in the ultimate growth of San Diego, and to-day holds real estate which he purchased when he first came here. He owns a good deal of city property and is largely interested in Pacific Beach, which is destined to be, probably, the most attractive of San Diego's suburbs. He has a residence on the southwest corner of Ninth and D Streets, which he erected two years ago. Mr. Hensley was married in this city in 1873 to Miss Hulda Bowers, sister of Senator W. W. Bowers. He has four children.

It is to men like George B. Hensley that San Diego is largely indebted for the rapid progress she has made during the past two or three years. Public-spirited, generous, progressive, he is an excellent type of the true American citizen.

WILLIAM E. HIGH.

MORE than twenty-five years ago a little book was published that attracted wide attention, and was the subject of considerable comment. It was entitled, "Ten Acres Enough," and was written to show how much the owner of ten acres of land in the State of New Jersey had raised; how he had supported his family, saved a considerable sum each year, and lived an independent and contented life. In the vicinity of San Diego there might be found a counterpart of this New Jersey farmer's experience on one-half the amount of land. The results that have followed the thorough cultivation of a plot of five acres of rich soil in the Cholla Valley have been often told, but there is comparatively little known of the man whose industry and judicious care caused the earth to yield such abundant returns.

William E. High was born in Berks County, Pennsylvania, on the first day of January, 1830. He remained on his farther's farm until he was twenty years old, attending the district schools as opportunity offered. Then he went to Chester County and lived with an uncle for two years. At the end of that time he returned to the old farm. About a year after this his father died, and then the place was sold and he hired out to work on a farm in the same county. He remained there for three years, and during that time taught the district school for one session. Afterwards he went to Bucks County and during 1856-57 ran a saw-mill. The latter part of 1857, however, saw him back again in Berks County, where he stayed until the following spring. These frequent changes in business had tended to unsettle him somewhat and he decided to seek a new country. He had heard much of California, and the fortunes that had been acquired in that distant land. Thither then he determined to journey. After two weeks spent in New York City he set sail on the *Star of the West* for Cuba, and from there took passage on the *New Granada* for Aspinwall. Crossing the isthmus he took the *John L. Stephens* at Panama, and after an uneventful voyage he arrived at San Francisco, the 15th of May, 1858. The same day he left for Sacramento, and from there went through Placer and El Dorado Counties. At Diamond Springs, in the latter county, he worked in a saw-mill for six months. Then he went to Nevada County, where he engaged in mining, following that business with varying degrees of success for nearly ten years. During this time he was located at Moore's Flat and at North San Juan. Early in 1868 he visited San Francisco,

BIOGRAPHICAL SKETCHES.

and while there made up his mind to come to the southern part of the State. He accordingly went back to Nevada County, settled up his business, and in the following spring started for San Diego, arriving here on the 2d of March. Being well pleased with the outlook he decided to remain. He located one hundred and sixty acres of land eighteen miles southeast of the city, but sold it in six months' time and

WILLIAM E. HIGH.

settled on another piece of one hundred and seventy-five acres adjoining the National Ranch Grant, ten miles from San Diego. He cultivated a small portion of this in fruit, and remained on it for four years, during which time he acquired a title, after some difficulty experienced, some parties claiming it as a Mexican grant. About the 1st of January, 1874, he moved to Cholla Valley, two and one-half miles from San Diego, where he purchased five acres of land, and there he and his brother engaged in raising fruit of different varieties. They experimented with various kinds until they found what was most suitable to the soil and climate, and those varieties they adhered too. The result was that they soon acquired the reputation of raising the finest fruits to be found in this section, and the product of their orchard commanded the highest prices.

Mr. High still remains on this famous place, and, with his brother, still cultivates it. In April, 1876, he went East to attend the Centennial and while absent was married. He returned in October with his bride. Two and a half years later she died; her maiden name was Susan Bechtel. For the last eight years Mr. High has been a member of the Cemetery Commission of San Diego; he was the first President of the San Diego Horticultural Society and is now its Vice-President. He was one of the Directors and Vice-President for two years of the Consolidated National Bank, and was a stockholder in the old San Diego Bank before the consolidation. He is interested in the San Diego and Cuyamaca Railroad, now in the course of construction. Four years ago he bought about two thousand acres of land in the Cuyamaca Grant, and he and his brother now own three thousand acres there, which is used for grazing purposes, and they have over two hundred head of cattle on it. Mr. High and his brother are equally interested in all their enterprises, and together they own considerable city and outside property. The site of Otay was sold by his brother to the present owners. Together they contributed one hundred and sixty acres of fine land as a bonus to the California Southern to induce them to build their road here. Mr. High has contributed liberally to all public movements, and although of a retiring disposition, he is in reality one of San Diego's most progressive and substantial citizens. It is to the earnest and well-timed efforts of men like William E. High that the present prosperous condition of this thriving city is largely due.

AARON PAULY.

A CALIFORNIA pioneer and one of the oldest residents of San Diego is Aaron Pauly. Mr. Pauly was born in Lebanon, Warren County, Ohio, May 24, 1812. His father died when he was five years of age. His youth and early manhood were passed in Warren County, and, until he was fourteen, on a farm. When thirty years old he started West and located in Quincy, Illinois, where he engaged in the mercantile business and remained until the spring of 1849. Gold had been discovered in California, and emigrants were flocking to the new El Dorado from all parts of the civilized world. Mr. Pauly formed a party and started across the plains for the Pacific Coast in the spring of that eventful year. Travelers and tourists of the present day, journeying overland in Pullman coaches, can have but slight conception of the fatigues, dangers, and delays that attended a journey to California in 1849. Each of the different routes had its hardships. The voyager by sea was tossed and buffeted about in closely-packed and ill-provisioned ships for months; those who journeyed by way of the Isthmus, in addition to the discomforts of a sea voyage, were compelled to pass through the fever-

AARON PAULY.

stricken districts of the Isthmus; the march across the plains was long and arduous; the trains were liable to attacks from Indians, their cattle often died from want of water and proper pasturage, and, in some cases, the emigrants themselves fell victims to the drought. There were twenty-five persons in the train with which Mr. Pauly crossed the plains. They came by the way of Salt Lake and the Truckee River, stopping finally at Coloma, a mining camp near Sacramento, built on the site of Sutter's Mill, in the race-way of which gold had been discovered two years before, by John W. Marshall. Mr. Pauly remained at Coloma during the winter of 1849-50, but in the spring went to the mines in Butte County, where he remained for two years. Having been quite prosperous in his ventures, he bought a large stock ranch at Spring Valley, Yuba County, twelve miles from Marysville. Here he made his home till 1865. He then disposed of the ranch and removed to Marysville, where he remained three years, engaged in the mercantile business with his sons, F. N. and C. W. Pauly. In 1869, on account of ill health, he disposed of his business in Marysville and moved to San Diego. Horton's Wharf had just been completed and Mr. Pauly landed the first stock of goods upon it. He opened a store, which was connected with the wharf, and had charge of the latter. At this time he had considerable trouble with Ben Holladay, who refused to allow his steamers to touch at Horton's Wharf. Finally, however, after threatening to charter a schooner and transport his goods independent of the steamship line, Holladay gave in and permitted his vessels to load and discharge at the wharf.

Mr. Pauly remained in the merchandise business until 1875, when he sold out and went into real estate, commission, and insurance with his son, C. W. Pauly. He has now retired from active business and devotes his time to conducting his private affairs. Mr. Pauly was a member of the Board of Supervisors in 1873-74. He was also Tax Collector for nine years, from 1875 to 1884, and was one of the organizers and first President of the Chamber of Commerce. During the time that he was at the head of this institution, the railroad was built into San Diego, and it is not too much to say that Aaron Pauly's labors did much to bring about that important event. He was one of the founders of the Baptist Society here, selected the lots and aided largely in building the present fine church edifice on the corner of E and Ninth Streets. Mr. Pauly owns considerable real estate in different parts of the city. In conjunction with D. C. Reed he built the fine business block on the corner of E and Sixth Streets, known as the Reed-Pauly Block; and with A. G. Gassen he will soon erect a magnificent four-story brick block on the northeast corner of E and Fourth Streets, which will cost, when completed, fully $100,000. He has lately finished a handsome and spacious residence on the corner of D and Eleventh Streets. It is the Queen Anne style of architecture, and is considered one of the most tasteful private residences in the city.

In addition to his interests in San Diego, Mr. Pauly has done much to further and develop the mines of the county, and the mining region of Julian is probably more deeply indebted to him, than to any other individual, for its present prosperous outlook. He was also one of the projectors and president of the company that built the wagon road from Yuma to San Diego. This road was of great benefit to San Diego, and a great deal of business was done over it, which continued until the opening of the Southern Pacific Railroad. Mr. Pauly was one of the organizers of the San Diego Benevolent Association, a society which is still in existence, and has for many years, in an unostentatious way, accomplished much charitable work.

Mr. Pauly was married in 1840 to Miss Elmira Nye, a native of Vermont. The result of this union was four children living, two sons and two daughters. Besides he had one daughter by his first wife, to whom he was married in 1834, but she died in a little more than a year afterwards. His eldest daughter is the wife of General Dustin, of Sycamore, Illinois, who served all through the War of the Rebellion. His sons are living in Southern California, one being employed in the First National Bank in Los Angeles and the other being engaged in the real estate business here. One daughter is married and living in Gridley, Butte County.

Mr. Pauly has fully realized his early expectations in the present wonderful growth and prosperity of San Diego. He is in excellent health, and bids fair to have many days of usefulness before him.

D. CHOATE.

It was a happy inspiration which led the fathers of the State of Maine to adopt as the motto of the young commonwealth, "Dirigo"—I direct. Situated on the northeastern confines of the Union, her territory reaches well towards the limits of a monarchial colony, and she stands as it were the most advanced sentinel of the host of Republican States. This position in the national sisterhood has had a marked effect in the formation of the character of her citizens, and they have inherited with the air they breathe an ardor, a courage, and a strength of will that is strongly marked, and is noticeable wherever they are found. In every enterprise requiring push and daring they are among the first; in every undertaking where brain and brawn united win the day, the hardy men of Maine are to be found. When gold was discovered on the Pacific Coast and the rush was made for the new El Dorado, the sons of Maine were in the van. They joined in the great caravans that toiled and struggled in the weary march across the plains; they enlisted in the army of gold hunters whose march over the isthmus was marked by a line of fever-stricken victims; they joined the fleet of argonauts that doubled Cape Horn and passed many weary months upon the sea—all seeking one goal, all bound for one haven. Among the men from Maine who joined the hosts of '49 was the subject of this sketch.

D. Choate was born in Kennebec County, Maine, on the 9th of September, 1827. His parents were farmers, and young Choate spent the early years of his life on the farm, availing himself of such educational advantages as were to be found in the district school until 1847, when he went to Lowell, Mass., to attend school. He remained there until the winter of 1848-49. In February of the latter year he joined a party of goldseekers, and on the first day of March sailed from Boston for Chagres, on the bark *Thames*. They had an uneventful voyage and reached the

D. CHOATE.

isthmus in safety. The journey overland to Panama was attended with the usual discomforts incident to the trip in those days, but the party were more fortunate than many. Here, however, they were detained for a month waiting for a vessel in which to obtain passage to San Francisco. Finally they embarked on board an English brig, the *Two Friends*. This portion of their journey was destined to be the most tedious of any. The vessel was small and overcrowded, the winds were light or adverse, and they were one hundred and sixty-seven days on the voyage. During this time the water and provisions got very low, and they were on short allowance for one hundred days of the time. Finally, on the 12th of October, or over seven months from the time they left home, they sailed through the Golden Gate and came to an anchor off the straggling settlement of Yerba Buena. The passengers of the *Two Friends* were not long in getting ashore, and after a brief stop started for the mines, Choate making Ophir his objective point. He remained there through the winter months and in April started for Yuba. During the summer he was engaged with others in turning the river from its bed, but the results were not up to the expectations of the prospectors. In the spring of 1851, Choate returned to Ophir and soon became engaged in mercantile business at this point. He remained at Ophir, carrying on a general mercantile business, for seventeen years until the mines were exhausted. He then came down to San Francisco, and in 1868 opened a dry goods house on Kearny Street, between California and Pine. In July of the following year he wanted a brief rest from business cares and a change of air, and having heard of the sanitary advantages of San Diego he made up his mind to visit it. Steamers were then running down the coast but once a month. Mr. Choate had not been many hours in San Diego before he had decided that here was the place for him to locate. He felt confident that upon the shores of this magnificent harbor would eventually arise a city that would equal San Francisco. He had seen that city when it was but a hamlet, and he saw no reason why San Diego should not in time increase in population and wealth as it had done. So sanguine was his faith that he did not even return to San Francisco to close up his business, but wrote to his brother to sell out and follow him. In August, 1869, he found himself permanently located in San Diego engaged in the real estate business. He made it a point to buy up land by the acre, from one to three miles out, and carry all he could of it, looking to the future for his profits. He had but one object in view—the accumulation of a fortune which he had come to California to gain, but had failed to acquire in the mines. His faith in the future of his adopted city never forsook him, and through all the fluctuations that have marked the progress of San Diego towards substantial prosperity, he held on to his real estate and added to it as he could. It is a singular fact that the land Mr. Choate bought in those early days, he holds now. He has laid out ten different additions to the city, each containing from forty to eighty acres, and he now has them all on the market. The lots are selling at from $200 to $500 each. The increase in the value of his property within the last year is over $300,000.

Mr. Choate is the promoter of the famous College Hill Loan Association, which is destined to be one of the most successful real estate projects ever undertaken in Southern California. The tract consists of one thousand six hundred acres situated just north of the city park. It is laid out in blocks and lots and now on the market. Every other block in the tract is given to the M. E. Church; and the first $200,000 realized from the sale of the church lands is to be used for building a college. The balance is to be sold from time to time and the interest alone can be used. This college (which is a branch of the Methodist Episcopal University of Southern California) will probably have an endowment fund of at least $5,000,000, greater than most of the great colleges of the Eastern States. The other half of the land is the property of the College Hill Land Association, which consists of ten members, all of whom reside in this city. The stock of the Association is now selling at $100 per share; its original cost was $5.00 a share. There are one thousand five hundred shares. The Association is still buying land. It is the intention of the Methodist people to begin the erection of a college of fine arts during the present winter. There will be a steam motor line running through the tract in a short time, and water pipes will be laid to every block by the same time. Mr. Choate put this great enterprise in operation by himself, contributing one hundred and fifty acres of land.

Mr. Choate is also interested in the Steiner, Klauber, Choate & Castle Addition, containing one thousand acres, two and one-half miles from the city and just east of the College Hill Tract. This tract was placed on the market September 1, 1887, and the sales the first day reached $87,000 in this city and $16,000 in San Francisco, at $100 per lot. Then they were raised to $125 for a week, and then to $150. The total sales to January 1, 1888, exceeded $250,000. The owners of the tract have entered into a contract with Babcock & Story for a motor line through it, around to the College Hill Tract and down Fifth Street, making a belt line from D Street.

Mr. Choate was one of the prime movers in the various efforts that were made to induce the building of railroads to San Diego, from the first Tom Scott boom to the final completion of the California Southern. In 1875 he was appointed postmaster and retained the office until 1882, when he resigned to attend to his private business. He has now retired from active business, but acts as an adviser in the development of his many important real estate enterprises. Mr. Choate has just completed a palatial residence on the corner of Fifth and Hawthorne Streets, on Florence Heights. He also contemplates erecting a number of substantial business buildings on several principal streets during the coming spring. Mr. Choate is a faithful and consistent member of the Methodist Church, and has given largely to many public charities. He is now in the possession of a princely fortune, yet he says he would gladly forego it all, rather than again pass through the anxieties, reverses, and disappointments he has experienced during his residence in San Diego.

JUDGE McNEALY.

ONE of San Diego's leading citizens, prominent alike as a lawyer and a jurist, is Judge W. T. McNealy. He is a native of Georgia, having been born in Thomas County, in that State, the 22d of January, 1848. When he was about two years old his parents removed to Jackson County, Florida, and located near Mariana. His youth was spent on his father's farm, and he attended the neighboring schools until he was fourteen. He had at that early age progressed so rapidly in his studies that, being without a teacher in the district school, young McNealy was called upon to take charge, and for six months he taught the pupils acceptably. He felt desirous, however, of continuing his studies and he went to the State military school at Marietta, Georgia, known as the Military Cadet School. He remained there one year, and then the students were attached as State troops to Joe Johnston's army during the last year of the war. Young McNealy then returned to Florida and taught school for a year. At the age of eighteen he began to read law in the office of Hon. A. H. Bush, the Circuit Judge. While a law student he acted as Deputy Clerk of Jackson County. On the 7th of January, 1869, after having studied law for three years, he started, by the way of Panama, for California, and arrived in San Francisco the 22d of February. He first came to Los Angeles, and after remaining there a few days started for San Diego by stage, reaching there the last day of March, in 1869. Soon after his arrival he was admitted to the bar, and that fall was nominated and elected District Attorney of the county on the Democratic ticket. Two years later he was re-elected without opposition.

In 1873 he was elected Judge for the Eighteenth Judicial District, then comprising San Diego and San Bernardino Counties, for a term of six years. In 1879 he was elected Superior Judge of San Diego County for a term of five years; in the same year he declined the nomination for Justice of the Supreme Court on the Workingmen's ticket. In 1884, when the nominating convention was about to meet, Judge McNealy's friends and the members of the bar insisted on his being a candidate for re-election. His health was such, however, that he hesitated a long time, but finally gave a reluctant consent, and was again elected Superior Judge. In September, 1886, his health became so bad that it was physically impossible for him to perform the duties of his office, and he sent his resignation to the Governor, to take effect on the first of the following October. He then retired from active business and endeavored to avoid all professional cares of every nature, in order to thoroughly recover his health. To a man of Judge McNealy's active disposition, however, this was well-nigh impossible, and he had to keep his mind employed. The result was that before many months he found himself engaged in the active practice of his

JUDGE McNEALY.

profession. The requirements of a general practice were such that it was not possible for him to limit his labors to his strength. Finally, however, a few months since, he decided to give up all his general law practice, and now he only acts as counsel in a few special cases and may be said to have practically retired from the profession.

Judge McNealy's career in San Diego County has been, in many respects, a remarkable one. Coming here as he did, an entire stranger, just arrived at man's estate, his ability as a lawyer, united with his personal popularity, at once made him a place in the community. His administration of the office of District Attorney during his first term, was such as to win for him the encomium of the best people in both parties. During his second term he merely emphasized in the minds of the public the opinion that had been previously formed of him. Of his career upon the bench during a continuous period of thirteen years it is impossible to speak in too high terms. He performed an immense amount of labor and rendered many important decisions, some of which involved large property interests. All of his rulings appear to have been made with but one object in view,—the strict administration of justice,—and when, at length, he retired from the bench the people felt that they had lost a champion, and the bar that they had been deprived of the services of an upright and impartial judge.

Judge McNealy was married in 1872, in San Diego, to Miss Lina E. Wadham. They have five children living, four boys and one girl.

ROBERT ALLISON.

ONE of San Diego's representative citizens is Robert Allison. He is a native of Ohio, having been born in Washington County, near Marietta, in March, 1814. His father was a farmer and Robert's boyhood was passed with his parents, living on the old farm and attending the district school, which was held in a log building, and the seats were rough slabs on which the pupils sat and learned their tasks. When twenty-one years old he started out into the world on his own account. He bought a flat boat and made the voyage down the Ohio and Mississippi to New Orleans, carrying country produce. His first venture was successful and he continued in the trade for eight or nine years. He then removed to Illinois, and went to steam milling first at Warsaw, and afterward at Nauvoo. After following this business for five years he started for Iowa, where he bought a farm on the Black Hawk Reservation. He purchased eight hundred acres from the Government and cultivated a good portion of it. In 1850 he crossed the plains with an ox team to California. On the way they ran short of provisions, but managed to pull through and finally arrived at Placerville in the latter part of September. After a brief stay he went down to Sacramento, where he opened a hotel, which he carried on for six or eight months. He then located one hundred and sixty acres of land in Sutter County, which he cultivated, raising hay principally. After farming there for three years he returned to Iowa, where he remained a little more than a year, and then again crossed the plains to California, bringing with him some six hundred head of cattle. He located near Vacaville, Solano County, engaging in raising cattle. Then, in 1868, his health being poor, he came to San Diego. At first he did not intend to locate, but he found that his health was so greatly benefited by the change, and the country pleased him so much, that he decided to remain. He therefore wound up his business in Solano County and came here to make it his home. He bought up a large number of cattle and went into ranching and butchering. He

ROBERT ALLISON.

purchased three thousand acres of the Cuyamaca and eight thousand acres of ex-Mission Grant, the latter situated about four miles from the city of San Diego. He still owns these lands, and is one of the largest cattle raisers in the county. He has now retired from active business, and devotes his time to the management of his private affairs, his three sons carrying on the ranching and butchering business. They now have over four thousand head of cattle on their ranges.

Mr. Allison has never held any public office, but has devoted his attention strictly to the conduct of his business interests. He has, however, been active in all public movements and has contributed liberally to all enterprises having for their effect the advancement of the city and county. He is one of the directors and a large stockholder in the San Diego and Cuyamaca Railroad, now in course of construction. He is much opposed to intemperance, which he looks upon as the greatest curse of the age, and is an earnest and consistent advocate of prohibition. Although over seventy years of age he is as active as many men ten years younger. His health is excellent and there is every prospect that he will be spared for many years of usefulness. His faith in the future of the county is great. He believes it will yet become one of the wealthiest and most progressive of the many great counties of the State. Mr. Allison was married in Ohio in 1838, to Miss Tempa Waterman. He has had eleven children, of which four are now living, three sons and a daughter, all of whom reside in this city.

PHILIP MORSE.

PHILIP MORSE was born in Fayette, Maine, May 23, 1845. His boyhood days were passed in the village, where he attended the district school. Later on he was a pupil in the Lewiston Falls Academy, where he prepared to enter Bowdoin College in the class of 1865. Failing health, however, compelled him to give up all thought of entering college, and he decided to come to California. Arriving in San Francisco in September of that year he secured a position as salesman in the lumber yard of Glidden & Colman, pier 20, Steuart Street, where he remained until March, 1869, when he accepted a position with McDonald & Co., to come to San Diego to take charge of their lumber business here. He arrived March 9, and has been identified with the interests of the city ever since. He was absent from San Diego from 1879 to 1883, in Arizona, where he had a mill and manufactured lumber for the mines. He was associated with Mr. Jacob Gruendike in this venture. Upon his return to San Diego in 1883, he went into business with his father-in-law, G. W. B. McDonald, under the firm name of McDonald & Morse. The firm continued in existence for one year, and then, in conjunction with several San Francisco capitalists, Mr. Morse organized the San Diego Lumber Company, of which he was elected general manager. The capital stock of the company was fixed at $75,000. The sales for the past year amounted to over $750,000. He is also a stockholder in, and was one of the organizers and first superintendents of, the West Coast Redwood Company of San Francisco. He is President of the San Diego Manufacturing Company, which is engaged in the manufacture of doors, sash, blinds, etc.

Although Mr. Morse is not a politician in the ordinary acceptance of the term, he has always taken a deep interest in municipal affairs, and for nearly three years he held the office of City Treasurer. He has been twice elected a member of the City Board of Education, and is now President of that body. He is Vice-President of the Y. M. C. A., and one of the leading members of the San Diego Natural History Society.

PHILIP MORSE.

In giving this brief sketch of Philip Morse, really but one side of his character has been exposed to view. We have seen how he has risen, through the exercise of exceptionally good business qualities, from a clerkship to a position of affluence and recognized prominence in the community. We have seen him successful in his business ventures, and honored and trusted by his fellow-citizens. But there is another phase of his character, which is seldom found combined with business acumen or financial ability. In the exercise of a wise economy nature but rarely endows the same mind with more than one of what may be called her cardinal gifts. Occasionally, however, when in a lavish mood, she departs from this general rule. The character of Philip Morse is an instance of this. Added to his ability as a business man he has a fine literary taste, and a talent for poetry, which has borne fruit in the production of some stanzas which will live in the annals of American verse. As a writer of descriptive prose, also, he has been quite successful. His sense of observation is keen and he writes of what he sees, in a bright, pleasant style that is both agreeable and instructive to the reader. One of the best of Mr. Morse's poetical efforts is entitled "Milking Time." It was first published in *Scribner's* for August, 1878, and besides being widely copied by the newspaper press has been included in a publication entitled, "Best Things by the Best Authors," and also in a collection known as "Perfect Jewels," illustrated. It is indeed a poetical jewel, and as the work of one of San Diego's best-known citizens, it is not inappropriate to find a place for it in this volume:—

MILKING TIME.

"I tell you, Kate, that Lovejoy cow
  Is worth her weight in gold;
She gives a good eight quarts o' milk,
  And isn't yet five year old.

"I see young White a-comin' now;
  He wants her, I know that.
Be careful, girl, you're spillin' it!
  An' save some for the cat.

"Good-evenin', Richard, step right in."
  "I guess I couldn't, sir,
I've just come down".—"I know it, Dick,
  You've took a shine to her.

"She's kind an' gentle as a lamb,
  Jest where I go she follers;
And though it's cheap I'll let her go,
  She's your'n for thirty dollars.

"You'll know her clear across the farm,
  By them two milk-white stars;
You needn't drive her home at night,
  But jest le' down the bars.

"Then when you've owned her, say a month,
  And learnt her, as it were,
I'll bet—why, what's the matter, Dick?"
  "'Tain't her I want—it's *her*!"

"What? not the girl! Well, I'll be blessed!
  There, Kate, don't drop that pan.
You've took me mightily aback,
  But then a man's a man.

CITY AND COUNTY OF SAN DIEGO.

> "She's your'n, my boy, but one word more:
> Kate's gentle as a dove,
> She'll foller you the whole world round,
> For nothing else but love.
>
> "But never try to drive the lass;
> Her nature's like her ma's.
> I've allus found it worked the best
> To jest le' down the bars."

a citiz̶Morse was married May 23, 1870, to Miss Sarah McDonald, been three ... W. B. McDonald, one of San Diego's most prominent Mr. Morse, which is situa... Supervisors. The fruit of this union has one of the finest in the city. The ... a son, is living. The residence of tractive, being done in the choicest of ... of Twelfth and E Streets, is ... 'wood.

R. G. CLARK.

R. G. CLARK, one of the old residents of San Diego County, was born in Greenville, Mercer County, Pennsylvania, May 1, 1832. He lived upon a farm and attended the district schools until he was eighteen years of age. He was then apprenticed to learn the trade of a moulder. He went to work in a foundry in Mercer County, where he remained two years. He then went to Springfield, Ohio, and worked in Leffell's foundry until he completed his apprenticeship. During this time he had also mastered the mystery of the steam engine, and was not only able to run one but understood its construction. This was to serve a good purpose in the future. From Springfield he went to Cincinnati and St. Louis, where he worked at his trade until 1854, when he started across the plains for California, joining a man who was bringing stock and wagons. They arrived at Salt Lake City in the fall of 1854, and remained there through the winter. In the spring they started again towards the Pacific slope with the first train. After leaving Salt Lake, the train was attacked by Indians several times, but they had a strong company and their assailants were repulsed. They arrived at Sacramento June 5, 1855. Then Mr. Clark went to Amador County. It was now that the knowledge of the steam engine he had acquired while working at his trade in Ohio came into play. A man was wanted to run the engine in the Oneida Quartz Mill. He applied for the position and obtained it. Afterwards he was foreman, during 1855 and 1856, of Tibbitt's foundry at Sutter Creek. Subsequently he engaged in mining on the Mokelumne River with varied success. He was for a ... General Superintendent of a large foundry at Silver City, Idaho, ...

ceiving, with one exception, the highest salary paid to any superintendent in the Territories.

When the Frazier River excitement broke out in 1858, Clark caught the fever and made the pilgrimage to British Columbia, returning, with thousands of others, poorer in pocket, but with an addition to his store of experience. For a short time after this he was foreman of

R. G. CLARK.

Worcester's foundry at Angel Camp, Calaveras County. Then in 1859 he went East and visited his old home in Pennsylvania, returning to California the following year. J. S. Harbison had previous to this time imported several colonies of bees from the East, and Mr. Clark and his brother bought some of him and established several apiaries in Ione Valley, Amador County. In this venture the brothers were very successful. One year afterward he went to Nevada and bought a farm called "Little Meadows," now known as Clark's Station, on the Truckee

River. He prospered in farming on the Truckee and remained there for seven years, but finally, on account of malaria, he was obliged to sell out and seek a change of climate. He decided to come to San Diego and arrived here in 1868. A few months after this he went back to Sacramento, and in company with his old bee friend, J. S. Harbison, engaged in silk culture. Their experiment, however, was not a success owing to a disease breaking out among the silk worms, and they gave up the business. Then in conjunction with Mr. Harbison he started for San Diego, bringing with them one hundred and ten hives of honey bees, arriving here November 28, 1869. From that time up to last spring Mr. Clark continued to be largely interested in bee culture, and did much to create the reputation which San Diego honey enjoys in the markets of the world.

In 1876 Mr. Clark began the culture of fruit and forest trees, and the making of raisins in the Cajon Valley. He owned at first two hundred and thirty acres, all under cultivation. Eighty acres were in trees and vines, and the balance in grain. He was the first man in San Diego to practically demonstrate the productiveness of the soil of El Cajon for raisin culture. He introduced a system of sub-irrigation in his vineyard, running a continuous concrete cement pipe, with outlets at convenient distances, under ten acres. His was the only vineyard in the valley that was irrigated, and although it was not necessary the experiment was one that proved not unprofitable. Mr. Clark has always shipped the largest portion of his raisins to the Eastern markets. For the last two years the house of Wm. T. Coleman & Co. has handled his crop. His raisins are pronounced by the best judges to be equal to any imported. When he first came to San Diego Mr. Clark was laughed at for bringing bees here, but before long he demonstrated the natural advantages of the county for bee culture. He was met with the same kind of encouragement when he first began growing grapes in the Cajon. People claimed that the soil was not suited for the purpose. Mr. Clark sold out all his interests in the Cajon in December, 1886, and came into San Diego. On the 13th of April following, in company with his family, he started for an Eastern trip, and traveled all through the Eastern and Middle States but found no place in which he could be content to live outside of San Diego County. He owns considerable real estate in the city, and will, in a short time, build a handsome residence on the corner of A and Thirteenth Streets. In the first years of his residence in San Diego County Mr. Clark labored very hard and surmounted obstacles under which men of less determination would have succumbed. When, however, his orchards and his vineyards were well under way, and he began to see some of his most cherished ideas realized, he felt amply repaid for all his trials and temporary disappointments. Ever since his first crop of raisins they have paid him on an average of $100 per acre net. Mr. Clark also planted the first Australian blue gum forest in the county. He is constantly in the receipt of letters from all parts of the country asking information in reference to vine and bee culture.

Mr. Clark was married in 1871 to Miss Anna L. Blake. They have one child, a boy eleven years old, Edgar Franklin, living. One child died.

DANIEL CLEVELAND.

In this country, where hereditary titles are unknown, and the only recognized aristocracy is that of ability or wealth, we are apt to value too lightly the pride of ancestry. This is accounted for when we bear in mind the fact that so few American families can climb the genealogical tree without meeting with a broken limb, or a branch that shows unmistakable signs of decay; in fact, with many families, the genealogical tree is nothing more or less than a shrub of very commonplace proportions. It will be generally admitted that there are many individuals among us who would be glad to be able to trace their descent through an unblemished channel for a dozen or more generations. There are a few American families, however, that have been so favored by fortune, for generation after generation, that they have never known any marked reverses, and their increase in wealth has been of such a healthy growth as to have caused neither demoralization nor that much-to-be-deplored condition of mind christened "purse pride," and so they have continued from father to son, for a century or more, occupying prominent yet not exalted positions in the walks of life, and respected and beloved by their acquaintances and neighbors. If we have in this country any aristocratic class, these families can properly claim to be members of it. And it is not such an aristocracy the Republic would ever have cause to fear; it would rather find there its firmest and most valued supporters. To such a family belongs the subject of this brief sketch.

Daniel Cleveland was born in Poughkeepsie, New York, March 21, 1838. His father, Stephen Cleveland, practiced law for many years in New York City and Poughkeepsie. He was eminent in his profession, and had as his clients some of the most distinguished citizens of the nation, including the Governor of the State, a Vice-President of the nation, and a Justice of the Supreme Court of the United States. Daniel Cleveland came from Revolutionary stock, his grandfather on both the paternal and maternal sides having fought in the war for Independence. His father was an officer in the last war with England. While attending college at Burlington, Vermont, he marched at the head of a company of his college students, as their captain, to join the American army, which met and defeated the British troops at the battle of Plattsburg, New York. Besides his eminence as a lawyer, he was prominent in politics in the Empire State, being always an earnest and consistent Whig. As a political speaker he was very able and convincing. For some years he owned the Poughkeepsie *Gazette*. He died in that city January 3, 1847.

DANIEL CLEVELAND.

Until he was twelve years of age Daniel Cleveland resided in Poughkeepsie, where he attended school. He then went to Biloxi, Mississippi, where he remained for five years attending school. At seventeen he removed to New Orleans, where for two years he was the head book-keeper in a commercial establishment. He then, in April, 1857, returned to Poughkeepsie, where he entered the office of Tallman & Paine and began the study of the law. In April, 1859, he was admitted to the Supreme Court of the State, after an unusually severe examination, lasting two days, and the following month went to San Antonio, Texas, and entered into a law partnership with his brother, William H. Cleveland, who was already established there.

In August, 1865, he was commissioned Mayor of San Antonio, on the petition of the leading business men of that city. He held the office about one year. He was the first officer in the State to admit the testimony of a negro against a white man. He had been a warm friend of the Union throughout the war, and soon after its close he took editorial charge of the San Antonio *Express*, the first Republican newspaper established in Texas, of which he was one of the founders. It is now one of the most prominent journals in the State. From the editorial chair and upon the stump he was earnest in the advocacy of Republican principles, which in Texas, in those days, was dangerous. Mr. Cleveland's frank utterances and his known stability of purpose did much to advance the Republican cause. He assumed the office of mayor, with a city badly demoralized, and deeply in debt. He surrendered the office with the city out of debt, and a considerable sum of money in the treasury. In October, 1866, finding his health failing from his arduous labors, he started for New York, where he remained a year. Then he left for San Francisco. He resided in the latter city for nearly two years, practicing his profession. In May, 1869, he came to San Diego and again entered into a law partnership with his brother, William H. Cleveland, who, during the Civil War, had come here and engaged in practice. He was a prominent citizen of San Diego, an able lawyer, a bank director and interested in the city's progress. He died in New Hampshire in 1873.

During his residence here Daniel Cleveland has invested largely in real estate and now owns the Cleveland Addition, a considerable tract of water front property, a large tract on the mesa, and property in different parts of the city. He has just begun the erection of a brick building on the corner of Sixth and E Streets, covering one hundred feet square, seven stories in height, and with a basement, provided with all the modern improvements, including elevators and incandescent electric lights at an estimated cost of about $150,000. While engaged in active practice, Mr. Cleveland was attorney for the Texas and Pacific Railway Company for five or six years, until it transferred its franchises to the Southern Pacific, and was also attorney for the Bank of San Diego while it existed. He has been identified with every public movement, and is always looked upon as one of San Diego's most public-spirited citizens. He is an earnest and consistent member of the Episcopal Church, and has been Senior Warden of St. Paul's Church almost continuously since 1869. He also officiated as lay reader in the church from 1870 until quite recently, often for many months at a time when there was no rector. He was one of the founders, and is one of the Directors and Vice-President of the San Diego Society of Natural History. He is an enthusiastic botanist and was the first resident of San Diego to engage in field botany. One genus and many species of plants have received his name in recognition of his services as a collector and discoverer.

Moses Cleveland, the founder of the family, came from England, and settled at Canterbury, Connecticut, in 1635. Among his descendants are the President of the United States; a Governor of Connecticut; the founder of the city of Cleveland, Ohio; the most distinguished mineralogist of America; Father Cleveland, the famous Boston missionary; some other eminent citizens, and the subject of this sketch. The Huntingtons—Daniel Cleveland's paternal grandmother's family—were among the Pilgrims of Plymouth, Massachusetts. Mr. Cleveland does not know of any intermarriage in his family with any person of foreign birth since 1640.

GEORGE W. HAZZARD.

ONE of San Diego's most enterprising and reliable business men is George W. Hazzard. Mr. Hazzard is a native of Indiana, having been born in Cambridge City, Wayne County, in that State, in February, 1845. His father died when he was an infant and George lived in Cambridge with his mother, attending the district school, until he was fourteen, when he removed to Delaware County. One year afterward his mother died, and at the age of fifteen he found himself alone in the world. He was then obliged to give up school and accepted a clerkship in a store in Muncie. Here he continued until he was twenty-two. Then, after a brief stay in Michigan, he started for California, arriving in San Francisco in November, 1868. After a short sojourn there he visited several places in Northern California, and finally, in December of that year, came to San Diego. He had heard good reports of San Diego as a place with a future before it, and this, together with the fact that his physician had advised him to seek a mild climate, had determined him to come here. The first thing he did was to take up a claim of one hundred and sixty acres of land in Otay Valley. After locating his claim and filing his papers, he found he was unable to improve it and therefore went to work for a gentleman in Paradise Valley. He worked there for four months, and during that time an offer being made him for his Government claim he sold it. With the proceeds he bought a piece of land in Paradise Valley containing ten acres, but by that time he came to the conclusion that farming was not his forte and he sold it, taking the proceeds and embarking in business in San Diego. In June,

BIOGRAPHICAL SKETCHES.

1869, Mr. Hazzard opened the first grocery store in the young city at the corner of Fifth and I Streets. San Diego then had a population of one hundred and fifty persons. He succeeded splendidly in his business enterprise, and as the place began to grow his business continued to increase. In 1871 National City began to come into prominence; and as it was understood that Tom Scott was to make that place the

GEORGE W. HAZZARD.

terminus of his overland railroad, he decided to remove there, being partly induced to make the change by a land consideration offered him by the Kimball Brothers. He remained in National City for three years. During this time San Diego was growing rapidly, and Mr. Hazzard, concluding that he might have made a mistake, returned here. He at once began the erection of a brick store, one of the first brick buildings in San Diego, at the corner of Sixth and H Streets, which cost him $14,000, and at that time was considered a great enterprise.

He continued to carry on a general merchandise business at this location until 1882, when he sold out to the firm of Francisco, Silliman & Co. During his fourteen years' business experience Mr. Hazzard had accumulated considerable ranch and city property, which he retained. During the last four or five years of his business career he had large dealings with the interior of the county and with Lower California. At times things looked rather blue, but his faith in San Diego's future had been unbounded from the start and he never lost heart.

When Mr. Hazzard opened an office and began handling his own property he naturally drifted into the business of handling property for other people, and he was soon engaged in a large real estate business. He had, through his large acquaintance, formed while engaged in the mercantile business, established a reputation for good judgment and reliability, and as a consequence found his advice sought by many people. Of late years most of the heavy real estate transactions in which he has been engaged have been on account of persons in the East. For one party in Cincinnati he has sold over $200,000 worth of real property, they leaving everything to his judgment.

While conducting business as a merchant Mr. Hazzard became interested in the mining industry of the county, and has aided largely in developing that portion of San Diego's wealth. In 1882 he bought the Hubbard mine, situated in the Banner District. He afterwards sold a one-half interest out and still retains the residue. He has great confidence in the county's mineral resources and predicts a bright future for them. Mr Hazzard has never held a political office, and has no taste for politics He has been prominent as a member of the Chamber of Commerce since its organization, and has served two terms as President of that body. He was one of the original incorporators of the San Diego Water Company and was for a number of years a Director. He was also one of the incorporators and a Director in the Gas Company for a number of years, until 1883. He is interested in the Artificial Stone Company, and the Marine Railway, and was one of the incorporators and is the largest individual stockholder in the Masonic Building Association.

In 1886 Mr. Hazzard built a handsome residence, in that charming section of the city, known as Florence Heights, at a cost of $20,000, where he now resides with his family. San Diego has no more ardent friend than Mr. Hazzard. He has always been ready to devote his time and means to every project tending towards the city's permanent advancement, and his reputation as a public-spirited, progressive citizen is proverbial.

WILLIAM JORRES.

PROMINENT among the older residents of San Diego is William Jorres. Mr. Jorres is a native of Hanover, Germany, where he was born on the 24th of August, 1824. After attending school he learned the carpenter's trade and followed it in the city of Hamburg until 1846, when he started for Monte Video. There he worked at his trade for about six months, when he went to Buenos Ayres, where he remained three years. While he was at Monte Video the port was blockaded by the combined French and English fleets for several months. In the latter end of 1849 he left Buenos Ayres on a ship bound round the Horn for San Francisco, where he arrived May 4, 1850. The first week after his arrival he went to the mines at Spanish Dry Diggings, on the Middle Fork of the American River. Then he went to Bear Creek and prospected that section pretty thoroughly for a year.

After the second fire in 1851 he went down to San Francisco, worked at the carpenter's trade for a while, and then started in for himself as a contractor, a business he followed with excellent success until 1869, when he came to San Diego.

During his residence in San Francisco Mr. Jorres in his business as a contractor superintended the erection of a large number of fine buildings. He put up four brick houses on Washington Street between Kearny and Montgomery in 1852–53; he built the large brick building on the southwest corner of California and Front in 1855, which is still standing; also the orthodox Jewish synagogue on Mason Street between Post and Geary. Most of his buildings, which were scattered about in different parts of the city, were substantial structures and are still standing.

After his arrival in San Diego Mr. Jorres formed a partnership with S. S. Culverwell and built the Culverwell & Jorres Wharf, situated at the foot of F Street. This was the first wharf started in New San Diego. It was not completed so soon as the Horton Wharf, as it was twenty feet wider and required more time to build it. It was made wide enough for carriages to be driven out to meet passengers from the steamers, who were landed at the end of the wharf. The cost of the wharf was $28,700. For the first year they ran it themselves and then leased it and Mr. Jorres again went into business as a contractor. This was in 1871, and the first contract he took was for the building of the present Court House on D Street. In 1873, after he had completed the Court

House, he took the contract for putting up the building for the Commercial Bank of San Diego, now occupied by the Consolidated National Bank, on the corner of Fifth and G Streets. He next put up the Central Market on Fifth Street between F and G. It was 200x60 feet and was fitted up with stalls, etc., for a market. After being used for this purpose a year it was leased by Charles S. Hamilton & Co., and has since

WILLIAM JORRES.

been occupied by them as a general merchandise store. He continued his business as a contractor here until 1877, when he went to Los Angeles, where he built the First National Bank, on Spring Street.

In the year 1872 Mr. Jorres bought out the interest of Culverwell in the wharf at the foot of F Street, and engaged in ballasting vessels and other business in connection with the wharf. He has recently begun the extension of the wharf, and it will, when completed, be one of the best wharves on the water front.

Mr. Jorres was for seven years County Treasurer, retiring from office in 1885. He was elected on the Democratic ticket. During his residence in San Diego he has always been alive to the interests of the city, and has done his full share towards its material advancement. He was an earnest advocate of the railroad and did all in his power to have it brought here.

Mr. Jorres was married in 1854, in Hanover, to Miss Sophie Kliengibel. He had gone to the old country from San Francisco to visit his parents, and while there met and was married to Miss Kliengibel. They came to San Francisco, arriving there in August, 1854. They have six children living, one son and five daughters; they have lost three sons. Their son, George W., was for two years postmaster, but resigned last fall to accept the position of assistant cashier in the San Diego National Bank.

Mr. Jorres owns considerable city property and has a very comfortable residence on the corner of Union and B Streets, which he built in 1869, previous to the arrival of his family from San Francisco.

CHARLES J. FOX, C. E.

No man has been more closely identified with San Diego County during the past eighteen years, and no name is better known to the early settlers and later residents, than that of Charles J. Fox. Mr. Fox was born in Boston, Massachusetts, October 12, 1834. He comes of a noted family and can trace his lineage back to 1640, when his ancestors settled in Massachusetts. Five generations back on his mother's side, Wheelock, the head of the family, was the founder and first President of Dartmouth College, where his portrait hangs in the art gallery, and Mr. Fox's father, grandfather, and great grandfather, were graduates of that famous institution of learning.

His paternal grandfather was a soldier of the Revolutionary War, and Mr. Fox has in his possession a book written and published by him, entitled, "Fox's Revolutionary Adventures." He was taken prisoner by the British troops and confined for some months in the old Jersey prison ship, in Wallabout Bay, in Long Island Sound.

Charles spent his boyhood days in Boston, and at the age of seventeen graduated from a scientific school, where mathematics and engineering were specialties. He had a natural taste for these pursuits, and the first work he did after graduation was as a member of a railroad survey party in Pennsylvania in 1851. In the spring of 1853 he went West, and until 1869 was engaged on different railroads throughout the Western States and Territories.

In the spring of 1860 he crossed the plains to where the city of

Denver now stands, and was one of the first settlers of that place, there being at that time but few houses, and they mere shanties. Most of the summer was spent in California Gulch, now the site of Leadville, in mining, prospecting and surveying. During a recent trip to the East he stopped at Leadville and saw the remains of a log house, which he helped to build in the summer of 1860. During 1864 and 1865 he was

CHARLES J. FOX, C. E.

in the U. S. Engineer service, having charge of the reconstruction of the Memphis and Charleston Railroad from Memphis to Corinth.

He continued to be engaged in railroad business in the South until his health failed, and in the spring of 1869 he came to California. After prospecting different parts of the State for six months he finally selected San Diego as his future residence, being attracted by the beauties of the climate and what he foresaw of its future commercial importance.

Having invested all his available funds in San Diego real estate, he opened an office for surveying and engineering, and has ever since devoted his best abilities to aid in building up the city and county. In pursuance of this object he took an active part in the organization of the San Diego and Fort Yuma turnpike road, two hundred miles in length, which was the first good road across the county to Arizona, and opened up a good deal of trade and travel. In 1875 he established a large apiary at Fallbrook, and the following year organized the Bee Keepers' Association, of which he was President, and established agencies for the sale of honey in various Eastern cities.

He was one of the incorporators of the San Diego Society of Natural History, and for ten years its Treasurer; also one of the stockholders of the Masonic Building Association, and a Director for several years; also one of the charter members of the San Diego Lodge, Knights of Pythias, serving a term as Chancellor Commander. He was in charge of surveys for the Memphis and El Paso Railroad, the San Diego and Los Angeles Railroad, and the Texas and Pacific, being the first engineer to call attention to and survey through the famous Temecula Cañon, now occupied by the California Southern.

Having for several years explored the county, including the Colorado Desert, he obtained an extensive and minute knowledge of the country, and was generally called on by new-comers for information, which he always cheerfully gave. He was active in protecting the rights of the settlers from the greed of land monopolists, and was several times elected County Surveyor and City Engineer, and filled these situations to the satisfaction of all. In connection with his partner, Mr. H. I. Willey, afterwards State Surveyor-General, he prepared and published the official and only map of San Diego County.

By appointment of the Judge of the Superior Court, he served as Commissioner in the partition of most of the Spanish grants, including the ex-Mission grant of fifty-two thousand acres, surrounding the city of San Diego.

He is now owner of considerable real estate in the city, and a good deal of county land, including a tract at Linda Vista, where he was the first to make improvements on Government land; and he also owns a large interest in the Junipero Land and Water Company, of which he is the President.

Mr. Fox is senior member of the surveying firm of Fox & Ryan, and is interested in many important enterprises. He has always been active and liberal in support of every important public measure, especially during San Diego's dark days, and has the respect of all the old settlers.

Mr. Fox married, in 1880, Mrs. A. A. Cosper, of San Diego. They have no children.

A. KLAUBER.

A. KLAUBER, the senior member of the firm of Klauber & Levi, was born in Austria in 1830, but emigrated to the United States when quite a young man. After a few years spent in the Eastern States he came to California early in the fifties. His first start was made in Volcano, Amador County. From there he went to Genoa, Nevada, where he engaged in the general merchandise business. In 1869 he came to San Diego, and in the fall of that year entered into partnership with Mr. Steiner, in the grocery business. Although Mr. Klauber is naturally of a conservative nature, he had no sooner become established in San Diego than the great natural advantages of the place so impressed him that he pushed his business just as rapidly as prudence would permit, and as profits accrued to him he invested largely in real estate. The result has justified Mr. Klauber's judgment, and he is to-day not only the head of one of the greatest wholesale business houses in Southern California, but his personal estate is very large.

One of the best evidences of the substantial character of the growth and permanent prosperity of San Diego is to be found in the fact that the mercantile house of which Mr. Klauber is the head has been in existence eighteen years, and has done a good business all through that time, steadily increasing year by year, until now, when its trade for 1887 will, it is estimated, reach the sum of one million dollars. The firm of Steiner & Klauber, of which Klauber & Levi are the successors, was formed in the fall of 1869. At that time the population of San Diego was very small, but the "back country" gave promise even then of its future, and the new firm was soon doing a good business with the mining district about Julian and the large ranches in this and San Bernardino Counties. In 1876 Mr. Levi acquired an interest, and the firm became known as Steiner, Klauber & Co. This was the style of the firm until the 1st of January, 1883, when Mr. Steiner retired and it became known by its present name. The principal part of the business of the old firm of Steiner & Klauber was retailing general merchandise, dry goods, etc. Gradually, however, this trade increased to such proportions that, after the retirement of Mr. Steiner, the firm began to give their attention more especially to wholesaling. It was not, however, until a year ago last March that they decided to quit the retail branch of their business entirely. By that time the development of the interior of the county and the rapid growth of the city made a change in their business imperative and they notified all their customers to that effect, sold out all their open goods of the retail class, and devoted themselves solely to the wholesale trade.

With this change in their business, enlarged facilities were demanded. Their old quarters on Fifth and H Streets were too contracted, and they decided to move into and occupy the whole of the large build-

A. KLAUBER.

ing on the corner of H and Fourth Streets. This was completed and the firm took possession in September last. The new building is of brick, four stories in height, and has a frontage of one hundred feet on H Street, and one hundred and fifty feet on Fourth. On the different floors and in a spacious basement, extending under the whole building, and well lighted and ventilated, are stored an immense stock of groceries, liquors, hardware, cigars, tobacco, wagon materials and agricultural implements. In addition to this building, the firm has two large

13

warehouses, one on the corner of Seventh and I, the other situated on the corner of Fourth and K. The former is 100x125 feet in dimensions and is used for the storage of agricultural implements; the latter contains an immense surplus stock of the heavier classes of merchandise, groceries, flour, etc., and is so arranged that the cars of the railroad company are discharged at its doors. The firm does a large business in San Diego and San Bernardino Counties and in Lower California. There is not a freight train leaving on the California Southern, a stage or mule team starting for the "back country," or a steamer departing for southern ports, but carries consignments from this firm.

Mr. Klauber has always been one of the live men of the city, and has done his utmost to advance its material interests. He was Chairman of the Board of Supervisors for two years, from 1878 to 1880, but has generally expressed himself as averse to holding public office. He is interested in the San Diego and Cuyamaca Railroad Co., now building a line to extend to Julian and open up a much-neglected but rich portion of the county. He is interested in what is known as the Steiner, Klauber, Choate & Castle Addition to San Diego, a tract placed upon the market last year, which met with a ready sale. He is also a large owner of timber lands in Mendocino County. He has a permanent home in this city, but, being the resident partner in San Francisco, he is obliged to spend most of his time there.

Mr. Klauber was married in Sacramento, in 1851, to Miss Theresa Epstein. They have nine children living and four have died. The eldest son, Melville M. Klauber, is with the firm in this city. Mr. Klauber is a prominent member of the Masonic Order. He is now in the best of health and bids fair to have many years of life before him.

S. LEVI.

THE junior member of the firm of Klauber & Levi is a native of Austria, in which country he was born December 26, 1850. When twelve years of age he came to this country, landing in New York City. From there he went to Syracuse, where he remained six months and then started for California. He arrived in San Francisco in March, 1863, and went directly to Auburn, Placer County. In that town he lived two years, turning his hand to whatever came in his way. In 1865 he returned to San Francisco and entered the employ of Sweitzer, Sachs & Co., with whom he remained until January, 1873, when he came to San Diego. After a brief stay here he went to Temecula, in this county, where he engaged in the general merchandise business. In 1876 he sold out his interest in Temecula and came to San Diego, where he was admitted into the firm of Steiner & Klauber. In January, 1883, Messrs.

Klauber and Levi bought out Mr. Steiner and he retired from the firm. It is since that time that the business of the house has reached such great proportions, and it is not improper to say that the rapid increase in business is owing largely to the energy, push, and personal popularity of the junior partner. Mr. Levi's career has been a remarkably fortunate one, but his success has been entirely due to his perseverance

S. LEVI.

and indomitable will. Coming to this country at an early age, he was thrown entirely upon his own resources, and in the battle of life no time was accorded him in which to study or obtain even a common-school education. It was not until he had become located in San Francisco that he had so far prospered in his worldly affairs that he could afford to set aside some time to the improvement of his mind. He then devoted his spare moments to study, attended evening school, and availed himself of every means in his power to make amends for his lack of early educational advantages. He is now considered one of the best-equipped and most thorough business men in the county. He has at different times taken an earnest interest in politics, and was elected Councilman from the First Ward, on the Citizens' ticket, at the election held last fall. This was the first election under the new charter giving the city a Mayor and twelve Councilmen. He was President of the Chamber of Commerce in 1882; was Master of the Masonic Lodge in 1882, '83 and '84; is now Vice-President of the San Diego Gas and Electric Light Co., Vice-President of the San Diego Telephone Co., and President of the Building and Loan Association. He is a thoroughly public-spirited citizen, and there is not an important public movement but finds in him an earnest friend and promoter.

Mr. Levi was married, in 1876, to Miss E. Meyer, of San Francisco. Their union has been blessed with three children, all of whom are living with their parents.

BRYANT HOWARD.

ONE of the best known and most respected of San Diego's citizens, is the President of the Consolidated National Bank, Bryant Howard. Mr. Howard is a native of New York, and is at the present time in the very prime of life. He first came to San Diego in 1870, and soon afterwards, in company with the late James M. Pierce and one or two others, founded the Bank of San Diego, of which he was the first cashier. The bank building was then located on the corner of Sixth and H Streets. A short time after this the Commercial Bank of San Diego was incorporated.

About 1873, Mr. Howard resigned his position as cashier, and started for Europe with his wife on an extended tour. Upon his return to this country he engaged in business in Los Angeles, dealing in paints, oils and glass. His house was soon in the front rank among the business houses of that city. Under the style of Howard & Co., the firm has, until recently, been in existence and doing a large trade. It is now consolidated with one of the leading firms on the Pacific Coast. Soon after locating in Los Angeles, a strong effort was made by some of the leading financial men there to induce Mr. Howard to take charge of a bank there which they would start. He had, however, a longing to return to San Diego, not only because he preferred it as a place of residence, but he foresaw its great commercial future.

About this time his old bank in San Diego and the Commercial bank were merged into one, and known as the Consolidated National Bank. Of this institution Mr. Howard became cashier. The capital stock of the bank was at first $100,000; but in August last it was increased to $250,000. For several years Mr. Howard has been President of the institution, and under his prudent management it has assumed a leading place among the financial institutions of Southern California. The bank has never speculated in real estate, nor have any of its officers engaged in any outside speculations. While strictly conservative in matters connected with the affairs of the bank, Mr. Howard is one of the most progressive of San Diego's citizens. Every movement for the advancement of the city or its people finds in him an able advocate and a substantial friend. When the first fire company was started here he made it a present of a fire bell, which is now in use. He is looked upon by the fire laddies as their especial patron and benefactor, and one of the companies is named after him.

The San Diego Benevolent Association, which has been in existence for some time, has done an immense deal of good in a quiet way toward ameliorating the condition of the deserving poor. One of its principal promoters and continued benefactors is Bryant Howard. When efforts were being made to induce the Texas Pacific to come to San Diego, Bryant Howard was among the foremost in holding out inducements, and as a member of the Citizens' Committee he worked early and late to bring about that object. When that project failed, and later on the Atchison people showed an inclination to build toward this city, Mr. Howard was equally as energetic in his efforts to induce them to come. The late James M. Pierce, who was a warm personal friend of Mr. Howard, as well as a business associate, left a munificent sum—$150,000—for the purpose of founding a home for boys and girls.

It is understood that Mr. Howard, in conjunction with two or three other gentlemen, who will each donate the same amount, contemplate the endowment of a chain of benevolent institutions, which will result in great benefit to San Diego. The plan, as proposed, includes the establishment of a Boys' and Girls' Aid Society (this is provided for by the will of the late James M. Pierce), an Orphans' Home, a Kindergarten, an Industrial School, a School of Technology and a Women's and Children's Hospital, all embracing the same scope; the object being to gather together all waifs and homeless children and give them a thorough education. Those too young to go to the public school will be sent to the kindergarten connected with these institutions. The sum of $600,000 has been already pledged to carry out this magnificent scheme of benevolence.

Mr. Howard has been twice married. He has two children, both boys, the eldest of whom, seventeen years of age, is a clerk in the bank. The youngest is four or five years of age

JOHN S. HARBISON.

There is no product of San Diego County that has done more to spread abroad her fame, than her honey. It has acquired a reputation in the markets of the world of the highest character. It is well known to the agriculturist that a section capable of producing such honey must possess superior advantages of soil and climate, and, as a result, the attention of a class of people has been directed hither who might have been influenced by the ordinary reports of the wonderful fertility of the country. Certainly, the man who was the pioneer in making known the fact that San Diego County was an apiarian paradise, is entitled to be classed as a public benefactor. It is concerning him that this sketch is written.

John S. Harbison was born in Beaver County, Pennsylvania, September 29, 1826. He comes of a sterling American stock, and can trace his lineage back through several generations. His grandfather, John Harbison, and his grandmother, Massey Harbison, were among the first settlers of Western Pennsylvania, locating near the town of Freeport, twenty-eight miles above Pittsburgh, on the Alleghany River, where the first grist-mill in that region of country was built and operated by his grandfather. In those days that part of the country was subject to many Indian outbreaks, and the Harbisons experienced their full share of the trials and sufferings incident to a life on the frontier. His grandfather acquired fame as an Indian fighter, and participated in numerous engagements in repelling the frequent murderous raids made on the settlers by the treacherous tribes of Indians inhabiting the country from the Alleghany Mountains on the east, Lakes Erie and Michigan on the north and west, and the Ohio River on the south; and as a volunteer soldier, took part in the several expeditions led by St. Clair and Wayne, which subsequently resulted in quelling all the Indian disturbances. Mr. Harbison's grandfather on his mother's side, William Curry, was a chief armorer in the Continental service, and was one of the memorable minute men of the Revolution, who were a picked body of men that could be relied upon under any circumstances and were detailed to execute the most hazardous and important undertakings. He fought in eight battles in that memorable struggle, and was with Washington when he crossed the Delaware on that stormy Christmas night and defeated the astonished Hessians encamped at Trenton.

The youth and early manhood of John S. Harbison were passed upon a farm, but in 1854, having an attack of the gold fever, he made up his mind to come to California. In October of that year he sailed from New York on the steamship *Northern Light*, via Nicaraugua, connecting on this side with the *Sierra Nevada*, which had taken the place of the *Yankee Blade*, the latter having been wrecked just after leaving

JOHN S. HARBISON.

San Francisco. He arrived in San Francisco November 20, and immediately started for the mining camp known as Campo Seco, in Amador County. Here he found that gold mining was not all his imagination had pictured, he worked hard and received very meager returns. Considerably discouraged he left the mines in a few weeks, and went down to Sacramento. Glad to turn his hand to anything, he secured work in the Sutterville saw-mill, where he stayed several months. In the meantime Harbison had made up his mind he would give up the avocations for which he had little taste, and devote himself to something with which he was acquainted. He sent home to Pennsylvania for a general assortment of seeds, and a small invoice of fruit trees. He received the first consignment in February, and secured ground in the town of Sutterville, near Sacramento City, where he started the first nursery of fruit and shade trees in the Sacramento Valley. During the fall and winter of 1855, and again in the fall of 1856, he made large importations of the choicest fruit trees from the most celebrated nurseries in the East. From these importations was started that great series of orchards which line the banks of the Sacramento River and adjacent country.

In May, 1857, he returned to his Eastern home, and began preparations for shipping a quantity of bees to California. He finally started from New York with sixty-seven colonies, and landed them safely at Sacramento, after a journey of about four weeks. This venture was so popular that he went East again the next fall, and obtained a second supply of bees, which also were safely brought to this State. He continued the business of nurseryman and apiarist near Sacramento until February, 1874, when he removed with his family to San Diego, where he has resided ever since.

In the fall of 1869, Mr. Harbison formed a partnership with Mr. R. G. Clark, for the purpose of introducing and keeping bees in San Diego County. They prepared a choice selection of one hundred and ten hives of bees from Mr. Harbison's apiaries at Sacramento, and shipped them by the steamer *Orizaba*, which landed in San Diego on the morning of November 28, 1869. Mr. Clark remained in charge of the bees, making all the explorations for the most suitable ranges for the location of apiaries and production of honey. Other importations were made by the firm, and the partnership was continued for the period of four years, at the end of which time a division of the apiaries and effects was made. Mr. Clark soon after disposed of his apiaries, purchasing land in the El Cajon Valley, where he established the first raisin vineyard in the county.

The great success attending the enterprise of Messrs. Clark and Harbison, and the world-wide fame of their San Diego County honey, very soon attracted the notice of bee-keepers and farmers of all parts of the States, and as a result, many were induced to come here, who took up public lands, established homes, and commenced the business of bee-keeping and tilling of the soil.

In December, 1857, Mr. Harbison invented the section honey box, an invention which has done more for the advancement of honey production than any other discovery in bee-keeping. For this he was granted a patent, January 4, 1859. At the California State Fair, held at Marysville, in September, 1858, Mr. Harbison exhibited the first section box honey.

In 1873 the firm of Clark & Harbison shipped the first car load of honey across the continent from California. Mr. Harbison was awarded a medal and diploma for his exhibit of San Diego County honey at the Centennial Exposition at Philadelphia, in 1876. Besides his labors as a practical horticulturist, a farmer and apiarist, Mr. Harbison has found time to contribute occasionally to current literature on those subjects with which he is familiar, and is the author of a book of four hundred and forty pages, entitled, "Bee Keepers' Directory;" it treats of bee culture in all its departments and is a recognized authority on the subject of which it treats. Although it was published in 1861, it is still considered the most practical work of the kind ever issued.

Mr. Harbison was married to Mary J. White, of New Castle, Pennsylvania, in 1865. The result of the union is one son, who died in infancy, and two daughters, both of whom are living.

COL. CHALMERS SCOTT.

ONE of the best-known citizens of San Diego is Colonel Chalmers Scott. He is a native of Louisiana, having been born in New Orleans, May 9, 1845. In 1854 he came with his parents to San Francisco, where his father, Rev. William A. Scott, was for many years pastor of St. John's Presbyterian Church. Chalmers attended the public schools until 1861, when he went to Europe with his parents. He attended college in Montauban, France, up to June, 1862, and then was a student in the University College, London, until May, 1863. His family then returned to the United States and he accompanied them. From June, 1863, to May, 1864, he attended the law department of the University of New York, graduating at the head, though the youngest of his class, at the age of nineteen, and having the degree of LL.B. conferred upon him. He then entered the law office of Blatchford, Seward & Griswold, where he remained until November, 1864, when he returned to San Francisco and for a year read law in the office of Haight & Pierson. He would have continued his legal studies but an injury to one of his eyes, received when at school, so affected the sight that he found close application to his books was using up his eyes completely. A sea voyage was recommended, and just at this time he met the late Thomas M. Cash, who was, at that time, the representative of the New York *Herald* on this coast. By him Mr. Scott was appointed special correspondent of the *Herald*, to make a trip to China and back.

He made the trip, was gone nearly three months, and on his return rushed through a two-thousand-word dispatch to the *Herald* before any other newspaper man could get a word of the news. A few days afterwards Mr. Bennett appointed him by telegraph resident correspondent of the *Herald* in China. This, however, he was obliged to decline. His eyes still troubled him and he went into the Sierras with an engineering party of the Central Pacific Railroad, remaining from June, 1867, to April, 1868. Becoming snow blind he returned to San Francisco.

COL. CHALMERS SCOTT.

The Spring Valley Water Company was then building their great San Andreas dam, and he joined the construction force under Colonel Elliott, U. S. Engineer Corps, as paymaster.

At the end of a year he resigned and again resumed the study of the law, entering the office of Gen. W. H. L. Barnes. In January, 1870, his attention was attracted to San Diego, and looking upon it as a coming city he came here and formed a law partnership with Col. G. A. Jones. He was admitted to the bar in July, 1870, and in March of the following year he was appointed County Clerk, to fill the unexpired term of Capt. Geo. A. Pendleton, deceased. He joined the Texas Pacific Survey as transitman under C. J. Fox, and made a survey from San Diego to San Gorgonino Pass.

In March, 1873, the party being called in, he resumed his law practice. In November, 1874, having married Maria Antonio Coutts, eldest daughter of the late C. J. Coutts, he moved out to the homestead on Rancho Guajome as legal advisor of the estate. In December, 1875, he accepted the position of Deputy State Treasurer under Don Jose Guadalupe Estudillo, but the climate of Sacramento not agreeing with his family he returned to Guajome. For a short time, in 1880–81, he was in the employ of the California Southern at San Diego, but in May, 1881, he was appointed Assistant Engineer on the Central Pacific Railroad, in charge of the survey from Yuma to Port Isabel, at the mouth of the Colorado. From Yuma he was transferred to Corinne, Utah, to survey a line by way of South Pass, of the Rocky Mountains, to Yankton, Dakota. The following year he went to Tucson, and in conjunction with Hon. S. R. De Long, Chief Engineer of the Tucson and Gulf of California Railroad Company, made a reconnoissance to Port Lobos, and afterward reconnoitered branch lines from Pacheco and Gila Bend to the Gunsight mine in Nigers District, Arizona. He was afterward in charge of the survey for the extension of the Vaca Valley and Clear Lake Railroad.

In August, 1883, he was sent to Guatemala as Chief Engineer of the Central American Pacific Railway and Transportation Co., to build an extension of the Guatemala Central Railroad from Escuintla to the city of Guatemala, a distance of thirty-eight miles. The previous management had wasted over two years of their time, and had graded only five miles of road, and laid three miles of track, leaving thirty-three miles to be surveyed, located, graded, and ironed in twelve months in order to save the concession. In thirteen miles of that distance the grade is continuous at the rate of two hundred and forty-six feet to the mile, and nine bridges from one hundred and eighty to two hundred and twenty feet in length and from eighty to one hundred and fifty feet high, and at Lake Amatitlan there was one solid fill seven hundred and fifty feet long and eighty feet deep in the lake, which had to be filled from one end, requiring over five hundred thousand cubic yards of dirt. It was in this work that the discipline of the Central Pacific Railroad proved its value, for with Colonel Scott as Chief Engineer and J. B. Harris as Superintendent of Construction, the locomotive blew its whistle in Guatemala City on July 19, 1884, the birthday of President Barrios, two months ahead of contract time.

That work completed, Colonel Scott returned to San Francisco, and after spending a year on other railroad work, resigned and followed civil engineering in Oakland and San Francisco, returning to San Diego in November, 1886, where he entered into the real estate business in April, 1887. He is a fine Spanish scholar and is considered the best authority on Spanish names in this locality. He deals largely in Lower California properties and is an authority on titles. Colonel Scott was a member of the National Guard of California for ten years, from 1865 to 1875. In the latter year he was appointed Chief Engineer with the rank of Colonel on the staff of Governor Irwin, and served in that capacity for four years.

As previously noted Colonel Scott married a Miss Coutts, who was an acknowledged belle. She was considered one of the most beautiful young women in Southern California, and to-day there are few matrons in the State who can equal her in queenly grace and attractiveness. Their union has been blessed with four children, one son and three daughters, all of whom are living. Colonel Scott is himself a notable man personally. He is six feet and three and one-half inches high and weighs two hundred pounds.

CHARLES HUBBELL.

ONE of the substantial and public-spirited citizens of San Diego is Charles Hubbell. Although he retired from active business some years ago, he takes a deep interest in everything that pertains to the advancement of the city. Mr. Hubbell is a native of the Empire State, having been born in Ballston in November, 1817. He lived until he was seventeen in Ballston and Oswego and then went to Rochester, where he became Assistant Teller of the Bank of Monroe. He remained in Rochester two years and then went to Pontiac, Michigan, to accept a position as Cashier of a bank there. He built and put in operation the first saw-mill in Clinton County, Michigan, and aided in cutting out the first road from Pontiac to Ionia, fifty years ago. He was one of the original incorporators of Saginaw City. He assisted in the first development of the Salt Springs of Northern Michigan and was identified with many other projects of importance in that State. In 1839 he returned to Rochester to act as Teller of the Commercial Bank. In 1846 he removed to Cincinnati, to become Teller of the Ohio Life and Trust Company. After one year in this position he went into the banking house of Ellis & Sturges as Cashier.

In 1853 he had a severe attack of hemorrhage of the lungs and spent a year and a half traveling about for the purpose of recovering his health. Then he settled at Keokuk, Iowa, where he remained fifteen years. There his natural taste for horticultural pursuits, a taste which he had never before had the opportunity to gratify, induced him to engage in fruit raising. He resided on a farm during the summer months and in the winter he lived in the city of Keokuk. During his stay there he filled several city and county offices.

In 1870, as his health was still far from rugged, on the advice of Professor Cleaver, who is now Surgeon-General of the Santa Fe Railroad Co., he started for California, coming direct to San Diego. Upon

CHARLES HUBBELL.

his arrival he was so pleased with the climate that he decided to make it his future home. He purchased one hundred acres of land on the National Ranch, and planted a vineyard and fruit orchard. In 1874 he accepted the position of Cashier of the Bank of San Diego and remained with that institution until it was merged with the present Consolidated National Bank. Mr. Hubbell was a member of the Committee of Forty, appointed by the citizens to induce the building of a railroad to San Diego. He was Corresponding Secretary of the committee, and labored zealously to bring about that much desired object—railroad communication with the outside world.

Mr. Hubbell was one of the original stockholders in the California Southern. He never sought public office here, but at the earnest solicitations of his friends he ran for, and was elected, School Trustee in 1872, and afterward in 1886, at the latter time being chosen President of the Board, which position he resigned last spring. He retired from active business in 1880, and has since been attending to his private affairs. Before coming to San Diego his health was so bad that he was not expected to live, but now, at the age of seventy, he enjoys perfect health, is active, and looks much younger than he really is. He has been prominently identified with the horticultural interests, and has been Secretary of the County Horticultural Society.

"In religion," Mr. Hubbell says, "I am a Baptist, having belonged to a church of that independent and democratic organization, nearly fifty years. I accept implicitly the doctrines taught by the Lord Jesus Christ, in their spirituality, and particularly as to purity, truth, love, universal benevolence, and the golden rule of sixteen ounces to the pound."

The ancestral motto of his family has always been, *Esse, quam videri*—be what you seem to be. Mr. Hubbell was married in 1843 in Rochester, New York, to Miss Anna M. Sage, who died very suddenly in 1881. During the thirty-seven years of her married life, she was never known to speak an unkind word to either her husband or children. He has had seven children, of whom five are living, four sons and one daughter. One of his sons is a lawyer, practicing in Rochester. One is a student in Crozer Seminary in Pennsylvania and two are connected with the First National Bank of this city. He is now building a residence, to cost about $10,000, on the corner of Eighth and Ash Streets, adjoining the residence of his son, O. S. Hubbell.

O. S. HUBBELL.

THE stranger visiting San Diego is naturally astonished at the progress made by the city during the past two years. If he was to be told that one of the leading spirits in designing and carrying out the improvements that meet his gaze on every hand,—the street railroads, the ferry, the motor lines, the beautiful suburban tracts,—was a young man, not yet thirty years of age, his astonishment would not be lessened. O. S. Hubbell has already accomplished in his brief business career far more than many men, who deem themselves favored by fortune, have done in the space of a long and laborious life-time. Mr. Hubbell was born in Keokuk, Iowa, May 29, 1859, but removed with his parents to

San Diego when he was twelve years of age. On his arrival here he attended the public schools, graduating at the high school. He made preparations to enter college, but his health failing he relinquished that object and entered the employ of the Bank of San Diego, the first bank established in this city, in the latter part of 1876. He first was book-keeper, then teller, and then was appointed assistant cashier.

O. S. HUBBELL.

He remained with this institution three years, and at the age of twenty-one was one of the incorporators and a stockholder of the Consolidated Bank of San Diego, and also an incorporator and stockholder in the Consolidated National Bank. He continued with this bank until 1885, when he resigned and became a stockholder and accepted the position of assistant cashier in the First National Bank. In 1886 he was elected a director and soon afterward cashier, a position which he still occupies. His wide acquaintance and well-known ability as a financier, added to his acknowledged integrity, aided very materially in giving the bank its present high position   The deposits when he first became connected with it were about $50,000, now they amount to nearly $2,500,000.

Mr. Hubbell is a half owner of Reed & Hubbell's Addition. This was the first addition of any size cut up from acre property into lots and put on the market with any success. It was first offered in August, 1886. It is situated on the bay between San Diego and National City, and originally consisted of 210 acres. They sold 80 acres in a body and cut the balance up into lots. The property is now very valuable. Among other land corporations with which Mr. Hubbell is connected, are the Escondido Land and Town Co., the San Marcos Land Co., the El Cajon Valley Co., the Morena Land Co., the Junipero Land and Water Co., and the Pacific Beach Co., in each of which he is an incorporator, a stockholder, and a director. He is a stockholder in the College Hill Land Association. He is a stockholder and Secretary of the Coronado Beach Co. He was one of the incorporators of the San Diego National Bank, and the Bank of Escondido, and a stockholder in the Bank of Elsinore and the Exchange Bank of Elsinore. He was one of the incorporators and is a director in the Coronado Ferry Co., an incorporator of the San Diego Street Railroad Co., and an incorporator and stockholder in the San Diego and Coronado Water Co., the San Diego and Cuyamaca Railroad Co., the San Diego, Old Town and Pacific Beach Railroad Co., and the West Coast Lumber Co. He is also a one-fourth owner in the San Diego Gas and Electric Light Co., the present stock of which is $500,000, and Treasurer of the company. He was one of the incorporators of the Marine Railway and Dry Dock Co. He was also an incorporator and is now a Director of the Cuyamaca Club, the leading gentlemen's club of San Diego. Last January he was elected a Director of the California Southern Railroad Co. He was one of the organizers of the San Diego City Guards, a crack militia company, in which he has served for six years.

He owns considerable city real estate besides his outside property. He has six lots on Sixth Street, which he intends to improve shortly; and about $200,000 worth of Fifth Street property. He intends to soon begin the erection of a block 100 feet square on Sixth Street, which will be six or seven stories in height, entirely fire-proof, and will be one of the finest structures in Southern California. He has in contemplation also the erection, in connection with other parties, of two or three business blocks, costing from $100,000 to $150,000 each. He is now building a handsome residence on the corner of Seventh and Ash Streets, occupying a whole block, and will cost when finished $50,000. The interior will be finished entirely in natural woods. The site of this residence is known as Groesbeck Hill, named after Mrs. Hubbell's father. Mr. Hubbell owns over 1,000 acres of land within the limits of the city of San Diego.

He was married in San Diego in 1881 to Miss Kate L. Groesbeck, a daughter of Gen. John Groesbeck, formerly of New York, who was at the time of his death the oldest member of the order of Odd Fellows in the United States. He has two children, both boys. It is not difficult to analyze the causes of Mr. Hubbell s success. Primarily, he has had the opportunity; secondly, he has improved it. Combining in a wonderful degree keen financial foresight with promptness of decision, failure is to him an unknown quantity. Personally, he is one of the most genial of men; affable in his manners, courteous to all, his popularity is not to be wondered at. It O. S. Hubbell has attained an extraordinary measure of success, the means by which he secured it were such that he has raised up friends rather than enemies along his pathway in life.

Mr. Hubbell has been very hard worked during the past few years, and will as soon as possible retire from any active part in the management of the many enterprises he is now engaged in, and devote his whole time to his duties at the bank, in which institution he deservedly takes a great deal of pride, leaving to his associates the conduct of all outside affairs with which his name is now connected.

JOSEPH FAIVRE.

In a city where the leading residents are remarkable for the eventful character of their lives, Joseph Faivre is entitled to take a prominent place. He was born in New Orleans, on the 4th of June, 1828. When Joseph was seven years old, his parents removed to Ohio, leaving him in charge of an acquaintace engaged in the cooperage business, to whom, six years later, their son was apprenticed. At the end of six years he was pronounced a master of his trade, and engaged in business on his own account as a trimmer of broken cargoes on the city levee. He was thus engaged for seven years, when he left the Crescent City and joined his parents at Dayton, Ohio, and went to work at his trade.

After coopering for a year he went to work quarrying stone and boating it down the Miami Canal to Cincinnati, where it was used for the Catholic cathedral being built by Archbishop Purcell. After completing his quarrying contract he engaged as a buyer of tobacco and grain for Henry Harmon, a well-known merchant of Dayton. After continuing at this business for eight years he returned to New Orleans, but only remained there a month when he left for Indiana, locating at the town of Adeka, on the Wabash, where for two years he kept a hotel. His venture as a landlord, however, was not a successful one. He lost all his savings, and removing to Otter Creek, six miles from Terra Haute, he went to work at his trade as a cooper. At the end of two years he availed himself of an opportunity to lease the Prairie House at Terra Haute, a large hotel, which he conducted for eight months. In the fall of 1856 he removed to Leavenworth, Kansas, where he kept a livery stable for two years, at the same time being engaged in buying and selling real estate. During this time he built seven or eight houses. He made a prospecting tour through the mountains of

JOSEPH FAIVRE.

Colorado, and at the end of three months located at Denver. There, during the years of 1860-61-62, he engaged in the wholesale and retail grocery business, doing the largest trade of any house in the city. He was at this time also doing business as a freighter of supplies from Leavenworth, St. Joe, Atchison, and Nebraska City to Denver. There were no railroads then, and Faivre's wagons were the equivalent of the freight trains of to-day.

In 1863 he sold out at Denver and went into the freighting business from Leavenworth to Salt Lake and Virginia, Montana. This trade was quite hazardous as, in addition to the ordinary dangers that befell his trains in the long journey across the plains, from the elements, they were liable to an attack from bands of hostile Indians, and Mr. Faivre was obliged to use the utmost care and tact to avoid these wily foes. While engaged in this business he also conducted an auction and commission house at Virginia, Montana. One of his trains met with a serious accident while descending the Bear River Mountain. An explosion occurred in one of the wagons, which was drawn by eight yoke of large Missouri cattle, and loaded with 5,500 pounds of powder and 75,000 feet of fuse. As may be imagined, the shock was terrific. The driver was blown to atoms and seven of the cattle were killed, their remains being scattered in all directions. During the same trip, one of the drivers of the train was struck by lightning on the Big Sandy River, in Wyoming. There was not a break upon his skin but the corpse was like a mass of jelly, and the sole of one of his shoes was split by the fluid.

In the spring of 1865 Mr. Faivre became snow blind, and he returned to Leavenworth, where he built a residence and made it his home. In 1870 he came to San Diego on account of his health. After a short sojourn here he liked the place so well that he went back to Leavenworth, settled up his affairs, and came on here to reside permanently in June, 1871. When he first came here in 1870, he bought considerable property, and upon locating here he purchased more and engaged in the business of real estate, brokerage, and loaning money, buying up school warrants, etc. About five years ago he retired from active business and devoted his attention to the conduct of his private affairs. In 1885 he made a trip to Europe, being absent four months.

Mr. Faivre has done a great deal to develop and beautify San Diego. He has built eight houses of his own and probably as many more as agent for others. One of his buildings is a three-story brick 50x100 feet, on E Street, between Fourth and Fifth, nearly opposite the First National Bank, costing $16,000. He is now erecting a fine building for business purposes, 75x100 feet in size, on the corner of Seventh and D Streets. One part will be four stories in height and the portion on the corner will be five stories. It will be provided with an elevator, have all the modern improvements, and cost over $40,000. Mr. Faivre was married in 1848 near Dayton, Ohio, to Miss Klyntick. They have had one child, who died of the cholera in New Orleans.

GEORGE WILLIAM BARNES, M. D.

IF a practical example of the benefit to be obtained from a residence in San Diego was wanting, it could be supplied from the experience of Dr. George William Barnes. He has been a resident of this city for seventeen years, and though formidable chronic maladies with which he has struggled through the greater part of his professional life, still continue, he finds, in this mild and equable climate, an immunity from acute attacks and generally an amelioration of chronic affections that makes existence comparatively a pleasure.

Dr. Barnes was born in Frederick County, Virginia, December 9, 1825, and at the age of ten removed with his parents to Newark, Ohio. Having decided to follow the profession of medicine, he became a student under the tutelage of Dr. A. O. Blair, of Newark, then one of the most prominent homeopathic physicians of Ohio. After attending courses of instruction in the Medical College of Ohio, the Eclectic Medical Institute of Cincinnati, and the Cleveland Homeopathic College, he was graduated in the latter institution in 1851. In the same year he located in Mt. Vernon, Ohio, where he pursued an extensive and lucrative practice for fourteen years. In 1865, having been elected to a professorship in the Cleveland Homeopathic Hospital College, he removed to that city. In 1869, however, he was obliged, because of failing health, to resign his position and seek a milder climate. He came to California and spent nearly a year in the State in the study and observation of its climatology. At the end of that time he decided that San Diego possessed in a larger degree the conditions favorable for his health and comfort than any place he had visited, and accordingly located here. Subsequent experience has convinced him of the wisdom of his choice. Several years since Dr. Barnes received a spinal injury which has interfered to some extent with physical effort, but notwithstanding this he continues to do professional and other work far beyond his apparent ability to perform. He is a man of immense vital force and strength of character, and besides his professional labors takes an active interest in all affairs pertaining to the social and material advancement of the city. While his ability as a physician places him in the front rank of his profession, his sterling personal qualities have served to endear him to a large circle outside of his professional clientele. He invested considerably in city property during the early years of his residence, and this having steadily enhanced in value has made him independent. He was largely instrumental in organizing the San Diego So-

BIOGRAPHICAL SKETCHES.   171

ciety of Natural History, and has labored zealously to promote its prosperity. He has continued as its President since its organization to the present time.

Dr. Barnes had associated with him in practice from 1881 to 1884, Dr. E. A. Clark, now of Los Angeles, and from the latter date to the 1st of November last, he had as his associate Dr. A. Morgan. He now

GEORGE WILLIAM BARNES, M. D.

has associated with him Dr. B. F. Gamber, late of Cleveland, Ohio, who has successively filled the positions of professor of anatomy, of physiology, of hygiene, and of sanitary science, at the Cleveland Homeopathic Hospital College.

Dr. Barnes' high professional standing is recognized throughout the country, and he retains many evidences of the esteem in which he is held by the medical fraternity. Among the positions of honor and trust he has held are the following: He has been a member of the

American Institute of Homœopathy, the oldest national medical association in the United States, since 1853; and since 1878, in consequence of a membership of over twenty-five years, he has belonged to the association of seniors of that body. He aided in the establishment of the first medical dispensary in Cleveland and the Homeopathic Hospital, still in successful operation, and was one of the consulting physicians of the latter. He was physician to the Cleveland Protestant Orphan Asylum, was Secretary of the Cuyahoga County Medical Society and Treasurer of the Western Institute of Homeopathy. He assisted in the establishment of the *Ohio Medical and Surgical Reporter*, and in its editorial management during its first volume. Ever since his resignation from an active professorship in the Cleveland College he has had the honorary title of Emeritus Professor of Materia Medica in that institution. He is now a member of the California State Homeopathic Medical Society, and an honorary member of the Los Angeles Homeopathic Medical Society. He is also a corresponding member of the St. Louis Academy of Science and of the Wisconsin State Historical Society. He has contributed to a great many medical journals and is the author of a seven-page pamphlet which has been very widely read, entitled, "The Hillocks and Mound Formations of the Pacific Coast."

THOMAS L. NESMITH.

It must be a source of pride to the old residents of San Diego, the men who gave the impetus to its growth, that started its "boom," to look around them and see the city of their creation, as it were, making such tremendous strides, and feel that to their individual efforts is largely due the change from a struggling hamlet to a thriving young metropolis. Thomas L. Nesmith is one of these early San Diegans, one of the men whose clear foresight and keen business sense foresaw that on the shores of this magnificent harbor must at no distant day arise a great commercial city. Mr. Nesmith is a native of New Hampshire, having been born in the town of Derry in that State, in 1811. His early youth was spent at the old Nesmith homestead, "The Lilacs," at Derry. The rudiments of his education were acquired at the district school, and he afterward attended the Pinkerton Academy at Derry. After leaving school he entered the employ of his Uncle Newcomb, in Haverhill, Massachusetts, as a clerk for a short time. He was not satisfied with the progress he had made in his studies, however, and he returned to the academy again and completed his course. He then entered the store of William Anderson, a cousin, in Derry, and made up his mind to become a merchant. He remained there for four years. He had now reached the age of twenty-one, and longed to go out

BIOGRAPHICAL SKETCHES. 173

into the world and fight the battle of life in earnest. His capital, measured by the usual standard, was not large, but it was substantial. It consisted of honesty, ability, and perseverance. Prepared as he was for the contest, he started for New York City, where he obtained an advantageous position in a large mercantile house. Here he remained for fifteen years, traveling, meanwhile, in the course of his business,

THOMAS L. NESMITH.

through the different States and West Indies. When he was thirty-eight years old he visited Europe, with his family, where he remained two years. He then returned to this country and located in the South, where he engaged in the mercantile business. Afterwards he went to Mexico. After passing two years in Mexico, where he established his son, Anthony Rutgers Nesmith, in business, he removed to Minnesota, where for two years he carried on banking. He had long desired to go to California, but circumstances had prevented. In 1870, however, he determined to go, and reached San Diego that year, with his family. San Diego has been his home ever since, and he was eight years at one time without leaving the county.

At the time of his arrival here the site of the present city of San Diego was covered with sage-brush and cactus, and there were not more than half a dozen buildings. The Horton House was in course of erection. There was little promise, then, of the great city of the future. Within a short time after his arrival he was elected President of the Bank of San Diego, which position he held until 1883, when he resigned. When the question of railroad communication was first thoroughly agitated, a committee composed of the leading citizens was formed for the purpose of negotiating with the different railway corporations and forwarding the interests of the city. Of this body, known as the "Committee of Forty," Mr. Nesmith was chosen President, and labored early and late to assure the building of a transcontinental railroad. In 1875 he resigned this post of honor upon being elected a Director of the Texas and Pacific Railway Company. Mr. Nesmith presided at the great railroad meeting held here in 1872, under the auspices of Col. Thomas A. Scott, when Prof. Louis Agassiz, Senator Sherman, and other distinguished men were present. He was one of the founders and the first President of the San Diego Benevolent Association, an organization that has done and continues to do a vast amount of good.

Mr. Nesmith married Maria Antoinette, a daughter of the late Anthony Rutgers Gale, of Natchez, Mississippi. She died at San Diego, in 1873. She was a woman of rare beauty, and most highly accomplished. He has two sons and a daughter living, having lost one son, Anthony Rutgers Nesmith, who died in Mexico, in 1880. Otto A. Nesmith is a lawyer residing in Minnesota, and Loring Gale Nesmith is cashier of the First National Bank of San Jose. His daughter, Henrietta, is the wife of Brig.-Gen. A. W. Greely, Chief of the Signal Service Bureau. When the news of the rescue of her gallant husband was received she was in San Diego, visiting her father. She hurried across the continent and arrived at Portsmouth, New Hampshire, just in time to welcome him upon his arrival there.

There is no citizen of San Diego more highly esteemed than Mr. Nesmith, and his kindly face and courtly manners are familiar to all. It is the earnest wish of those who know him that he may yet be spared many years to enjoy the contentment that follows a career so honorable and ennobling as his has been.

While Mr. Nesmith has fulfilled well his duties to the living, he has not been unmindful of those who have gone before. He has placed three memorial windows in St. Paul's Church, in this city, in memory of his family who are deceased. They are as follows One to his wife, Maria Antoinette Nesmith, "Christ Blessing little Children;" one to his son, John Wadsworth Nesmith, "The Wise Men;" one to his son, Anthony Rutgers Nesmith, "The Angel at the Tomb." The windows were made at Munich, in Bavaria, and as works of art they are very perfect.

MRS MARY J. BIRDSALL.

WHEN the advocates of female suffrage advance arguments in support of their cause they are too apt to appeal to sentiment, and to overlook one of the most forcible arguments. That is the ability with which women direct those branches of business that are popularly supposed to fall within the special province of men. When we find a woman who combines executive ability with attention to detail, who has a talent for direction as well as a faculty for managing—who is, in fact, a thorough woman of business, the most ultra opponent of equal rights to the gentler sex is apt to surrender his opinions. When we find a specimen of this stronger type of womanhood, she not only excites our admiration but commands our respect. We admire the gifts with which nature has endowed her, and respect the manner in which she has applied them. Among that body of able, enterprising, and progressive pioneer residents that gave the impetus to San Diego's growth, there is to be found the name of a woman—Mrs. Mary J. Birdsall. Coming to San Diego when it was but a hamlet, she has lived to see it advance to a bustling, commercial city, and by her business prescience she has been enabled to participate in the general prosperity that has attended its wonderful growth.

Mrs. Birdsall was born near Jefferson City, Missouri, but was raised in Tennessee, and educated at the Young Ladies' Model School in Summerville, Tennessee. She graduated at the age of fifteen, and within a year afterward was married. About twenty years ago she came to California, by way of the Isthmus, and for two years lived in the northern part of the State. Then, in 1870, she came to San Diego. At that time what is now the city of San Diego contained but a few board houses. The erection of the Horton House, the first brick building, had just been commenced, and it gave little promise of the great future before it. In company with her husband, Mrs. Birdsall started the Home Restaurant on the ground where the Commercial Hotel now stands. It was afterwards known as the Lyon Restaurant. In 1880–81 she kept a hotel known as the Commercial, situated below the Horton House, on the ground now occupied by the Chadbourne Furniture Company. In 1881 she began the erection of the fine house at present occupied and managed by her, the Commercial Hotel, on the corner of Seventh and I Streets. It contains one hun-

MRS. M. J. BIRDSALL.

dred and fifteen rooms, and is admirably arranged for the purpose for which it was designed. It is strictly a temperance house, and no liquor has ever been sold in it. It is especially popular with the old residents of this section of the State. Being cast upon her own resources, Mrs. Birdsall cultivated her natural business ability, and by strict attention to her duties she has acquired a most enviable position in the community. While directing her hotel in an admirable manner she has, by the exercise of judicious investments, acquired a handsome competency. Besides the Commercial Hotel she owns considerable city real estate and county property. During San Diego's darkest days, Mrs. Birdsall never lost faith in the future—her confidence in the city's ultimate importance was unbounded.

Mrs. Birdsall has two sons and one daughter, the latter being married. One son is attending college, and one resides in Arizona. Her father died here in 1880. Mrs. Birdsall is a lady of retiring disposition, never seeking publicity. She is, however, very charitable, and has contributed liberally to all good objects.

DR. D. CAVE.

ONE of the most promising signs of the healthful condition and assured permanency of the Republic is the deep interest manifested in its institutions by our adopted citizens. Many of the most progressive members of the body politic are men who were born under monarchial Governments. When transplanted to the free soil of America they seem to imbibe the spirit of our institutions intuitively and become leaders in every social and business enterprise. A good type of this class of citizens is the subject of this sketch.

Dr. D. Cave was born in Strasburg, France, in 1846. When a child he removed with his parents to Vienna, Austria. At the age of twelve he began work in mercantile business, in which he continued till he was eighteen years old. Then, having a taste for natural science and mechanical work, he commenced the study of dentistry. At the age of twenty-three he began the practice of his profession and continued with success for about four years, when a bronchial affection which he had contracted compelled him to abandon practice and he began to travel for his health.

He visited America for a twofold purpose—first, in search of health, and secondly, for the purpose of seeing the cradle of scientific dentistry, and to satisfy his desire for improving himself in his profession. Ill health compelled him to cut short his stay in the principal Eastern cities, and he soon started for the Pacific Coast. Upon arriving in San Francisco he consulted with several acquaintances as to his future movements.

BIOGRAPHICAL SKETCHES. 177

They advised that he go by steamer as far as Los Angeles, as it was a good locality for business and an excellent climate for throat troubles. They also told him that San Diego had a good climate, but that the place was dead; that there was nothing but sand hills there, and that jackrabbits fed in the streets. He determined, notwithstanding their reports, to go as far as San Diego, and then if he did not like it he

D. CAVE, D. D. S.

would return to Los Angeles or Santa Barbara. He accordingly purchased a ticket for San Diego and left on the steamer *Orizaba* on the voyage down the coast. After visiting Santa Barbara and Los Angeles, during the time the steamer stopped at those places, he landed in San Diego on the 14th day of April, 1872. He was in poor health, hardly able to speak the English language, without friends, and his whole capital had dwindled down to one solitary twenty-dollar gold piece. He went to the Horton House, and in a few days his throat began to improve, and his voice, which had been lost for nearly six months, returned like magic. He determined to advertise his profession and begin work at the hotel with what few instruments he had. He met with such success that in a short time he was able to establish himself in the business part of the town, in one of the best localities, and to furnish his offices in the best style. He was thus enabled to do the finest kind of work, and soon gained a reputation as a skilled operator that was not confined to the limits of San Diego. He is the only dentist that has remained here through all the ups and downs of the community for fifteen successive years. His practice has steadily increased until he retired from business a short time ago, when he turned over to his successors a practice of over one thousand dollars cash receipts per month.

Dr. Cave has been the tutor of two of San Diego's young men, and so high was his reputation that they were granted licenses by the California Board of Dental Examiners without attendance at any college of dentistry. Both now have a lucrative practice of their own, and have gained a reputation for their skill. He is an active member of the California State Dental Association, and also of the Southern California Odentological Society. He aided, too, in organizing the San Diego Dental Society, of which he is President. Dr. Cave has not confined his usefulness to his profession, however, but has been prominent in all movements having for their object the advancement of San Diego. To him belongs the credit of having organized the San Diego County Immigration Association, in the latter part of 1885. He was President of the Committee of Celebration at the time of the completion of the Atchison system to the Pacific Ocean *via* San Diego. He served a term as President of the Chamber of Commerce, in 1885, and while occupying that position, demonstrated the advantages of the soil of San Diego for raising cereals, fruit trees, plants, etc., by showing what had been produced on his own land. He was at this time, *ex-officio*, a member of the Board of Pilot Commissioners. He has been President of the San Diego Fire Company and is now an exempt member. He has been Chancellor Commander and is a charter member of San Diego Lodge No. 28, Knights of Pythias; and Master of San Diego Lodge No. 35, F. and A. M. He is now President of the Board of Directors of the Free Public Library, and Vice-President of the Society for the Prevention of Cruelty to Animals, which he aided in organizing. He is a Director in the San Diego Building and Loan Association ; Treasurer of the Morena Land and Town Co.; a member of the San Diego Horticultural Association, in the work of which he has taken an especial interest; a member of the San Diego Natural History Society; a member of the San Diego Benevolent Association, and, in fact, is identified with about every public organization in the city.

Dr. Cave was naturalized in 1877, and has always been an earnest and consistent Republican. He has taken an active part in political affairs, but has steadily refused, although repeatedly urged to do so, to be a candidate for any political position. He was married in San Diego, June 19, 1878, to Miss Rosa Meyer, a native of France, and a graduate of a high school in Paris. He has two children. He is the largest stockholder in the new town of Morena, and contemplates erecting a fine residence there the coming season.

DR. W. A. WINDER

Few residents of San Diego are better known or more highly respected than Dr. W. A. Winder. A veteran of two wars, his life has been an adventurous one. He was born in Baltimore, Md., December 5, 1824. His father was an officer in the regular army, and the greater part of his early boyhood was passed with his parents at the different military posts between North Carolina and Maine. Up to the time he was nine years of age he attended school in North Carolina, and then went to Baltimore, where he continued in school until sixteen years old. Having a fondness for medicine he now began to study it, and fit himself for practice. He attended lectures in Philadelphia. When the Mexican War broke out, he volunteered his services, and just after the battle of Buena Vista was commissioned a Lieutenant of Artillery. He served during the rest of the war and continued in the service for eighteen years, resigning at the close of the Civil War. Just after the Mexican War, in 1848, he was sent with part of his regiment to Florida, to assist in quelling the outbreak of the Seminole Indians, and he remained there thirteen months.

In 1854 he sailed from New York with his regiment, the Third Artillery, for California on board the ill-fated steamship *San Francisco*. Thirty-six hours out of New York, when in the Gulf stream, the ship was caught in a hurricane and disabled. For fourteen days she drifted about on the ocean in a helpless condition. There were 750 soldiers and thirteen officers, some of whom had their families, besides a number of civilian passengers. During this time cholera broke out on board and nearly one hundred died from that dread disease. Perhaps the most terrible of their misfortunes occurred during the height of the storm, when an immense sea struck the ship and carried away the upper saloon, on which were crowded over two hundred soldiers. Finally, when hope had well-nigh given way to despair, a vessel hove in sight, and in answer to their signals of distress replied that she would stand by them. The following day the sea had gone down sufficiently to permit the transfer of most of the passengers to the vessel, which proved to be the Scotch bark *Three Bells*, of Glasgow. Another vessel also came to their assistance, and all were rescued before the doomed steamer sank beneath the waves. For his heroic conduct during those dreadful days of trial on board the *San Francisco*, and the part he took in securing the safe transfer of the women and children to the *Three Bells*, Lieutenant Winder was accorded a vote of thanks by the Legislature of his native State, Maryland.

DR. W. A. WINDER.

He started again with his regiment for the Pacific Coast, and was sent with a detachment to the Mission San Diego, where he remained for three years, during which time he made ten expeditions among Cahuila Indians, living in the northern part of the county. At times they displayed hostile traits, and the presence of the troops was necessary to prevent an outbreak. He was then stationed at Fort Yuma for a year, during which time that post was threatened by Indians. During the War of the Rebellion he served about six months in the Army of the Potomac, commanding Battery G, Third Artillery, and then was ordered to this coast and placed in command of Alcatraz, in San Francisco harbor. There he remained three and a half years, until the close of the war. He then resigned his commission and entered civil life. Soon after this he engaged in a mining venture below Ensenada, in Lower California, for a while, and afterwards was interested in a mine at Lyttle Creek, near San Bernardino. He then went to Los Angeles, where he remained until 1872. In the latter year he came to San Diego, where he has made his home ever since. He has practiced medicine until about three years ago, when he retired from active practice. He now has charge of the Marine Relief Hospital, an institution which he has built himself, and is but just completed.

Dr. Winder was married in 1850, in Portsmouth, New Hampshire, to the daughter of Governor Goodwin, of that State. He has one son, who is now a lieutenant in the navy and attached to the United States steamer *Marion*. Dr. Winder is the owner of Winder's Addition. He is a liberal-spirited citizen, and a representative man.

JUDGE M. A. LUCE.

ONE of the best-known and most prominent men in every movement to advance the best interests of San Diego, is Judge M. A. Luce. He comes of good New England stock, and is of a right possessed of those attributes which are strongly characteristic of the better type of the American character,—energy, ability, and probity. His father is a native of Maine, is a preacher in the Baptist Church, and now, at the age of seventy-eight years, is living in Poway Valley, a hale and hearty old man. His mother was born in New Hampshire.

The subject of this brief sketch first saw the light in Quincy, Illinois, in the year 1842. He lived with his parents in Central Illinois until he was fourteen years of age, when he left home to prepare for college at Hillsdale, Mich. Here he spent a part of each year in advancing his own education, and the residue of the time in educating others, that is, in teaching school. Thus passed nearly four years of his boyhood. Then came that eventful April day in 1861 when the call "to arms" resounded through the land. The response that came forth from the loyal North was something unparalleled in the history of mankind. The ink was scarcely dry with which the President's proclamation for volunteers was written when the tramp of battalions was heard throughout the land. From no section of the North was the patriotic response more immediate and hearty than from the great States of the West. Foremost among them was the commonwealth of Michigan. Young

Luce, brimming over with loyalty, dropped his schoolbooks, and enlisted in the Fourth Michigan Volunteer Infantry. During the war he took part in the following engagements: Bull Run, New Bridge, Hanover, Court House, Mechanicsville, Gaines Mill, Savage Station, Turkey Bend, White Oak Swamp, Malvern Hill, Second Bull Run, U. S. Ford, Chancellorsville, Kelly's Ford, Ashby Gap, Brandy Station, Middle-

JUDGE M. A. LUCE.

burg, Gettysburg, Williamsport, Wapping Heights, Culpeper, Bristol Station, Rappahannock Station, Mine Run, Wilderness, Laurel Hill, Spottsylvania, North Anna, Tolopotomy Creek, Jericho Mills, Bethseda Church, Cold Harbor, and Petersburg. Was wounded slightly at Spottsylvania, while with the forlorn hope in the assault of May 12.

At the close of the war Luce, now a bronzed young veteran, after paying a brief visit to his parents, returned to Hillsdale and resumed his collegiate studies, which had been so rudely interrupted four years before. He graduated in 1866, and having decided to devote himself to the legal profession, attended the Law University at Albany, where he graduated a year later. With his diploma in his pocket he returned to his native State, and began practice in Bushnell, of which he was the first City Attorney. He was afterward Attorney of the First National Bank of Bushnell and local Attorney of the Chicago, Burlington and Quincy R. R. Co., and in 1872 was the candidate of his party for the State Senate. In 1873 the first of Southern California's booms began to be heard of. In these days it would be called a very small boom, a kind of a "Northern Citrus Belt" affair; but then it made quite a stir, not only on the Pacific Coast but was felt all over the East. That was the time when Col. Tom Scott was building his Texas Pacific (on paper) across the continent, to have its terminus on the shores of San Diego Bay. One result of this agitation was to direct attention to the harbor, which had lain neglected and unthought of since the day the great empire of California became a part of the Republic. Tidings of the promising future of this Pacific Coast city came to Luce in his Illinois home, and as at that time his health was apparently failing, he decided to emigrate. He arrived in San Diego in May, 1873, and immediately opened a law office, and engaged in the practice of his profession. In the fall of 1875 he was elected Judge of the county court, and held the office until the new constitution went into effect and terminated the jurisdiction of that court in 1880. Judge Luce took an active part in the movement to bring the Atchison, Topeka and Santa Fe road to San Diego, and was a member of, and acted as counsel for, the Citizens' Committee. In the fall of 1880 the California Southern Railroad Co. was organized and he was elected Vice-President. He was also appointed Attorney of the road and has continued so up to the present time. He is still a member of the Board of Directors. Judge Luce's law practice has been very large, he having acted as Attorney for a majority of the heaviest local corporations, while the Pacific Steamship Co. and other important organizations have intrusted their legal business to his care. Judge Luce is now preparing to retire from the active practice of his profession, his private business interests having become so numerous and important as to require his entire time and attention. Ever since the day of his arrival in San Diego Judge Luce has had an abiding faith in the future of the city. Firm in his convictions on that point he has from the first, as opportunity offered, invested in real estate, and he is now one of the heaviest holders of real property. Unlike some other men of like business instincts the aggregation of property has not served to lessen his interest in the growth of the city, but he is to-day as keenly alive to everything that tends to develop and enlarge its importance as he was ten years ago. He has been identified with every public improvement, and is willing at all times to give freely of his means towards the material advancement of San Diego. He has been interested in the mining development of the county, and is a principal shareholder in the Shenandoah mine at Mesa Grande, in this county. He is of the opinion that the future wealth and importance of San Diego will be largely due to the development of its mines. In the past profitable operations have been retarded by the crude machinery employed in working the ore and insufficient means of transportation. With the completion of a railroad to the mining center, and the introduction of new and approved machinery, all this will be changed, however.

Judge Luce is one of the executors of the trust of the late James M. Pierce, donating $150,000 to the establishment of the Boys' and Girls' Aid Society. He has been President of the Unitarian Church Society ever since its organization. In December, 1870, he was married, at Bushnell, to Miss Adelaide Mantania, of Avon, Illinois, who was at the time Assistant Principal of the public schools at Bushnell, Illinois. Uniting personal attractions and all the female accomplishments to a richly stored mind, Mrs. Luce has proven a worthy helpmate to her husband in the battle of life. Six children have blessed their union, of which four, two boys and two girls, are living; two have died, and are buried in the cemetery here.

Judge Luce is six feet in height, slight figure, and a face that has more the look of a student than a professional man, or one immersed in business. He has a strong taste for literature, and possesses a well-appointed library. Now that he is getting rid of some of his professional cares he will probably find solace from the demands of business in the society of his books.

GEORGE A. COWLES.

GEORGE A. COWLES, who died last fall at the Florence Hotel, in this city, was one of the thoroughly representative men of San Diego County. Mr. Cowles was born in Hartford, Connecticut, April 5, 1836. His early days were spent upon a farm near Hartford. His father was engaged in manufacturing, and was the first man to make broadcloth in this country. When he was fourteen years old he entered the dry goods store of B. & W. Hudson, in Hartford, as errand boy. Five years later he had become first salesman of the establishment. During these years, however, he had not neglected his education, but attended night school faithfully, and took a course in the Commercial College. He remained with the Hudsons until he was twenty-one, and then engaged in the business of manufacturing cotton goods, on his own account. He was burned out, however, soon afterward. At the age of twenty-five we find him in the city of New York, carrying on a commission business and holding an interest in the manufacture of cotton goods at several places. When thirty years of age he was elected President of the New York Cotton Goods Exchange. He retired from the cotton business in 1869, and in 1872 became interested in Government contracts, in which he continued for three years. For several winters he visited this coast on account of his wife's health, and one

GEORGE A. COWLES.

winter he spent in Florida. This was unfortunate for him, as he contracted malarial fever, which nearly broke him down. He first came to San Diego in 1873. He had journeyed between this city and San Francisco a number of times by stage and by private conveyance, stopping in the different valleys and making himself familiar with the various localities. In 1877 he concluded to locate in San Diego County permanently. At that time the outlook for communication with the outside world was very poor. Mr. Cowles, however, had strong faith in the natural resources of the county, and believed firmly in the future commercial importance of the city of San Diego.

Having decided to make this his home he went, in the spring of 1878, to El Cajon and began farming operations. He then owned between six and seven hundred acres of land in the heart of the valley, but he acquired more, from time to time, until he had between three and four thousand acres. The first year he planted about everything in the shape of tree and vine, in order to test what could be grown to the best advantage. When his grapes matured he found that the finest Muscats could be grown in El Cajon that were to be found in the State, and when his olive trees began to bear, the fruit rivaled any that he had ever seen. He therefore decided to devote himself especially to these two products. The result proved the wisdom of his choice, for to-day the raisins produced on the Cowles Ranch are sent all over the United States, and they are without doubt superior to any grown either in this country or Europe. In one of his vineyards Mr. Cowles raised the largest quantity of Muscat grapes on record on one acre. This season there were shipped from eight to ten thousand boxes of raisins from this vineyard, which is but five years old. It is situated in the center of the valley. Besides grapes, and olives, and other fruits, there are about one thousand acres in grain, while the ranch is stocked with one hundred head of fine horses, and about three hundred head of choice, graded cattle.

It is conceded that in placing upon the market the finest raisins grown on American soil, Mr. Cowles perhaps did more than any one man in directing attention to the wonderful fertility and productiveness of San Diego soil. By his individual efforts in another direction, he finally accomplished a task that will result in untold benefit to the Cajon Valley. Reference is made to the extension of the Atchison system from San Diego into the valley. He personally guaranteed to the Chief Engineer of the company the free right of way from Twenty-second Street Station in San Diego to the north end of the Cajon Valley. This offer was accepted, and the road is now well under way, and will be completed in a short time. From the Cajon the line will be extended to Poway, Bernardo, Escondido, San Marcos, and Oceanside, connecting at the latter point with the California Southern. In this undertaking Mr. Cowles gave another evidence of his indomitable push and energy—the same qualities that made him successful as a merchant. Indeed, his great success as an agriculturist was largely due to the fact that he always conducted his farm matters on strict business principles. He was as much in earnest in curing raisins as he formerly was in manufacturing cotton goods.

Mr. Cowles was one of the organizers of the Consolidated National Bank, and continued a Director up to the time of his death. He was also a Director in the old Commercial Bank, and was Vice-President of the San Diego County Savings Bank. He was the organizer of the San Diego Marine Ways and Dry Dock Company, of which he was Vice-President, having declined to accept the Presidency. He raised a subscription of $50,000 in six and one-half hours for this enterprise. He was a Director in the California Southern Railway Company, and such confidence had the railroad people in his judgment that they left the direction of the construction of the Cajon branch entirely to him. He was married in 1861 to the second daughter of Hon. Roswell Blodgett, of Hartford, a gentleman who has done as much for the advancement of educational interests in Connecticut as any other man. Mr. Cowles demonstrated, in a practical way, that San Diego had something more to boast of than bay and climate, and the work that he did for the advancement of the county will be more and more appreciated as the years roll by.

DR. P. C. REMONDINO.

Few citizens of San Diego have had a career more replete with incidents than Dr. P. C. Remondino. Born in Turin, Italy, on the 10th of February, 1846, he was sent as a child to a Catholic seminary, where he remained until nine years of age. In 1854 he left Italy with his father, and crossing the Atlantic landed in New York City. From the latter city father and son journeyed westward until they came to Minnesota. At Wabeshaw, a thriving town in that State, the father engaged in mercantile business, and young Remondino attended the public schools. At sixteen years of age he entered Jefferson College, at Philadelphia, and began the study of his chosen profession, medicine. During the summer of 1864, while still attending college, the Battle of the Wilderness occurred, and there was such a call for army surgeons that Remondino, with several other students, volunteered his services. They were accepted, and for some time he continued doing hospital duty at Annapolis and City Point. In March, 1865, he graduated at Jefferson College. The very evening of his graduation he left the reception party tendered his class, for Fortress Monroe, having received his commission as Acting Assistant Surgeon attached to the Third Pennsylvania Heavy Artillery. He served in that capacity up to the time the regiment was mustered out in November, 1865. He then returned to Minnesota, and entered upon the practice of his profession with his former preceptor, Dr. Milligan. At the breaking out of the Franco-German war Dr. Remondino was enjoying a lucrative practice in his adopted town, but his fondness for adventure, and desire to become skilled in his profession, induced him to seek employment in the French service. Accordingly, being provided with flattering credentials, both from the Governor of the State and from officials in Washington, he sailed for Brest. He arrived in safety and at once started for Tours, which was then the seat of government. Here he presented his credentials and was cordially received by Leon Gambetta, who provided for his appointment as an army surgeon. He was

DR. P. C. REMONDINO.

attached to a regiment just formed, called "Franc Tireurs du Nord," Colonel Rondeau Commander, which was recruited in the French departments bordering on Belgium. He served with this regiment during the campaign in the north of France against the First Prussian Army Corps under the command of General Manteufel, until the dissolution of all the volunteer corps in the French army. He was then detailed for service with the Artillery Legion of Havre, and was Post Surgeon of Fort Saint Adresse, the principal fort on the heights of

Havre, overlooking both the city and harbor. He remained there until peace was concluded. After the discharge of the troops, Dr. Remondino traveled through Italy and Switzerland, for pleasure and instruction, and afterwards extended his journeyings to England. He then returned to Minnesota and resumed the practice of his profession in 1871.

The winter of 1871-72 was an unusually severe one in Minnesota, and his health, which had been somewhat undermined because of the exposure he had undergone in the French service, warned him that he should seek a more genial climate. He accordingly started for San Diego, reaching California in December, 1873, and arriving here in January following. He had intended engaging in the cattle business, but on looking the ground over the prospects did not strike him favorably, and meeting an old classmate, Dr. R. J. Gregg, he opened an office adjoining his, and once more settled down to active practice. He was City Physician in 1875-76; County Physician for several consecutive terms; Surgeon for the California Southern Railroad Company up to the time of his retirement from practice; Surgeon of the Marine Hospital, and did all the surgical work for the Pacific Coast Steamship Company. In 1879 he built a large hospital here in conjunction with Dr. T. C. Stockton. They had accommodations for fifty patients, but owing to the light charges of charitable institutions they found it impossible to compete with them and the experiment was abandoned. In the spring of 1887, finding that his private business affairs were interfering with his professional duties, he retired from the active practice of his profession. Recognizing the great want of hotel accommodations in San Diego he built the St. James Hotel, which was opened for business in February, 1886. Since that time it has received some additions, and the entire cost will aggregate $250,000. Besides this fine building he owns considerable real estate in the city and county, and has invested liberally in every enterprise that he believed tended to advance the material interests of San Diego. Dr. Remondino returned in October from an extended Eastern tour, during which he attended, as a delegate, the International Medical Congress, at Washington, where he took a leading part in the proceedings, and read a paper on San Diego's climate, which attracted wide attention.

Dr. Remondino is Major and Surgeon of the Third Regiment Uniformed Rank Knights of Pythias of the State of California; a member of the Blue Lodge of Masons, San Diego Lodge; and a member of California Consistory F. and A. M., Thirty-third degree. He was United States Pension Surgeon for nine years, up to last year. Although retired from practice as an active member of the San Diego County Medical Society, he still takes an active interest in everything pertaining to its prosperity. He was married, in 1877, to Miss Sophie Earle, in

San Diego, and has four children, two girls and two boys, all living here. He is looked upon as one of the most public-spirited and progressive citizens in a community where push and enterprise are the eading elements of popularity.

N. H. CONKLIN.

ONE of the leading members of the San Diego Bar is N. H. Conklin. Although yet a comparatively young man, his life has been a busy one. In turn a soldier, journalist, and lawyer, he has achieved prominence in every profession with which his fortunes have been identified. Mr. Conklin was born in Wyoming County, Pennsylvania, June 6, 1839. His father, a native of New York, was a member of the famous Conklin family, whose members have added luster to the annals of jurisprudence and occupy a high place on the roll of forensic fame. His mother came from the State of Connecticut. His boyhood was passed with his parents in the town of Tunkhannock, on the Susquehanna, where he acquired such an education as was to be had in the public schools. In 1859 he began the study of the law in the office of Judge Peckham, Judge of the Court of Common Pleas. He was stil immersed in his studies at the time of the breaking out of the war. Those who are not yet arrived at middle age have little idea of the scenes that followed the firing upon Sumter,—the ebullitions of patriotic fervor, the mustering to arms, the hurried march to the field. Throughout the loyal States the response to President Lincoln's proclamation for troops was instantaneous—there was no hesitating then. Young Conklin heard the summons, and throwing aside his law books, began raising a company of volunteers. Within less than a week from the time of the issuing of the proclamation, his company was full and he made a tender of it to the Governor. But the quota of the State was filled and the offer was declined. The Government and many of the people then believed with Senator Seward that the whole "affair" would be over in ninety days. Suffering under his disappointment, young Conklin went to Cincinnati to visit some friends. He could not, however, resist the impulse to give his services to his country, and within a week after his proffer had been rejected by the Governor of Pennsylvania, he enlisted in Cincinnati in Company D, Second Kentucky Volunteers. He had been walking along the street when the beating of a drum again roused the fires of patriotism within his breast; he went upstairs, where a war meeting was being held, and enlisted as a private, not knowing at the time what the regiment was or where it was going; he only knew that his country needed his services, and right freely he proffered them. He was sent with his regiment to the Kan-

BIOGRAPHICAL SKETCHES

awa, in Western Virginia, and remained there until the spring of 1862. His regiment was then ordered to Kentucky, and then into Tennessee. He participated in the terrible battle of Shiloh, and was at the siege of Corinth. He then went back to Kentucky, and was in that State at the time of Bragg's raid. At Louisville he was discharged for promotion, having been commissioned Second Lieutenant in the Eighty-third Ohio.

N. H. CONKLIN.

When he reached Cincinnati, he found that his regiment had been ordered into the field. This was in November, 1862. He then returned to his home in Pennsylvania, where he remained until the following spring, reading the neglected law books. But he could not be content in such a peaceful avocation, and having a strong taste for the navy, he applied for and was appointed Master's Mate. He was immediately ordered to report on board the *Kenwood*, attached to the Mississippi squadron. He took part in the siege of Vicksburg, and saw much active service while on the *Kenwood*, which was one of the fastest steamers on the river and was generally used as a dispatch boat. In the spring of 1865 he was ordered to the *Chilicathe*, an iron-clad. As soon as he was mustered out of service at the close of the war, he again returned to Pennsylvania and once more renewed his law studies. He had two brothers in the Union army, both of whom are now living, one residing in Northern California and one in Missouri.

As soon as he had been admitted to the bar, he started west and located at Warrensburg, Missouri, where he began the practice of his profession. He remained at Warrensburg until the fall of 1874. During this time he was engaged in publishing the *Johnston Democrat*, a weekly newspaper. In October, 1874, Mr. Conklin started for San Diego. Upon his arrival here, he assumed editorial control of the San Diego *World*, a daily, in connection with Mr. Julian, at present one of the proprietors of the *San Diegan*. In 1877 he was elected District Attorney of the county, and held the office two years. Since then he has been engaged in the practice of the law. Mr. Conklin has the largest general law practice of any attorney in San Diego. He is the legal adviser of most of the large corporations here; is a stockholder in and attorney for the San Diego and Cuyamaca Railroad Co., and is one of the principal stockholders of the Mission Valley Water Co. He is a Past Post Commander of Heintzleman Post G. A. R., and is at present Commander of San Diego Commandery Knight Templars. He was instrumental in bringing the railroad here and has been interested in all public improvements. He has a handsome residence lately completed in Florence Heights, on the corner of Fifth and Ivy Streets.

Mr. Conklin was married in 1867, to Miss Myra J. Reese, of Warrensburg, Missouri, in Pleasant Hill, a short distance from the former place. Their union has been blessed with eight children, three of whom are living.

R. A. THOMAS.

In considering the phenomenal progress that has attended San Diego during the past two or three years, the most important factor in her development will be found to have been the class of business men who have invested their capital in the various enterprises that have lifted her from a quiet town into a bustling, thriving city. It is to the progressive spirit of these citizens that she is indebted for the handsome buildings that are ornamenting her streets, and the motor lines that make rapid communication with her charming suburbs a pleasure. They are, as a rule, men who have come from the young States of the West, and they have brought with them the vigorous spirit, the prompt and accurate judgment that seem characteristic of that portion of the Union. The subject of this sketch is an excellent type of this class of San Diego's citizens.

R. A. Thomas was born in Waukesha County, Wisconsin, July 10, 1847. His early boyhood was spent on his father's farm in Fon du Lac County. The first rudiments of education he acquired in the

R. A. THOMAS.

district school. At the age of sixteen he entered the high school in the city of Fon du Lac, and remained there four years. After this he went to Kansas and taught school for about three years in Atchison. For two years following, he was engaged in a Government survey in Western Kansas, and after that he went into the lumber business in Atchison County. In 1876 he went to New Mexico and engaged in the raising of cattle. This, however, was not to his liking and he returned to Kansas and went to dealing in lumber and hardware in

Onaga. A year afterward he, in company with his brothers, opened a private bank known as Thomas Brothers' Bank. In 1882, contemplating a change, they turned their thoughts to San Diego, and Mr. R. A. Thomas came hither to "spy out the land." Although the San Diego of that day was not apparently a very promising place for the investment of capital, yet Mr. Thomas' keen judgment foresaw the future possibilities and he decided upon locating here. He accordingly wrote to his brothers to close up their business in Kansas and come out here.

In the following year they arrived here, and in June purchased the ground on which the First National Bank now stands, and organized and opened a bank there. Since that time Mr. Thomas has been one of the most active and public-spirited of San Diego's citizens He has been the leading spirit in most of the important enterprises that have been organized here. He was one of the original incorporators of the San Diego Street Railroad Co., of the San Diego and Coronado Ferry Co., of the San Diego Lumber Co., of the West Coast Lumber Co., and of the San Diego and Old Town Railroad Co. He has also been largely interested in a great many land companies, including Escondido Land Co., the San Marcos Land Co., the Cottage Hill Land Association, and the Pacific Beach Co. He still owns stock in these corporations, but has dropped out of the management, and now devotes himself exclusively to his duties as President of the First National Bank. He held the position of cashier of that institution until last June, when he was elected President.

In a short time he will erect a six-story brick building in connection with Mr. I. A. Sheriff, on the southeast corner of Fifth and E Streets, which will cover one hundred feet square. This will be one of the finest buildings in the city and will cost not less than $120,000. He will also erect another building in connection with O. S. Hubbell, a five or six-story brick, covering 125x100, that will cost about $150,000, on the corner of Sixth and D Streets.

Mr. Thomas was married in March, 1875, to Miss Mary Beven, of Atchison, Kansas. He has two children, both daughters.

JUDGE JOHN D. WORKS.

A son of Indiana who has won for himself a proud position in the young metropolis of the Pacific Coast is Judge John D. Works. He was born in Ohio County in that State, in the year 1847. His father was a lawyer by profession, and had for many years practiced in Ohio and Switzerland Counties. Young Works lived on a farm till he w seventeen years of age, availing himself of such educational adv; tages as were afforded by the district schools of the neighborhood. e the spring of 1861 came the attack upon Sumter, the call for volt

BIOGRAPHICAL SKETCHES.   195

teers, and the mustering of troops. Like the other Western States, Indiana sent regiment after regiment to the front, and her troops were seen on every battle-field from Donelson to Vicksburg and from Atlanta to Savannah. The fire of patriotism in those stirring days burned not only in the bosoms of men of mature years, but it stirred the youth of the country; they left their tasks unfinished, their farm-work undone.

JUDGE JOHN D. WORKS.

John Works felt the infection that was in the air and longed to shoulder a musket and march to the war. But he was yet too tender in years to be mustered by the recruiting sergeant, and he had to curb his longing for military service. Finally, however, when he had reached \: age of seventeen, he enlisted in the Tenth Indiana Cavalry, and from A; time on until the the close of the war he was in active service. the:as most of the time with his regiment attached to the Army of the reuberland. He took part in the battle of Nashville, in December,

1864, when Hood, who had raised a new army in northern Alabama, and penetrated into middle Tennessee, was signally defeated by General Thomas. Immediately after this, Works went with his regiment down the river to New Orleans, and thence across to Mobile, where he participated in the siege of that place. During most of this time he was engaged in outpost and scout duty.

When the city capitulated to the Union forces under General Canby, his regiment rode across the country from Mobile to Vicksburg, a distance of one thousand six hundred miles. The bridges had all been destroyed and the country pretty well laid waste by General Wilson on his last raid, and Works and his fellow-troopers had to do some pretty lively foraging to get enough feed for their horses and themselves, as their rations were very short. After being mustered out he returned home, and for a time attended school, but he had decided to become a lawyer, and he was soon devoting all his energies to the study of his chosen profession in the office of Hon. A. C. Downey, formerly one of the Judges of the Supreme Court of Indiana. As soon as he was admitted, he began the active practice of his profession without intermission, except that he served one term as a member of the State Legislature in 1879, until 1883, when he came to San Diego. Here he opened an office and began practice. He served one term as City Attorney, and in October, 1886, was appointed by Governor Stoneman to the Superior bench to fill the vacancy caused by the resignation of Judge W. T. McNealy. At the general election, Judge Works was nominated for the unexpired term of Judge McNealy, and elected without opposition. In September of the last year, owing to the laborious duties of the position, and the inadequate compensation allowed by law, Judge Works tendered his resignation to the Governor and was succeeded by Hon. Edwin Parker. He then at once formed a partnership with ex-Congressman Olin Wellborn and John R. Jones, and is now engaged in the active practice of his profession.

If anything was wanting to show the high opinion entertained of Judge Works by his legal associates, it could be found in the resolutions adopted by the members of the bar, on the occasion of his retirement from the bench. During nearly all the time that Judge Works has been engaged in the practice of his profession, and while he was discharging the arduous duties of a judicial office, he has found time to engage in legal literature, and has produced a number of very valuable law books. His "Indiana Practice and Pleading," in three volumes, is a thorough and exhaustive work on code practice and pleading. A volume published some months since on the "Removal of Causes from the State to the Federal Courts," gives, in a convenient form, the law and practice relating to methods necessary to be adopted in such cases. He is now engaged in the preparation of a work entitled, "The Principles of Pleading and Practice," which will aim to give, in a clear and practical form, the general principles of pleading and practice as they exist, as effected by the rules of pleading at common law, and in equity and the codes and statutes of the several States.

Although Judge Works came to San Diego on account of a bronchial affection, he is now in the enjoyment of excellent health. He is a laborious student, and as a Counsellor stands in the very front rank of his profession. Personally, he is one of the most genial of men and is deservedly popular with all. He has a fine residence on Fifth Street, and has invested some of his means in real estate. He has unbounded faith in the future of San Diego and expects to see it a great and thriving commercial city. Judge Works was married in Bevay, Indiana, in November, 1868, to Miss Alice Banta. The fruit of this union has been six children, all living with their parents, and making one of the happiest family circles one can wish to see.

L. S. McLURE.

ONE of the best-known citizens of San Diego, on account of his public spirit, wealth, and social position, is L. S. McLure. He was born in Marshall, Saline County, Missouri, September 23, 1848. Mr. McLure's father was born in Charlottesville, Albemarle County, Virginia, but was raised in Pennsylvania. His mother, who was a Miss Parkison, was born in Williamsport, Pennsylvania, and is still living. When he was three years of age his parents removed to the city of St. Louis. He attended the public schools there until he was twelve years old, and afterwards went to Pleasant Ridge College. The war was raging at this time, and young McLure's ardent temperament drew him, as might be expected from his birth and early training, to espouse the cause of the South. So pronounced was he in the utterance of his sentiments, that he was, in the summer of 1863, banished from St. Louis. He immediately went into the Confederate lines and enlisted in the First Missouri Brigade, in which he served till the close of the war, in 1865. He then returned to St Louis, where he remained until 1869, when he started for Montana. There he was engaged in mining until 1875, when he went to Puget Sound, locating at Seattle. He resided in Seattle for six years, devoting himself to the insurance business, representing twenty-one companies, and doing the largest business of anyone north of San Francisco. During this time he was elected City Treasurer, and was appointed a Trustee of the Hospital for the Insane, at Steilacoom. In 1882 Mr. McLure decided to remove to San Diego. Here he engaged in the business of insurance and was the representative of a number of companies of fire, life, marine and accident insurance.

He has invested considerably in city property, but still retains his interests in mines in Montana. He has retired from active business, and now devotes himself entirely to the management of his property interests here and in the North. He finds time, however, to take part in every enterprise that has for its object the advancement of his adopted city, and is a most liberal contributor to every worthy public object. He is

L. S. McLURE.

a thorough San Diegan in his sentiments, and says he would not live anywhere else.

Mr. McLure was married in July, 1880, while living in Seattle, to Miss Ella Tibbits, who is a native of Minnesota. Mr. McLure's ancestors were Scotch, and although recognizing no aristocracy but that of merit he is justly proud of his own lineage. He can trace his descent on his father's side in an unbroken line to the time of William the Conqueror.

GOVERNOR ROBERT W. WATERMAN.

AMONG those who have largely aided in the wonderful development of San Diego County during the past three years is the present Governor of the State, Robert W. Waterman. Governor Waterman's career has been in some respects a peculiar one. Although always active in the councils of his party and earnest in the performance of those duties that pertain to good citizenship, unlike most men who have risen to prominence in public affairs, he never held a political office until after he was fifty years of age.

He was born in Fairfield, Herkimer County, New York, in 1826, but when very young removed with his parents to Illinois. There he remained until 1850. Gold had been discovered in California and the new El Dorado was attracting the most adventurous and progressive spirits of the country. Waterman was then twenty-four years old, and as might be expected his sanguine temperament was easily affected by the stories of fortunes to be acquired on the shores of the far-away Pacific. He joined a party of emigrants and made the journey across the plains. He did not remain long in the gold fields, and finally returned to his home in Illinois. Just at this time the Western States were in a red glow of excitement caused by the border warfare in Kansas. The "dough-face" policy of President Pierce, largely moulded and directed by his Secretary of War, Jefferson Davis, had permitted affairs to assume such a condition that the anti-slavery element in the new Territory was thoroughly terrorized and overawed. The feeling in the State of Illinois finally took shape, in the spring of 1856, in the calling together of a convention of the "Anti-Nebraska Party," that was destined to be a memorable one in the history of American politics. The convention assembled at Bloomington on the 29th of May, adopted the Republican name, formulated strong Republican resolutions, appointed delegates to the coming Republican convention, and nominated a full ticket of presidential electors, with Abraham Lincoln at their head. To this remarkable deliberative body Robert W. Waterman was sent as a delegate. There he found himself surrounded by men of all shades of political belief,—Whigs, Democrats, Free-soilers, Know-nothings, Abolitionists,—all willing to pool their issues, and unite in the formation of a new party having for its cardinal principles liberty of conscience and equality of rights to all. That grand convention was practically the birthplace of the Republican party, and he stood with Abraham Lincoln, Lyman Trumbull, Richard Yates, David Davis, Owen Lovejoy, and

Richard Oglesby as sponsors to the political infant which was thenceforth to prove itself so stalwart a guardian of the liberties of the nation. Having assisted at the baptism of the Republican party he has ever since faithfully fulfilled the vows he then assumed.

In 1873 Mr. Waterman returned to California and purchased a ranch near San Bernardino. His experience in farming at that time,

GOVERNOR ROBERT W. WATERMAN.

however, does not appear to have proved remunerative, for in the following year we find him prospecting in the great Mojave Desert. He felt certain that the section toward which he bent his steps was rich in mineral deposits, and to find it he bent all the energies of his determined nature. After a long and weary search, and surmounting obstacles beneath which a man of less resolute nature would have succumbed, he located a silver-bearing ledge, which was subsequently developed into the Calico Mining District. The Waterman mine, on the line of the Atlantic and Pacific Railroad, he owns in conjunction with Mr. J. L. Porter. Feeling strong faith in the richness of the Julian District in this county, Mr. Waterman in the fall of 1886 paid a visit to the Stonewall mine and was so forcibly impressed with what he saw that he purchased it, paying the sum of $45,000 therefor. He at once began a system of extensive improvements, expending over $50,000 in the construction of a mill, shafts, etc., and soon had the mine on a paying basis. Finding necessity for a saw-mill he built and equipped one of first-class capacity, which supplies lumber for the use of his mine and the neighboring community. The revenue received from his mining ventures is quite large, and the major portion of this is invested in lands in Southern California. His home ranch, situated in a cañon some five miles east of San Bernardino and within sight of the famous Arrowhead Hot Springs, is one of the most beautiful places in California. Sheltered from the winds, at an altitude of over two thousand feet above the sea, the air is pure and delicious. The soil is rich, water is abundant, and everything that goes to make farm life agreeable is at hand. On this ranch he has a fine herd of cattle, and the product of his dairy is famous throughout all Southern California. It is not to the development of mines, the tilling of the soil, and raising of choice cattle, however, that Governor Waterman has confined his energies and his capital, but he is identified with every movement tending to advance the material interests of his section. He was one of the projectors and is largely interested financially in the magnificent structure known as the Stewart Hotel, now completed at San Bernardino, and is a heavy stockholder in the proposed motor railroad line to be built from San Bernardino to Arrowhead Springs. He is, also, heavily interested in San Diego County. Besides the mine and saw-mill near Julian, to which reference has been already made, he has recently purchased twenty thousand acres of land in that vicinity, which, by the opening of railroad communication, is bound to become very valuable. For the purpose of getting the ore from the Stonewall mine to market and developing the rich agricultural section of the Cuyamaca, Governor Waterman has interested himself in the San Diego and Cuyamaca narrow-gauge railroad line, the construction of which has been already commenced. The completion of this road will mark another era in the development of this county, opening up, as it will, a section rich in agricultural and mineral resources which has heretofore lain dormant. A few months since Governor Waterman purchased four fine residence lots in the vicinity of Florence Heights, San Diego. As a member of the committee appointed to secure the erection of a monument to the gifted patriot and eloquent preacher, Thomas Starr King, he has taken a warm interest and has contributed liberally from his own purse.

As previously stated Governor Waterman has ever since the formation of the Republican Party, been one of its most earnest followers, and, while he had not the inclination to seek political preferment, and his business cares debarred him from accepting official position, he has always taken a lively interest in its welfare. During the last presidential campaign he, in company with Richard Gird, a former miner and now a large land-owner, built a Republican wigwam at San Bernardino and equipped three companies of plumed knights.

On the 27th of August, 1886, the Republican State convention assembled at Los Angeles. It was felt that the nomination of a strong ticket was necessary if California was to be kept in the Republican column. While to the northern part of the State was generally conceded the honor of nominating the head of the ticket, it was decided that the candidate for Lieutenant-Governor ought to come from Southern California. Numerous names were placed before the convention, but when George A. Knight, of San Francisco, sitting as a delegate for Mendocino County, nominated Robert W. Waterman in a speech as brilliant as it was convincing, the first ballot showed him to be a prime favorite, he receiving two hundred and twenty-nine votes, within ten and one-half of the number necessary to a choice. His speedy nomination followed. At the polls he ran far ahead of his ticket—as was shown by the election of a Democratic Governor—defeating his rival, M. F. Tarpey, by a vote of ninety-four thousand nine hundred and sixty-nine, to ninety-two thousand four hundred and seventy-six. This was the first political office he ever held. By the death of Washington Bartlett, which occurred on the 12th of October last, the duties of Chief Magistrate devolved upon Mr. Waterman. The manner in which he has thus far discharged the duties of his high position indicate that his administration will be one of the most successful that California has ever experienced. His enlarged views, unswerving integrity and high-minded strength of purpose, give ample promise to the people that the man who now fills the gubernatorial chair will zealously guard their interests, and fulfill the duties of his position with credit to himself and honor to the State.

Among his first appointments, illustrating his knowledge of men and his desire to cut loose from all entangling alliances, was the selection of Hon. Marcus D. Boruck, of San Francisco, to be his private Secretary. Perhaps no better choice than this could have been made. Mr. Boruck is a firm adherent of Republican principles and has a large acquaintance with men and affairs. It was during his long service as Secretary of the State Central Committee that the Republican party achieved its greatest triumphs in California, and it is not improper to say that those successes were largely due to Mr. Boruck's sound judgment and sage advice.

Personally, Governor Waterman is one of the most genial of men; simple in manners, he is easily approached, and has a kind word and a happy salutation for all. He is generous to a fault and his many excellent qualities of head and heart have, during his career in California, raised up for him an army of friends who are not confined to party lines, but are as numerous among his opponents as among those of his own political sect.

Governor Waterman was married in Belvidere, Illinois, September, 1847, to Miss Jane Gardner. The fruit of their union was seven children. The eldest son is dead, but two sons and four daughters are now living.

COLONEL W. H. HOLABIRD.

ACCORDING to Webster, one of the definitions of boom is, "to make a loud noise;" another, "to move rapidly." If San Diego's boom was started with a loud noise, it has certainly moved rapidly, and gathered stability and strength as it progressed. The boom, then, has been a good thing for San Diego; all will admit that. It is not with the boom itself, however, that we have to deal, but with the man who started it—the "Father of the Boom," as he has been termed, W. H. Holabird. Colonel Holabird is a native of the Green Mountain State, having been born in Chittenden County, in 1845. Just after having graduated at the Williston Academy he went with his father to Atchison, Kansas, where the latter had been appointed agent of the Hannibal and St. Joseph Railroad, then just completed to the Missouri River. He entered the office of the company with his father, where his active mind soon found time, while attending to his clerical duties, to devise a system for supplying the train on the road with periodical literature. This was the beginning of the newspaper and periodical train service now in operation on the railroads of the country. During the exciting contest in Kansas that raged between the Lecompton and Free State parties, that preceded the great Civil War, young Holabird was an earnest and active opponent of slavery. On the occasion of the visit of William H. Seward to Atchison he was one of the most prominent of a company of young men who erected a triumphal arch in honor of the advent of "the defender of Kansas." He was agent of the C. O. C. and P. P. Express Company that carried the mails across the plains and the Sierras to the Pacific in much less time than had ever been known before. At the outbreak of the war he returned to Vermont and enlisted in the Twelfth Vermont Volunteer Infantry. In the same regiment was H. L. Story, the well-known capitalist of San Diego. They served together during the first three years of the war. After the battle of Gettysburg, Holabird was transferred to the navy, and ordered to service on board the monitor *Monadnock*. After the bombardment of Fort Fisher, in which his vessel took part, he was promoted to be Paymaster. In the winter of 1865-66 he made the eventful voyage in the *Monadnock* around the Horn. On the way up the coast the vessel came into San Diego Bay, and anchored for a few days off La Playa. After being mustered out of service at Mare Island Navy Yard, Colonel Holabird returned East, locating in Chicago,

COLONEL W. H. HOLABIRD.

where he was engaged a short time in commercial pursuits. He soon tired of this quiet life, however, and went back to railroading. For seven years he was in the service of the Atchison, Topeka and Santa Fe as general traveling agent.

When Babcock & Story became interested in the Coronado Beach property, and began to lay plans for improving it, they looked about to find a man whom they could rely upon to take immediate charge and assist in its development. At this juncture Mr. Story bethought him of his old comrade-in-arms, W. H. Holabird. He sent for him and engaged his services as general agent of the company. In two weeks' time Colonel Holabird had copies of a map of the property and a descriptive pamphlet in every city and town in the United States and Canada. At the great sale, in November, 1886, he acted as auctioneer, and as an incentive to the bidders he unrolled a plan of the Hotel del Coronado that was to be and is. Many thought his descriptions too glowing, his picture of the future too highly colored. Those persons now wish they had invested more heavily in the lots then offered by the auctioneer to the highest bidder. This was the beginning of the San Diego boom, and for his services on that occasion, Colonel Holabird has been known as the "Father of the Boom." After this Colonel Holabird laid out and boomed all the towns along the line of the California Southern Railroad, and for a time made his headquarters at Los Angeles. The superior advantages of San Diego, however, brought him back, and last year he located here again, this time, as he says, for good.

COLONEL JOHN A. HELPHINGSTINE.

ALTHOUGH not an old-time resident of San Diego, there is no citizen more highly appreciated for his enterprise and public spirit than Col. John A. Helphingstine. Colonel Helphingstine was born in Crawford County, Illinois, October 12, 1844. His father was a farmer, and his boyhood was passed on the farm until he was seventeen years of age. Then came the War of the Rebellion; Sumter was fired on, and the North, rising like a giant in his might, flew to arms. The loyal citizens of the country responded with alacrity to President Lincoln's call for volunteers, but from no section was the response more general than from the broad prairies of his own State. Men past the prime of life took their places in the ranks, and school-boys dropped their books to enlist in the service of the Union. Young Helphingstine bade his parents farewell, left the farm, and enlisted as a private in the Sixty-second Illinois Volunteers. He served through the war, in the Army of the Cumberland for two years and then was transferred to the West, and was mustered out as Quartermaster of his regiment. During his spare moments while in the army, Helphingstine had studied law, and at the close of the war he attended the high school in Crawford County. Having graduated, he resumed his law studies under Judge Harrison, in Independence, Kansas. In 1870 he was admitted to the Kansas bar and successfully practiced his profession for ten years in Independence. He served one term as Police Judge of the town, and for five years was County Clerk of Montgomery County.

In 1880 he went to New Mexico, where he engaged in mining, continuing in that calling for three years. He then turned his attention to journalism, and established a daily newspaper, the *Chieftain*, at Socorro. He conducted this paper for three years, with ability and energy, and in that time made it a power in the community. He was largely instrumental in securing the appointment of E. G. Ross as Gov-

COLONEL JOHN A. HELPHINGSTINE.

ernor of the Territory. The circumstances attending his connection with this appointment are so strongly characteristic of the man—of his loyalty to friends and his indomitable perseverance—that it is worth recounting. Ross was an old Kansas man, and at one time, during Andy Johnson's administration, had represented the State in the United States Senate. His candid views openly expressed, and his independent conduct, however, during those stirring times, injured him with his party (the Republican), and upon his return home from the Senate, he was politically ostracized. Disappointed at the treatment he had received at the hands of his party, and reduced in means, he left Kansas and went to New Mexico. There Helphingstine found him working at a case in a newspaper office. The two men had formed a friendship in other days, and Helphingstine came to his assistance now. Knowing his thorough executive ability and his stubborn honesty, he boldly advocated Ross' appointment as Territorial Governor in the columns of the *Chieftain*. This indorsement proved of eminent service, and Ross was made Governor. During his administration, Helphingstine served as Inspector-General on his staff with the rank of Colonel.

On the twentieth of October, 1886, Colonel Helphingstine came to San Diego. He had intended resuming his law practice here, but was wooed from his profession by the brighter opening he found in real estate. He took charge of the lands of the Coronado Beach Company as their general agent, February 1, 1887, and remained in that position until the 1st of September last. During this time his sales of real estate amounted to about one million dollars. While connected with the Coronado Company, he formed a syndicate and purchased a large tract of land within the city limits, which he has placed on the market, under the name of Helphingstine's Addition. He also has the agency of the El Cajon Valley Company. Colonel Helphingstine, some months since, secured the premises formerly occupied by the Commercial Bank of San Diego, and has there fitted up the finest set of offices to be found in San Diego. On the tenth of October last, he was presented, by Mr. E. S. Babcock, Jr., on behalf of the Coronado Beach Company, with an elegant gold watch, as a token of their appreciation of his efforts in their behalf when general agent of the company. Colonel Helphingstine is interested quite largely in city real estate, and, besides, has a valuable ranch property. Colonel Helphingstine was married, in Fredonia, Kansas, in February, 1872, to Miss L. E. Lowe, daughter of Rev. Boyd Lowe. Their union has been blessed with one son, now twelve years of age, and in their beautiful residence on Florence Heights, Colonel and Mrs. Helphingstine have an ideal home.

San Diego has no citizen more devoted to her interests, or whose faith in her future greatness is stronger, than Colonel Helphingstine. He is popular with all classes of people, and his friends are legion.

WILLARD N. FOS.

As has been stated in the introduction to this work, the publishers have sought to confine the biographical portion of it to the older residents of the city and county, those who have been identified with San Diego in its days of patient waiting, and those who have aided in starting it upon its wonderful career of progress. There are, however, citizens who, though their residence has been comparatively short, are to-day as thoroughly identified with the growing city, and through their active energy and public-spirited enterprise are helping to develop its great advantages as though they had been many years residents within its gates. Prominent among this class is Willard N. Fos. If for no other reason, he is deserving of a place in this work as an example of what youth, combined with energy, pluck, and brain has accomplished in San Diego. Mr. Fos is a native of Ohio, having been born in Berlin, February 25, 1863. When he was eight years old his parents removed to South Lincoln, Massachusetts, and there Willard obtained the first rudiments of his education. Three years later he went to Manchester, New Hampshire, where he entered the public schools, and continued until he graduated at the high school, in 1883. He then entered Gaskell's Commercial College, where he remained as a student for a year. Then so apt a scholar had he proven himself, so thoroughly had he mastered the details of all that was taught in the institution, that at the age of twenty-one he was selected as Principal. He had now thoroughly acquired the theory of business, and was soon to make a practical test of his qualifications. The Page Belting Company, of Concord, New Hampshire, offered him a handsome salary to engage as a traveling salesman for them. He was very successful and brought to the firm a large increase in custom. Not content with being an employe, however, he started in the same business on his own account at Manchester. In 1886 Mr. Fos had his attention directed to Southern California, and noting the superior geographical position of San Diego, its fine harbor, and its great climatic advantages, he pressed his inquiries further. He learned of the great progress that was being made by the means of capital and energy to develop these advantages, and he decided that he would come hither and lend the aid of his youth and push toward building up this young city. He came and has prospered, probably even beyond his most sanguine expectations. He opened a banking office, and bought a large tract of land along the shores of the bay, between the present city and Old Town. A steam motor line is now running through the property, and it is being rapidly covered with tasteful dwellings. From the upper portion of the tract a most magnificent view can be obtained, and it is bound to become one of the most attractive portions of the city. Mr. Fos' reputation for business sagacity and probity, which he acquired in his New England home, served him

WILLARD N. FOS.

in good stead when he came to locate on the Pacific Coast, as he has been called upon to invest large sums for his acquaintances in the East, they trusting implicitly to his judgment. Mr. Fos is a member of the Masonic Order, is an Odd Fellow, a Knight of Pythias, and belongs to several other fraternal societies. He has a fine residence on Florence Heights, and owns considerable city as well as suburban property outside of his addition. He was married in Manchester, New Hampshire, February 2, 1885, to Miss Charlotte Maud Whittier, a cousin of the poet,

John G. Whittier. He has one child, a daughter. Mr. Fos owns property at Kendle Green, just outside of Boston, where his parents reside, but he says there is no place like San Diego, and here he intends to make his home for life.

MORSE, WHALEY & DALTON BUILDING.
[See illustration opposite page 14.]

THE first building thoroughly metropolitan in appearance erected in San Diego, was the Morse-Pierce Block on the corner of Sixth and F Streets. This was completed in August last, and attracted many favorable comments from visitors. So well satisfied with the success that attended this building was Mr. E. W. Morse, its part owner and projector, that he proposed to his partners, Messrs. Thomas Whaley and R. H. Dalton, that they should join him in putting up another to equal it in architectural beauty and the substantial character of its construction. This was agreed to and a very eligible location having been secured on Fifth Street next to the First National Bank, the work of construction was begun in September, and lately completed. This building is one of the most beautiful, for its size, on the Pacific Coast. It has a frontage of fifty feet on Fifth Street, with a depth of ninety-five feet. It is four stories in height and the front of the roof is surmounted by a pediment in the center, flanked on either side by a railing of terra cotta. In the center of the pediment is the monogram of the proprietors, and directly underneath the figures "1887." The front of the building is of the finest pressed brick, ornamented with granite, terra cotta, marble and onyx. All of the capitols, keystones, ballisters, panels, and sprendels are in terra cotta; the sills, skewbecks and corbels are in granite; the cornices are in galvanized iron, and at different points blocks of white marble and black onyx set in, lend a tone of richness and finish to the front that is admirable.

The lower floor is divided into two stores, extending the whole depth of the building. The entrance to the upper floors is by means of a wide doorway, which opens into a large vestibule paved with tiles. The stairways are built in double flights, having a landing-place half way in each story. They are semi-circular, and an arcade extends from the ground floor to the roof. The stairs are built of solid oak. The halls, corridors and stairways have a dado of lincrusta walton and are amply lighted. The hinges of the doors are of bronze, and all the door knobs are of ebony. The window glass in the entire front of the building is the finest imported plate. The rooms on the second floor are to be used for offices and are so arranged that all of them are provided with an abundance of light and fresh air. The third story is divided up into suites of rooms and will be let for lodging purposes. These suites have every convenience that experience can suggest, and will, when furnished, make luxurious apartments for bachelors or small families. The fourth floor, which, in reality, consists of two stories, having a height between the floor and roof of over twenty feet, is finished up into two magnificent halls for secret societies. With the great height of the ceilings and an abundance of light, these rooms rank with the finest of the kind in the State. The building is lighted throughout with the Edison incandescent light, and on the sidewalk in front are four ornamental iron electric light lamp posts. The sidewalk in front of the building is made of artificial stone. In addition to the stairways provision is made in the center of the building for an elevator. This will be built on the most approved plan and run by hydraulic power. The completion of the Morse, Whaley & Dalton Block marks an era in architectural progress in San Diego, and the energy and public spirit of its projectors cannot be too highly commended. It is to the efforts of such men that San Diego will be largely indebted for the substantial appearance of its business edifices.

FIRST NATIONAL BANK.
[See illustration opposite page 40.]

THIS institution was organized in July, 1883, as the Bank of Southern California, but on the 1st of October following it was reorganized as the First National Bank of San Diego. The original incorporators and stockholders were Jacob Gruendike, President; R. A. Thomas, Vice-President; John Wolfskill, W. L. Parker, and John R. Thomas. C. E. Thomas was cashier, but was not a stockholder. The capital was then $50,000, but it has since been increased twice. In October, 1885, it was increased to $100,000, and E. S. Babcock, Jr., and H. L. Story were added to the Board of Directors, and in June, 1887, it was again doubled, making the capital now $200,000, with a surplus of $75,000. The present officers of the bank are: R. A. Thomas, President; H. L. Story, Vice-President; O. S. Hubbell, cashier; M. T. Gilmore, assistant cashier. These four, with E. S. Babcock, Jr., Jacob Gruendike, and J. R. Thomas, constitute the Board of Directors. The deposits of the bank are now something over $2,100,000, and the amount of cash carried on hand about $1,000,000. The total assets are $2,500,000, and they are increasing at the rate of $200,000 a month. The bank has on its books over two thousand, five hundred actual accounts, and does a business of from $400,000 to 600,-000 a day. The business increased during the last year about two hundred per cent. There are now twenty-five persons employed in the bank in various capacities. The banking room occupied for the past two years had grown totally inadequate to accommodate the great increase in business, and accordingly, several months since, it was decided to utilize the store adjoining. The partition wall was torn down and the whole lower floor of the building has been prepared for the use of the bank. This now makes a commodious banking room, fifty by sixty feet in size, and abundantly lighted. Three new vaults are being put in, one of which will be burglar-proof, and the others will be used for the storage of books, etc. The interior of the room is finished in mahogany, and the walls and ceiling are elaborately frescoed. In arranging the interior, the lobby, or space allotted to customers, is in the center and the desks and working room are on the outer edge, which afford the clerical force the benefit of plenty of light. The cost of these improvements has been about $30,000.

The bank has been conservative in its management, and not less than fifty per cent of the deposits are carried in hand. It has attained a very wide popularity and the great increase in its business is one of the marked features of San Diego's rapid growth. If its present enlightened management is continued there is no question that it will retain the position it now occupies, that of one of the most prosperous, as it is one of the most popular, banking institutions on the Pacific Coast.

The following is the report of the condition of the First National Bank of San Diego at the close of business December 8, 1887.

RESOURCES.

Loans and discounts		$1,400,888 17
United States bonds		71,000 00
Real estate and furniture		38,442 47
Expenses		9,398 52
Due from United States Treasurer		2,250 00
Cash on hand	$372,103 21	
Cash with banks	623,009 93	995,113 14
Total		$2,517,092 30

LIABILITIES.

Capital	$ 200,000 00
Surplus and profits	106,603 77
Deposits	2,156,468 53
Circulation	54,020 00
Total	$2,517,092 30

THE CONSOLIDATED NATIONAL BANK OF SAN DIEGO.

[See illustration opposite page 46.]

THIS bank is the oldest bank in the county, being the successor of the Bank of San Diego, which was established in 1870, with T. L. Nesmith as President, and Bryant Howard as cashier and manager. In 1879 this bank consolidated with the Commercial Bank, taking the name of the "Consolidated Bank," with Judge O. S. Witherby as President, and Bryant Howard as cashier and manager, and in 1883 was nationalized with the same officers.

Its stockholders are among the oldest residents and wealthiest people of the county, some of whom have been residents of the county since the cession of the State to the Union. Its Directors are men of experience in the business of this coast, and its present President and manager, Mr. Howard, is one of the best known bankers on the Pacific slope.

Its management is very conservative, confining itself strictly to legitimate banking business, and furnishing temporary aid, not capital, to its customers. Its employes are prohibited, by its by-laws, from dealing in stocks, or taking any part whatever in any speculative schemes.

While this bank has kept clear of any entangling alliances, it has lent its hearty assistance to every legitimate commercial enterprise, and has aided in the establishment of nearly every industry in this county. It has been the leading factor in the commercial development of this section of the State, and while prudent and cautious, has always been liberal in its aid where safety was assured, and has never pushed a deserving customer.

A bank so conservative, yet so liberal and just, cannot fail to command the confidence and respect of the business public, and this bank and its officers possess it to the fullest extent. Its commercial success is evidenced by its last statement at the close of business, December 7, showing a cash reserve of nearly $900,000, deposits of over $2,000,000, and capital surplus, and profits of $350,000.

A brief description of its office will be of interest to those of our readers who have not been so fortunate as to have seen it. The bank is located in the massive two-story building at the corner of Fifth and G Streets—one of the busiest corners in the city. Its office proper is fifty by sixty feet, besides which there are a Directors' parlor and a reading-room for its employes. It has four large vaults, and over one hundred feet of massive walnut counters, over which eighteen clerks, besides its officers, attend to the wants of its customers. The walls and ceilings are beautifully frescoed in the style of the Italian renaissance, the same style being observed in all of the interior decoration of the building. Taken all in all, it is the finest and best equipped banking room in the State, and has few peers in the country.

To all who may visit San Diego we commend this bank as a safe depository for their funds, and for the courtesy of its officers, who are ever ready to give new-comers truthful and valuable information.

THE PIERCE-MORSE BLOCK.
[See illustration opposite page 60.]

ONE of the finest buildings in Southern California is the Pierce-Morse Block, on the corner of Sixth and F Streets. It is 50x100 feet, five stories high, and is fitted up with every modern improvement. It has a first-class passenger elevator that makes the rooms in the upper stories as easy of access as those on the ground floor. It is lighted by incandescent electric lights throughout, and four large ornamental iron lamp posts are erected on the street in front of the building, which contain each a group of electric lamps; and these, when the fluid is turned on at night, render the vicinity of the building as light as day. In the cellar is a fine engine that runs the elevator, the electric lights, etc. The ground flour is occupied by first-class stores, and the floors above are all rented for offices. The building is a monument to the enterprise of its projectors, James M. Pierce, now deceased, and E. W. Morse, and is a credit to San Diego.

VILLA MONTEZUMA.
A MAGNIFICENT AND ARTISTIC HOME, DEVOTED TO MUSIC, ART AND LITERATURE.

SITUATED on a gently sloping hill-side on the corner of Twentieth and K Streets, and commanding a magnificent view of San Diego and its incomparably lovely surroundings, stands a private residence that the citizens may look upon with pardonable pride. It is the Villa Montezuma, the home of the world-famed pianist and vocalist, Jesse Shepard, whose wonderful performances have thrilled the music-loving of two continents. There is something so very peculiar, something so very striking, about even the exterior of the building that the passer-by cannot but stop and admire its extreme unostentatious eccentricity.

The odd windows, in peculiar shapes and sizes, some of which are of stained glass; the inscription printed in quaint old English: "A. D. MDVVVLXXXVII;" the harmonious blending of colors—at once command attention, and the observer longs to see what one who planned the exterior of a mansion so unique would do for its interior embellishment.

The moment the hall is entered one is made acquainted with the artistic purpose, the effects of universal culture to be seen at every turning. At once it becomes apparent that nothing is copied here, nothing imitated. The art student, while yet standing in the hall, recognizes at a glance that here is a study which cannot be properly appreciated and appropriated at a single visit, but that the masterly *ensemble* of light and shade in positive and negative colors, must be studied with as much serious consideration as would be required in the study of a picture by Raphael or a portrait by Rubens.

THE DRAWING ROOM.

Under an arabesque art transom hang the *portières* separating the red room from the drawing-room. This far surpasses in elegance anything yet seen in the mansion. Everything has the appearance of riches, art, and love for the beautiful; the dark shades here modify and subdue the light ones there—everything is strictly in keeping with the artistic intention, the furniture being selected with a special view to the arrangements and designs on floor and ceiling. Perhaps the great feature of this room is the splendid bay-window eighteen feet deep, of bent glass, the upper sashes containing life-size heads, in art glass, of Shakespeare, Gœthe, and Corneille, these heads representing the poetry of England, Germany, and France. The ceiling is exquisitely silvered and bronzed, relieved by deep panels of redwood. A large Persian rug of rich pattern gives this room an oriental as well as a home-like and most inviting air, appreciated at a glance by persons of broad culture and experience. The bay-window is separated from the main room by a beautiful arch in carved wood, from which hang three large lace curtains, which show the jeweled and arabesque glass behind in the most artistic manner possible.

THE MUSIC ROOM.

In the music-room, which may be entered through heavy *portières* either from the pink room or the drawing-room, everything is so severe, so simple, yet so grand, that one cannot but admire the most exquisite taste that Mr. Shepard has displayed in its arrangement. The first things that catch the eye are the art windows, through the many-hued glasses by which the room is lighted. In the figures there delineated, every feature represented, every expression, every tint is perfect. Indeed, they seem to lack only the spark of life to make them flesh and body. They are most wonderfully life-like, and one thinks that in them art has accomplished a work almost divine. In the first moments of day, the rays of the rising sun illumine a life-sized portrait of Sappho, the Greek poet. Reclining upon a couch, and with a wrap thrown loosely about her form, she sits idly picking a lyre. Beside her are two Cupids, who accompany Sappho's playing, with flutes. The forms of the figures are exquisitely moulded and the proportions are perfect. Through an open portal a marine view, with rays of sunlight and great rolling storm clouds, is pictured. Over the portrait is a heavy black and white *sgraffito* border, beneath which and about the picture is a crazy patch of Venetian, opalescent and cathedral glass of rich colors. Throughout this and in the borders of all the figures in the room are interspersed heavy sapphires, rubies, emeralds, garnets, opals, and other jewels, all cut and highly polished. These gleam and sparkle like dew on a bed of pansies in the morning sun. To the left of Sappho's portrait is a life-size one of L'Allegra, representing Milton's poem. Corresponding with this is a portrait of La Penserosa, another of Milton's creatures, who stands admiring some blossoms she holds in her hands. Over these windows, which occupy the front of the bay-window in which they are situated, is an arch of carved black walnut, resting upon columns of similar material. In the north end of the room, in circular windows, are life-sized bust portraits of Beethoven, and Mozart. These are marvelous works of art; Beethoven, to the left, with hair disheveled, his prominent forehead wrinkled, small, deep-set eyes, has a dreamy look, as if his mind was in another sphere; Mozart's handsome features, to the right, snow-white hair, prominent nose, features particularly kind and benevolent, and eyes large and bright, that are lighted up as if he is about to speak. At the other end of the room, portraits of Raphael and Rubens correspond with those of Beethoven and Mozart. These, like their companion pictures, are masterpieces, and as the sunlight strikes them at different times of day, the faces are filled with life-like expressions that no painter's brush could ever portray. Beneath the portraits of Rubens and Raphael are allegorical representations of the Orient and the Occident, each consisting of a man dressed in the costume of his respective clime.

Reluctantly the eye leaves the marvelous figures constituting the windows, and looks about to observe the next surprise. Art, pure and simple, is found in everything. No two chairs in the room—or in the building, in fact—are alike in either shape or hue. There are no pictures in the music-room, save those in the art-windows, but the hard-finished redwood walls are relieved by ebony panels inlaid with bas-relief figures of ivory and mother-of-pearl, that are hung at intervals. The ceiling is of redwood panels and lincrusta walton in silver-gray figures, and from its center depends an elaborate oriental candelabra containing on the outer circle six pale blue wax candles, and within is a heavily jeweled metallic shade that contains a single wax candle. In addition to the six heavy Persian rugs that cover the highly waxed floor, an immense Polar bear skin is in its center. Opposite Sappho's portrait is the mantel. It is of medieval design, and is built of imported English tiles, heavily glazed, and porcelain bricks. The design of the mantel is purely original. It represents the roof of a tower of one of the old German castles, like those found along the Rhine, and extends over halfway up to the ceiling. Small black walnut shingles of odd shapes cover it from top to bottom, save at one place, where a portico, also of walnut, is placed. This bears a bronze bust of Diana, who seems to look down from the height as if charmed with the beautiful surroundings. The furniture in the room is all art furniture of the most recent designs, and its varied hues and tints are all in perfect harmony with the windows, rugs, walls and everything. Pushing aside the maroon *portières* a cozy little retreat, probably eight feet in diameter, is found. The windows are in art glass, representing the four seasons. A jeweled and artistically ornamented window occupies the center, and over each window is a transom, also of jeweled art glass. In the center of the mosaic floor is an ebony stand, bearing a life-size figure of an Egyptian head in gold bronze.

ST. CECELIA.

One of the finest art glass windows in the villa is that of St. Cecelia, situated so as to catch the last rays of the setting sun. The quiet dignity and sublime resignation which are portrayed in the face and form of this martyr saint, strike one at once as being an admirable rendering of the subject as originally portrayed in the *cinque-cento* period by Carlo Dolce. Indeed, one could almost imagine that this beautiful window possesses the power of the "Vocal Memnon" at Thebes, which is reputed to have awed the entranced spectator by its production of sweet music.

MAGNIFICENT PRESENTS.

The interior decorations are greatly enhanced by the large number of valuable presents which Mr. Shepard has received from his friends in all parts of the world. On the second floor is a superb room 25x22, containing ten windows of irregular form overlooking the mountains to the east, and Mexico to the south, while to the west are spread out the ocean, with the Coronado Islands and Point Loma in the distance. This is Mr. Shepard's sanctum, where he converses with intimate friends, reads, writes and lives. Perhaps there is not in the world another room like this. A Spanish cedar stairway leads from it to the observatory directly above, and it is one of the most strikingly original features of this unique house.

Every square foot of the walls is covered with pictures, both large and small, of some celebrity, living or dead, Mr. Shepard's friends, acquaintances and favorites. And here the visitor to "Villa Montezuma" is initiated into the intimate environments, tastes and inclinations of the celebrated writer and musician who inhabit it.

In this room are displayed, in a prominent and positive manner, Mr. Shehard's personal characteristics as an individuality in art and literature. Over a beautiful organ is a large steel engraving of Meyerbeer, with his five chief operas represented by figures in the background; the picture, a master-work of itself, is set off to advantage in a deep bronze frame. Below this, to one side of the organ, is a beautiful portrait of Mrs. Siddons, the greatest of England's tragic queens, and Felicia Hemans; the Princess D'Ursini, on the other side, with Richard Wagner, George Eliot, and Rossini. A bust of Beethoven, in bronze, occupies a niche near Wagner. In other portions of the room are portraits, pictures and busts of men and women of genius, numbering nearly one hundred, and the room is a veritable gallery of celebrities. Portraits, photographs and prints from Russia, Germany, France, Italy, England and Australia are reminders of Mr. Shepard's friends in those countries, with inscriptions of esteem and affection from composers, singers, poets, painters and writers. Beauty and utility combine to render this residence a model of the ideal and the real, and the cultured visitor from foreign ports finds a solution for this extraordinary display of taste in the fact that Jesse Shepard himself evolved the leading ideas herein set forth. There is not a single detail, from the first drawing of the plans to the hanging of the last picture on the walls, that has not been closely scrutinized and criticized from an artistic standpoint, and wherever there seemed to be the slightest error against good taste, or in harmony of color and good effect, changes were made, in many instances a dozen times over, until the arrangement seemed, in Mr. Shepard's eyes, to be at last perfect. Throughout the entire house this kind of work has been done, to the great strain of nerve and physical endurance, until it seemed at times that part of this great work must be given up.

Villa Montezuma is exclusively a private residence consecrated to music, art and literature. Mr. Shepard gives no concerts or other entertainments in his home, but he gives receptions and musicales from time to time to his friends and those especially invited, for which no charges are made.

www.ingramcontent.com/pod-product-compliance
Lightning Source LLC
Chambersburg PA
CBHW021345230426
43666CB00006B/419